The Stark Law:
A User's Guide to Achieving Compliance

Sonnenschein Nath & Rosenthal LLP

The Stark Law: A User's Guide to Achieving Compliance is published by HCPro, Inc.

Copyright 2005 HCPro, Inc.

All rights reserved. Printed in the United States of America.   5 4 3 2

ISBN-13: 978-1-57839-635-1
ISBN-10: 1-57839-635-2

HCPro, Inc., provides information resources for the healthcare industry. A selected listing of our newsletters and books is found at the back of this book.

HCPro, Inc., is not affiliated in any way with the Joint Commission on Accreditation of Healthcare Organizations, which owns the JCAHO trademark.

Gina M. Cavalier, Esq., Author

Christopher G. Janney, Esq., Author

Albert M. Shay, Esq., Author

Gadi Weinreich, Esq., Author

Howard J. Young, Esq., Author

Melissa Osborn, Executive Editor

Paul Singer, Layout

Jacqueline Diehl Singer, Layout Artist

Brenda Rossi, Cover Designer

Jean St. Pierre, Director of Operations

Bob Croce, Group Publisher

As with most emerging or developing legal issues, many different arguments and perspectives can and should be presented and examined in any thoughtful and responsible discussion. Consequently, the discussions of the issues in this book do not necessarily reflect the views of the authors, the authors' law firm, or of any clients of the authors or the authors' firm. In addition, this book should not be considered as, or as a substitute for, legal advice and it is not intended to nor does it create an attorney-client relationship. Because the information provided herein is general, it may not apply to your individual legal or factual circumstances. You should not take (or refrain from taking) any action based on the information you obtain from this book without first obtaining professional counsel. This disclaimer is an integral part of this book, and the book cannot be cited fairly or in context without including an explicit reference to, and quotation of, this paragraph.

Arrangements can be made for quantity discounts. For more information, contact:

HCPro, Inc.
P.O. Box 1168
Marblehead, MA 01945
Telephone: 800/650-6787 or 781/639-1872
Fax: 781/639-2982
E-mail: *customerservice@hcpro.com*

Visit HCPro at its World Wide Web sites:
www.hcpro.com, www.hcmarketplace.com

About the Authors

PRINCIPAL AUTHORS

Gina M. Cavalier

Christopher G. Janney

Albert W. Shay

Gadi Weinreich

Howard J. Young

CONTRIBUTING AUTHORS

Eric M. Baim

Ramy Fayed

Jacqueline Finnegan

Chris Kanagawa

Kashmira Makwana

Betsy McCubrey

Scott Memmott

Jordana G. Schwartz

Janice Ziegler

About the Authors

The authors are attorneys in the Health Care Group of Sonnenschein Nath & Rosenthal LLP. Founded in 1906, Sonnenschein has 700 attorneys and other professionals in nine U.S. offices. The Firm's Health Care Group, which includes over 40 full-time health law attorneys, provides legal advice and counsel to hundreds of the nation's most prominent health care providers, suppliers, practitioners and payers. Thumbnail sketches of the principal authors are provided below.

Gina M. Cavalier (Georgetown University Law Center, J.D., 1996) is a partner in Sonnenschein's Health Care Group. Ms. Cavalier provides advice and counseling on the Stark Law, the Anti-Kickback Law, and HIPAA — as well as health care fraud and abuse, compliance and Medicare regulations more generally — to a wide variety of providers, payors, manufacturers and other health care organizations. She regularly writes and speaks about these and other health care compliance matters.

Christopher G. Janney (Harvard Law School, J.D., 1991) is the National Vice Chair of Sonnenschein's Health Care Group. Mr. Janney provides counseling in the health care fraud and abuse and corporate compliance areas to hospitals and hospital systems, academic medical centers, insurers, group purchasing organizations, pharmaceutical manufacturers, and a broad array of other health care organizations. Mr. Janney writes and speaks extensively on the Stark Law, as well as a host of other regulatory and compliance issues.

Albert W. Shay (Saint Louis University School of Law, J.D., 1987) is a partner in Sonnenschein's Health Care Group. Mr. Shay provides regulatory and corporate advice to a wide variety of health care organizations, including hospitals (general acute care and specialty), hospital systems, academic medical centers, ancillary service providers and large multi- and single-specialty medical groups. He regularly counsels clients in connection with the formation of clinical service joint venture arrangements, including the fraud and abuse, self-referral, and Medicare reimbursement implications of such arrangements. Mr. Shay is the Vice Chair of the Fraud and Abuse, Self-Referrals, and False Claims Practice Group of the American Health Lawyers Association and he writes and lectures frequently on these issues.

Gadi Weinreich (Harvard Law School, J.D., 1987; Cambridge University, LL.M, 1992) is the National Chair of Sonnenschein's Health Care Group. Mr. Weinreich counsels academic medical centers, hospitals and a wide variety of other providers, suppliers, manufacturers, practitioners and payors with respect to health care corporate transactions and strategies, as well as fraud and abuse, regulatory and compliance matters. Mr. Weinreich has published numerous articles and lectured extensively on the Stark Law, as well as a wide range of fraud and abuse and regulatory developments.

Howard J. Young (Duke Law School, J.D., 1993) is a partner in Sonnenschein's Health Care Group, and a former Deputy Branch Chief for the U.S. Department of Health & Human Services Office of Inspector General. Mr. Young works extensively with hospitals and health systems, pharmaceutical and device manufacturers, durable medical equipment suppliers, dialysis clinics, pharmacies and physician groups. Mr. Young provides advice and counseling to these organizations with respect to a range of fraud and abuse and regulatory issues and matters, including those relating to the Stark Law, the Anti-Kickback Law, the False Claims Act, compliance program development and implementation, provider self-disclosure, and internal investigations. He also speaks regularly on fraud and abuse, regulatory and government investigation matters.

* * *

The authors would like to thank the following individuals, without whose support this project would not have been possible: Charlene Anderson, Mariela Edwards, Lily S. Farel, Michael K. Gottlieb, Drenda Henley, Arlene James, Frances K. Jenkins, H. Lauren Kim, Anna Libetti, Gay MacLean, Megan McGovern, Regina Pruitt, Jane Hyatt Thorpe and Dionne Rothwell.

Contents

Contents

Contents

Contents

Contents

Introduction

Midway upon the journey of our life

I found myself within a forest dark,

For the straightforward pathway had been lost.

Ah me! how hard a thing it is to say

What was this forest savage, rough, and stern,

Which in the very thought renews the fear.

The Divine Comedy, Inferno, Canto I

Dante Alighieri

The federal physician self-referral law—commonly referred to as the "Stark Law"—establishes two basic prohibitions:

1. For certain types of services, a physician may not refer a Medicare beneficiary to a healthcare entity with which the physician (or one of his or her immediate family members) has a financial relationship, unless an exception applies.[1] We will refer to this as the Stark Law's "referral prohibition."

2. A healthcare entity may not bill for improperly referred services, unless an exception applies.[2] We will refer to this as the Stark Law's "billing prohibition."

The Stark Law's principal policy objectives are straightforward. The Centers for Medicare & Medicaid Services (CMS), formerly known as the Health Care Finance Administration (HCFA), is the federal agency principally responsible for implementing and enforcing the Stark Law. According to CMS, the Stark Law's referral and billing prohibitions are necessary because (1) physicians may "overutilize by ordering items and services for patients that, absent a profit motive, they would not have ordered," (2) a patient's choice "can be affected when physicians steer patients to less convenient, lower quality, or more expensive providers of healthcare" based on financial considerations, and (3) "where referrals are controlled by those sharing profits or receiving remuneration, the medical marketplace suffers since new competitors can no longer win business with superior quality, service, or price."[3]

The Stark Law's basic prohibitions and policy objectives can be easily summarized, but almost every other aspect of the Law is quite complex. Moreover, the consequences flowing from a Stark Law violation can be severe. This book will help healthcare providers, suppliers, and practitioners understand the Stark Law. It does so by untangling and explaining each of the Stark Law's many moving parts, providing a simple and logical system for identifying financial relationships, and, wherever possible, offering suggestions for "safe harboring" these relationships under one or more of the Law's exceptions.

The book is organized as follows:

- **Chapter 1: Background.** This chapter provides background information relating to the Stark Law and sets forth the authors' three-step process for determining whether an arrangement implicates the Stark Law and, if so, whether it also violates the law. These steps are then addressed in greater detail throughout the book.

- **Chapter 2: Definitions.** This chapter discusses a number of terms and phrases, such as "physician," "immediate family member," "fair market value," and "set in advance" that appear throughout the book and that are critical to understanding and applying the Stark Law.

- **Chapter 3: Designated health services.** This chapter describes the various healthcare items and services—commonly referred to as "designated health services," or DHS—that are covered by the Stark Law.

- **Chapter 4: Referrals.** This chapter provides the framework for determining whether a physician will make a "referral" "to" an entity for the "furnishing" of DHS, which are prerequisites for triggering Stark Law liability.

- **Chapter 5: Financial relationships.** This chapter provides the framework for determining whether a physician (or a physician's immediate family member) has a "financial relationship" with an entity that furnishes DHS, also a prerequisite to Stark Law liability.

- **Chapter 6: All-purpose exceptions.** This chapter addresses the Stark Law exceptions that are available regardless of the type of financial relationship that a physician or immediate family member has with an entity furnishing DHS.

- **Chapter 7: Ownership interest exceptions.** This chapter addresses five Stark Law exceptions that are available when the financial relationship at issue takes the form of a direct or indirect ownership or investment interest.

- **Chapter 8: Direct compensation arrangement exceptions.** This chapter addresses 18 of the 20 Stark Law exceptions that are available when the financial relationship at issue takes the form of a direct compensation arrangement.

- **Chapter 9: Indirect compensation arrangements exception.** This chapter addresses the Stark Law exception that is available when the financial relationship at issue takes the form of an indirect compensation arrangement.

- **Chapter 10: Recruitment and retention exceptions.** This chapter addresses the two direct compensation arrangement exceptions that are available when the compensation at issue is furnished in connection with a physician recruitment or retention arrangement.

- **Chapter 11: Sanctions, collateral consequences, and reporting requirements.** This chapter addresses the potential consequences of a Stark Law violation, both under the Stark Law itself and under several other statutes—most notably, the federal civil False Claims Act (FCA). This chapter also addresses the reporting requirements that the Stark Law imposes on entities that furnish DHS to Medicare beneficiaries.

- **Chapter 12: Advisory opinions.** This chapter explains the process by which a provider, supplier, or practitioner may seek an advisory opinion from CMS concerning whether a physician has a financial relationship with an entity that furnishes DHS and, if he or she does, whether any Stark Law exceptions apply.

We also have included in the CD-ROM accompanying this book, copies of the Stark Law, the Stark Regulations, and several of the most important and frequently cited Stark-related *Federal Register* sections, including those setting forth the preamble to (1) the 1995 Stark I Regulations, (2) the 1998 proposed Stark II Regulations, (3) the 2001 Stark II, Phase I Regulations, and (4) the 2004 Stark II, Phase II Regulations.

The challenges of analyzing the Stark Law

Before turning to our step-by-step approach to analyzing an arrangement under the Stark Law, let's discuss the need for such an approach. As noted above, it is much easier to articulate the Stark Law's basic prohibitions and principal policy objectives than it is to implement them. Indeed, those who counsel providers, suppliers, and practitioners about how to apply the Stark Law have found the task to be difficult and, at times, quite frustrating, for several reasons:

The Stark Law's breadth

Both as written and as interpreted by CMS, the Stark Law's referral prohibition is quite broad. For example, one could argue that (1) each and every physician in the United States has a "financial relationship" with each and every hospital to which the physician refers patients, and (2) as a result, no physician may refer a Medicare patient to any such hospital without implicating—and, in the absence of an applicable exception, violating—the Stark Law. This is no exaggeration. For Stark Law purposes,

- a physician has a "financial relationship" with any hospital with which the physician has a "compensation arrangement,"[4]

- a compensation arrangement includes "any arrangement" between a physician and hospital that "involves remuneration,"[5] and

- "remuneration" means that "any payment or other benefit made directly or indirectly, overtly or covertly, in cash or in kind."[6]

Thus, if a hospital provides a physician with anything of value, regardless of how small (e.g., notepads and coffee mugs),[7] then the hospital and physician have a "financial relationship" and, in the absence of an exception, the physician may not refer Medicare patients to the hospital, and the hospital may not bill anyone for DHS furnished to such patients, without violating the Stark Law.

Proliferation of exceptions

Because its prohibitions are so broad, the Stark Law is overinclusive and implicates hundreds of thousands of common, everyday provider-physician arrangements, none of which offends any of the Stark Law's underlying policy objectives. For example, nobody actually believes that, in exchange for a free coffee mug, a physician would refer a Medicare beneficiary to a hospital for a medically unnecessary inpatient or outpatient admission or procedure.

For this reason, Congress and CMS have created almost three-dozen separate exceptions to the Stark Law's prohibitions. The "compensation under $300" exception, for example—which might cover the free coffee mug—protects "compensation from an entity in the form of items or services (not including cash or cash equivalents) that does not exceed an aggregate of $300 per year," provided that multiple conditions are met (for example, the compensation at issue "may not be solicited by the physician or the physician's practice").[8]

The Stark Law's other exceptions cover the following:

• Publicly traded securities
• Mutual funds
• Specific providers
• Space rental
• Equipment rental
• Employment
• Personal services arrangements
• Physician recruitment
• Isolated transactions

- Remuneration unrelated to designated health services
- Group practice arrangements with hospitals
- Payments by a physician
- Fair market value compensation
- Medical staff incidental benefits
- Risk-sharing arrangements
- Compliance training
- Indirect compensation arrangements
- Charitable donations
- Referral services
- Obstetrical malpractice insurance
- Professional courtesy
- Retention payments in underserved areas
- Community wide health information systems
- Physician services
- In-office ancillary services
- Pre-paid health plan services
- Academic medical center services
- Implants (in ambulatory surgery centers)
- Dialysis-related drugs (end-stage renal disease)
- Preventive screening tests and immunizations
- Post-cataract surgery eyeglasses and contact lenses
- Intra-family rural referrals

Stark's complexity

In addition to the Stark Law's overbreadth and the many resulting exceptions, the Law can be difficult to navigate for a third reason: many of the elements of the Stark Law's basic prohibitions and exceptions are complex, counterintuitive, and, in some cases, have been defined, interpreted, redefined, and reinterpreted on multiple occasions by CMS over the past 15 years. For example, (1) the Stark Law definition of the word "referral" is more than 370 words long;[9] (2) a flat fee that does not change may violate the "volume or value" standard,[10] but a per service fee that is tied directly to DHS referrals may not;[11] and (3) the term "indirect compensation arrangement" was undefined by CMS until 1998,[12] was defined by CMS in 2001,[13] and was redefined by CMS in 2004.[14]

Intermittent guidance

A fourth factor has made compliance with the Law difficult for healthcare organizations: CMS has provided only sporadic and relatively limited Stark Law guidance. The original Stark Law was enacted in 1989 ("Stark I"),[15] and it was expanded in 1993 ("Stark II"),[16] but CMS did not issue final regulations covering the expanded law until 2001[17] and 2004,[18] respectively. Congress sought to address this lack of guidance in 1997, when it set up an "advisory opinion" process.[19] Through the end of 2004, however, CMS had issued only a handful of Stark Law advisory opinions.

Strict liability

To raise the compliance stakes still higher, the Stark Law is a "strict liability" statute. That is, unlike one of the Stark Law's cousins—the federal healthcare program anti-kickback statute,[20] which is violated only if the defendant acts with the requisite state of mind (i.e., "knowingly and willfully")—the Stark Law may be violated even if the parties do not intend to violate the Law and are not aware that they are doing so.

For example, assume that a physician and a hospital have a financial relationship (because the hospital has given the physician a coffee mug) and that this financial relationship does not fit into an exception (because the physician "solicited" the mug from the hospital). Under these circumstances, each and every time the physician refers a Medicare patient to the hospital, the Stark Law's referral prohibition may be violated; and each and every time the hospital bills Medicare (or anyone else) for items or services furnished to such patients, the Stark Law's billing prohibition may be violated—regardless of whether the physician or the hospital intended to violate the Stark Law or were even aware that such violations were occurring.

Enforcement

All of these factors that make the Stark Law so challenging from a compliance standpoint would probably be manageable for the healthcare industry if the federal government had exclusive jurisdiction to enforce the Stark Law. Unfortunately, this is not the case.

Although the jurisprudence in this area is evolving and relatively limited, and although there are no U.S. Supreme Court cases directly on point, several lower federal courts have concluded that when a provider submits a claim for services that were furnished as a result of a referral that violated the Stark Law, that submission may constitute a "false claim" for purposes of the FCA. The FCA, in turn, has a *qui tam* (or "whistleblower") provision, which allows private individuals and organizations to bring FCA actions in the name of (and on behalf of) the federal government.[21] If the whistleblower prevails, he or she is entitled to keep as much as 30% of the proceeds of the litigation (which may include treble damages and a fine of up to $11,000 per claim), as well as reasonable expenses and attorneys' fees.[22]

For all of these reasons, providers, suppliers, and practitioners must be extremely careful to comply with the Stark Law and, thus, need clear and practical guidance for doing so. This book is intended to provide such guidance.

Notes

1. More specifically, in the absence of an applicable exception, a "physician" who has a "financial relationship" with an "entity" (such as a clinical laboratory or a hospital), or who has an "immediate family member" who has such a financial relationship, may not make a "referral" "to" that entity for the "furnishing" of "DHS" for which payment may be made under the Medicare program. 42 United States Code (USC) §1395nn(a)(1)(A); 42 Code of Federal Regulations (CFR) §411.353(a).

2. In the absence of an applicable exception, an entity that furnishes DHS pursuant to a prohibited referral may not "present" or "cause to be presented" a claim or bill for such services to the Medicare program (or to any other individual or entity). 42 USC §1395nn(a)(1)(A); 42 CFR §411.353(b).

3. Stark II Proposed Regulations (Preamble), 63 *Federal Register (FR)* 1659, 1662 (1998).

4. 42 USC §1395nn(a)(2)(B); 42 CFR §411.354(a)(1).

5. 42 USC §1395nn(h)(1)(A); 42 CFR §411.354(c).

6. 42 USC §1395nn(h)(1)(B); 42 CFR §411.351.

7. Stark II Proposed Regulations (Preamble), 63 *FR* 1659, 1699 (1998).

8. 42 CFR §411.357(k).

9. 42 CFR §411.351.

10. Stark II, Phase I Regulations (Preamble), 66 *FR* 856, 878 (2001); 42 CFR §411.354(d)(4).

11. 42 CFR §411.354(d)(2).

12. Stark II Proposed Regulations (Preamble), 63 *FR* 1659, 1705-1706 (1998).

13. Stark II, Phase I Regulations, 66 *FR* 856, 958-959 (2001), setting forth 42 CFR §411.354(c)(2).

14. Stark II, Phase II Regulations, 69 *FR* 16054, 16134 (2004), setting forth a revised 42 CFR §411.354(c)(2).

15. Section 6204 of the Omnibus Budget Reconciliation Act of 1989 (Public Law 101–239, enacted on December 19, 1989).

16. Section 13562 of the Omnibus Budget Reconciliation Act of 1993 (Public Law 103–66, enacted on August 10, 1993).

17. Stark II, Phase I Regulations, 66 *FR* 856 (2001).

18. Stark II, Phase II Regulations, 69 *FR* 16054 (2004).

19. 42 USC §1395nn(g)(6).

20. 42 USC §1320a-7b(b).

21. 31 USC §3730.

22. 31 USC §3730(d).

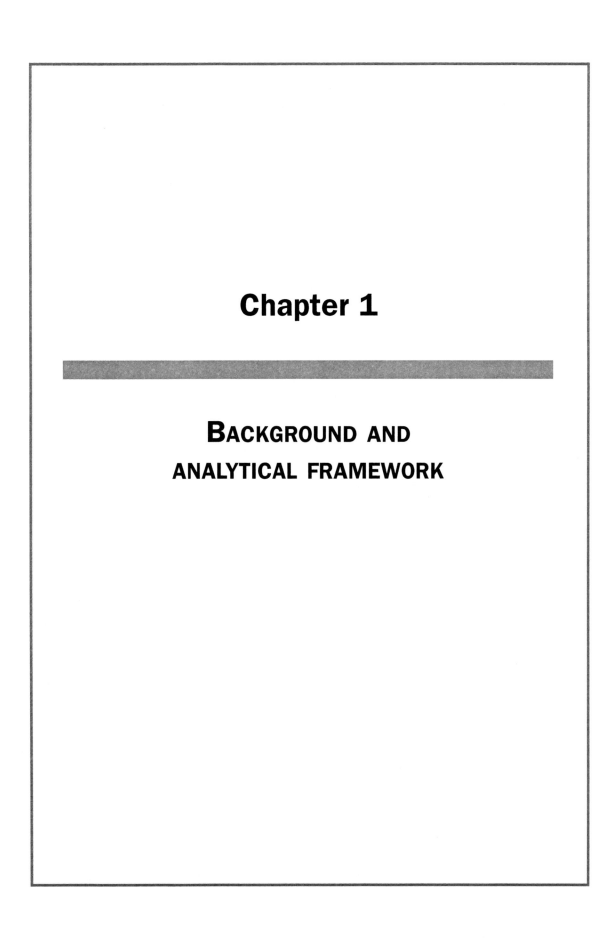

Chapter 1

BACKGROUND AND ANALYTICAL FRAMEWORK

Chapter 1

BACKGROUND AND
ANALYTICAL FRAMEWORK

This chapter is organized into two sections. Section I summarizes the Stark Law's basic prohibitions, sanctions, policy objectives, and evolution. Section II sets forth a framework for determining whether a particular arrangement implicates or violates the Stark Law.

I. Background

A. Basic prohibitions

The Stark Law has two basic prohibitions: a referral prohibition and a billing prohibition.

1. Referral prohibition

Pursuant to the referral prohibition, absent an applicable exception, a physician who has a "financial relationship" with an "entity," or a physician with an "immediate family member" who has such a financial relationship, may not make a "referral" "to" that entity for the "furnishing" of "designated health services" (DHS) for which payment may be made by the Medicare program.[1]

Example 1.1

A physician owns a clinical diagnostic laboratory. This financial relationship does not meet an exception. The physician refers a Medicare beneficiary to the laboratory for blood tests, which are DHS reimbursable by Medicare.

Commentary: This referral violates the Stark Law's referral prohibition.

---

2. Billing prohibition

Pursuant to the billing prohibition, absent an applicable exception, a healthcare provider may not bill for improperly referred services. More specifically, an entity that furnishes DHS pursuant to a prohibited referral may not "present" or "cause to be presented" a claim or bill for such services to the Medicare program or to any other individual or entity, including secondary insurers and the patient.[2]

Example 1.2

This example includes the same facts as Example 1.1. In addition, the clinical laboratory submits a claim for $100 to Medicare for the services it furnished to the Medicare beneficiary.

Commentary: This claim for reimbursement will violate the Stark Law's billing prohibition. Note that the laboratory could not avoid the billing prohibition by foregoing Medicare reimbursement and billing the patient.

Note: Both the referral and billing prohibitions are discussed further in Chapters 2–10.

B. Sanctions

Where a physician has violated the referral prohibition and an entity has violated the billing prohibition, a variety of sanctions may be imposed. These sanctions are highlighted below and discussed in more detail in Chapter 11.

1. Refunds

An entity that collects payment for DHS performed pursuant to a prohibited referral must refund all collected amounts on a timely basis.[3]

Example 1.3

This example includes the same facts as Example 1.2. In addition, Medicare has reimbursed the laboratory $100 for the services it furnished to the improperly referred Medicare beneficiary.

Commentary: The Stark Law requires the laboratory to refund the $100 to Medicare.

---

2. Civil monetary penalty/assessment/exclusion

Any person "who presents or causes to be presented a bill or claim" for improperly referred DHS and "knows or should know" that the claim is for improperly referred DHS is subject to the following:

- A civil monetary penalty (CMP) of up to $15,000 per service
- An assessment (in lieu of damages) of up to three times the amount claimed
- Exclusion from participation in any federal healthcare program[4]

Example 1.4

This example includes the same facts as Example 1.3.

Commentary: In addition to its refund obligation, the laboratory (and the referring physician) may be subject to a $15,000 CMP and an assessment of three times the amount claimed, and may be excluded from participating in Medicare and other federal healthcare programs.

---

3. Circumvention

Any physician or entity that knowingly participates in a "scheme" to circumvent the operation of the Stark Law is subject to a CMP of up to $100,000 and may be excluded from participation in federal healthcare programs.[5]

C. Policy objectives

According to the Centers for Medicare & Medicaid Services (CMS), the Stark Law reflects Congress' concern that a physician with a financial stake in determining whether or where to refer a patient may be "unduly influenced by a profit motive," thereby undermining efficient utilization, patient choice, and competition among participants in federal healthcare programs.[6] More specifically, CMS believes that:

- physicians can "overutilize by ordering items and services for patients that, absent a profit motive, they would not have ordered,"[7]

- a patient's choice "can be affected when physicians steer patients to less convenient, lower quality, or more expensive providers of healthcare, just because the physicians are sharing profits with, or receiving remuneration from, the providers,"[8] and

- where referrals are "controlled by those sharing profits or receiving remuneration, the medical marketplace suffers since new competitors can no longer win business with superior quality, service, or price."[9]

Example 1.5

An orthopedic surgeon has a 50% ownership interest in a physical therapy (PT) company (PT Company A) that is located 25 miles from the surgeon's office. A representative from a second company (PT Company B) meets with the surgeon and states that it charges less than PT Company A and is located in the same building as the surgeon. After this meeting, the surgeon continues to refer all of her patients to PT Company A.

Commentary: CMS might be concerned that the surgeon is steering patients to PT Company A—a more expensive and less convenient provider—not because PT Company A provides better quality medical care than PT Company B, but because the surgeon shares in the profits of PT Company A.

D. Medicare v. Medicaid

Many federal fraud and abuse laws—including one of the Stark Law's older "cousins," the federal healthcare program anti-kickback statute[10]—apply to Medicare, Medicaid, and a host of other federally funded healthcare programs. The Stark Law, however, only prohibits referrals for DHS that are covered by Medicare. Although there is a common misconception that the Stark Law has been "extended" (in its entirety) to cover Medicaid referrals and billing, the relevant statutory provision does not do so.[11] Rather, the Stark Law generally prohibits the use of federal funds to pay for services furnished to a Medicaid patient that would be considered improperly referred services under the Medicare program.[12] That is, the Law's prohibitions and sanctions do not attach to Medicaid referrals, but arrangements that would be improper under the Stark Law may prevent the relevant state from receiving federal money for those services.

Example 1.6

A physician who has a financial relationship with a hospital (to which no exception applies) refers a Medicare patient to the hospital for outpatient hospital services. The hospital furnishes the services and, notwithstanding its knowledge of the physician's financial relationship, submits a claim to Medicare, which results in a payment of $1,000 under the applicable ambulatory payment classification code.

Commentary: The physician and hospital have violated the Stark Law's referral and billing prohibitions and may be subject to sanctions.

Example 1.7

This example includes the same facts as Example 1.6 except that the patient is neither entitled to nor eligible for Medicare. Instead, the patient is a Medicaid recipient residing in Pennsylvania.

Commentary: Neither the physician nor the hospital has violated the Stark Law. The federal government, however, could refuse to pay Pennsylvania the federal government's share of the state's payment to the hospital (or, if this share already has been paid, the federal government might seek to recoup it).

E. Evolution of the Stark Law and Stark Regulations

The original Stark Law was enacted in 1989, and CMS issued its first set of implementing regulations (Stark Regulations) in 1991. Since then, the Law has been amended, and CMS has issued additional Regulations on several occasions. The timeline below summarizes major developments relating to the Stark Law and Stark Regulations. The specific provisions of these authorities (e.g., the definition of "immediate family member," the requirements of the exception for employment arrangements, etc.) are discussed, analyzed, and applied throughout this book in the sections to which they relate.

- **1989:** Congress enacts the first Stark Law, commonly referred to as "Stark I."[13] Stark I's referral and billing prohibitions apply only to referrals for clinical laboratory services.

- **1990:** Congress amends Stark I, clarifying certain definitions and reporting requirements.[14]

- **1991:** CMS issues interim final regulations that relate to one component of Stark I (concerning reporting requirements).[15]

- **1992:** CMS issues proposed regulations implementing Stark I (Stark I Proposed Regulations).[16]

- **1993:** Congress extensively revises the Stark Law.[17] Most notably, these amendments—commonly referred to as "Stark II"—expand the referral and billing prohibitions beyond clinical laboratory services to cover 10 additional types of DHS.

- **1994:** Congress amends the Stark Law's reporting requirements and alters some of Stark II's effective date provisions.[18]

- **1995:** Stark II becomes effective on January 1, 1995. CMS issues final regulations implementing Stark I (Stark I Regulations).[19]

- **1998:** CMS issues proposed regulations implementing Stark II (Stark II Proposed Regulations).[20]

- **2001:** CMS issues final regulations implementing a portion of Stark II. These are commonly referred to as the "Stark II, Phase I Regulations."[21]

- **2002:** With a few exceptions, the Stark II, Phase I Regulations become effective on January 4, 2002.

- **2004:** CMS issues interim final regulations implementing the remainder of Stark II. These are commonly referred to as the "Stark II, Phase II Regulations." These regulations become effective on July 26, 2004.[22]

II. Analyzing arrangements under the Stark Law

Determining whether an arrangement violates the Stark Law is a three-step process. The first two steps address whether the arrangement at issue *implicates* the Stark Law. In general, an arrangement implicates the Stark Law if—in the absence of an applicable exception—DHS referrals made pursuant to the arrangement would violate the Law's referral prohibition and the submission of any claims relating to such referrals would violate the Law's billing prohibition. The third step addresses whether the arrangement at issue *violates* the Stark Law. An arrangement violates the Stark Law if the arrangement both implicates the Law *and* does not qualify for protection under any Stark Law exception. A more detailed discussion of each of these steps is set forth below.

A. Step one: Referrals

Step one requires answering the following question: Does the arrangement involve a "physician" making a "referral" "to" an "entity" for the "furnishing" of "DHS" covered by Medicare? If the answer is "no," then the arrangement does not implicate (and, therefore, cannot violate) the Stark Law. If the answer is "yes," then the arrangement *may* implicate the Stark Law, and one must proceed to step two. *Note:* The various components of the step one inquiry are discussed in detail in Chapters 2–4.

B. Step two: Financial relationship

Step two requires answering the following question: Does the physician (or one of his or her immediate family members) have a "financial relationship" with the entity furnishing DHS? As discussed more fully in Chapter 5, the Stark Law and Regulations create four categories of financial relationships.

1. Direct ownership interest

If a physician has an ownership or investment interest in an entity that furnishes DHS, then the physician has a financial relationship with the entity in the form of a "direct ownership/investment interest."

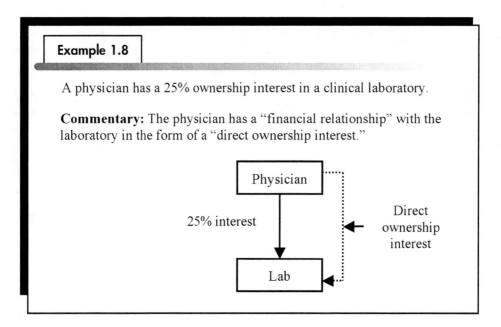

Example 1.8

A physician has a 25% ownership interest in a clinical laboratory.

Commentary: The physician has a "financial relationship" with the laboratory in the form of a "direct ownership interest."

2. Indirect ownership interest

If a physician has an ownership or investment interest in an entity that, in turn, has an ownership or investment interest in an entity that furnishes DHS, then the physician has a financial relationship with the DHS entity in the form of an "indirect ownership/investment interest."

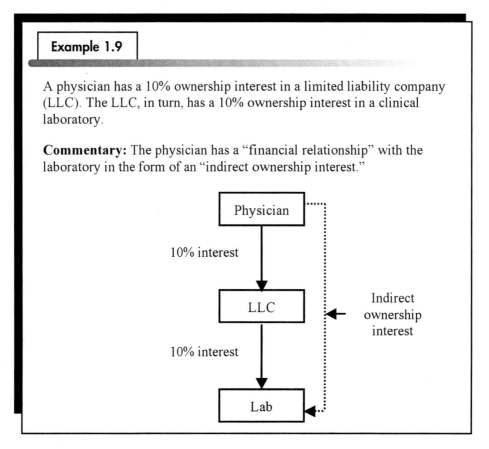

Example 1.9

A physician has a 10% ownership interest in a limited liability company (LLC). The LLC, in turn, has a 10% ownership interest in a clinical laboratory.

Commentary: The physician has a "financial relationship" with the laboratory in the form of an "indirect ownership interest."

3. Direct compensation arrangement

If a physician receives remuneration directly from (or gives remuneration directly to) an entity that furnishes DHS, then the physician has a financial relationship with the entity in the form of a "direct compensation arrangement."

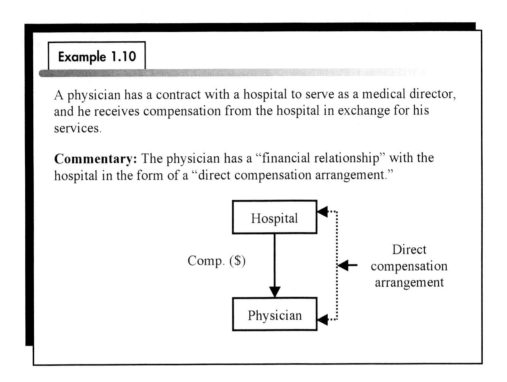

Example 1.10

A physician has a contract with a hospital to serve as a medical director, and he receives compensation from the hospital in exchange for his services.

Commentary: The physician has a "financial relationship" with the hospital in the form of a "direct compensation arrangement."

4. Indirect compensation arrangement

If a physician receives remuneration indirectly (i.e., through one or more intervening individuals or entities) from an entity that furnishes DHS, then the physician *may* have a financial relationship with the DHS entity in the form of an "indirect compensation arrangement." We use the term *may* because of the four types of financial relationships that a physician may have with an entity for purposes of the Stark Law, determining whether a relationship takes the form of an indirect compensation arrangement is by far the most complicated.

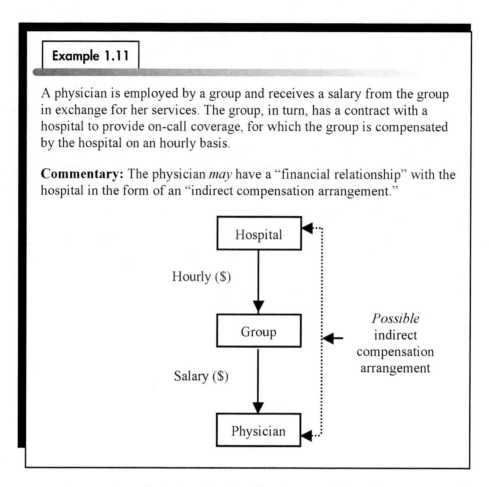

Example 1.11

A physician is employed by a group and receives a salary from the group in exchange for her services. The group, in turn, has a contract with a hospital to provide on-call coverage, for which the group is compensated by the hospital on an hourly basis.

Commentary: The physician *may* have a "financial relationship" with the hospital in the form of an "indirect compensation arrangement."

If the answer to the question of whether the physician (or any of his or her immediate family members) has a financial relationship with the entity furnishing DHS is "no," then the arrangement does not implicate (and, therefore, cannot violate) the Stark Law, and the physician is free to refer Medicare patients to the entity for DHS—and the entity is free to bill for such DHS—without violating the Stark Law. If the answer to this question is "yes," however, then the arrangement *does* implicate the Law, and one must proceed to step three.

C. Step three: Exceptions

Step three requires answering the following question: Does the arrangement qualify for protection under one or more of the Stark Law's exceptions? These exceptions generally fall into four categories:

1. **All-purpose exceptions** (Chapter 6). These exceptions are available for all four types of financial relationships: (1) direct ownership interests, (2) indirect ownership interests, (3) direct compensation arrangements, and (4) indirect compensation arrangements.

2. **Ownership/investment exceptions** (Chapter 7). These exceptions are available for two types of financial relationships: direct ownership interests and indirect ownership interests.

3. **Direct compensation arrangement exceptions** (Chapter 8 and Chapter 10). These exceptions are generally available for one type of financial relationship: direct compensation arrangements.

4. **Indirect compensation arrangements exception** (Chapter 9). This exception is available for only one type of financial relationship: indirect compensation arrangements.

If the arrangement at issue fits within one or more exceptions, then the Stark Law will not be violated. If the arrangement does not fit within at least one exception, then the Stark Law will be violated if a prohibited DHS referral is made.

Notes

1. 42 United States Code (USC) §1395nn(a)(1)(A).

2. 42 USC §1395nn(a)(1)(B).

3. 42 USC §1395nn(g)(2); 42 Code of Federal Regulations (CFR) §411.353(d).

4. 42 USC §1395nn(g)(3); 42 CFR §§1003.102(a)(5), 1003.102(b)(9), 1003.105.

5. 42 CFR §1395nn(g)(4); 42 CFR §1003.102(b)(10).

6. Stark II, Phase II Proposed Regulations (Preamble), 63 *Federal Register* (*FR*) 1659, 1662 (1998).

7. Stark II, Phase II Proposed Regulations (Preamble), 63 *FR* 1659, 1662 (1998).

8. Stark II, Phase II Proposed Regulations (Preamble), 63 *FR* 1659, 1662 (1998).

9. Stark II, Phase II Proposed Regulations (Preamble), 63 *FR* 1659, 1662 (1998).

10. 42 USC §1320a-7b(b).

11. 42 USC §1396b(s).

12. Specifically, the Social Security Act denies any federal financial participation payment to a state under its Medicaid program for services that would have been prohibited by Medicare under the Stark Law if Medicare covers the services to the same extent as the state's Medicaid plan. 42 USC §1396b(s). See also Stark II, Phase II Proposed Regulations (Preamble), 63 *FR* 1659, 1704 (1998).

13. Section 6204 of the Omnibus Budget Reconciliation Act of 1989 (Public Law 101–239, enacted on December 19, 1989).

14. Section 4207(e) of the Omnibus Budget Reconciliation Act of 1990 (Public Law 101–508, enacted on November 5, 1990).

15. 56 *FR* 61374 (1991).

16. 57 *FR* 8588 (1992).

17. Section 13562 of the Omnibus Budget Reconciliation Act of 1993 (Public Law 103–66, enacted on August 10, 1993).

18. Section 152 of the Social Security Act Amendments of 1994 (Public Law 103–432, enacted on October 31, 1994).

19. 60 *FR* 41914 (1995).

20. 63 *FR* 1659 (1998).

21. 66 *FR* 856 (2001).

22. 69 *FR* 16053 (2004).

Chapter 2

DEFINITIONS

Chapter 2

DEFINITIONS

As discussed in Chapter 1, determining whether an arrangement violates the Stark Law is a three-step process. The first step requires determining whether the arrangement involves a "physician" making a "referral" "to" an "entity" for the "furnishing" of "designated health services" (DHS) covered by Medicare. If the answer is "yes," the second step requires determining whether the referring physician or one of his or her "immediate family members" has a "financial relationship" with the entity furnishing DHS. If, the answer is "yes," the third (and final) step requires determining whether the arrangement qualifies for protection under one or more Stark Law exceptions.

Before turning to these steps in Chapters 3–10, we will address several terms that appear throughout the Stark Law and Stark Regulations. In some cases (e.g., "physician" and "immediate family member"), the definitions are fairly straightforward. In other cases (e.g., "fair market value," "set in advance," and "volume or value"), the definitions, interpretations, and historical background are more complicated. In every case, however, understanding these terms is critical to determining whether an arrangement implicates or violates the Stark Law.

I. 'Physician'

The Stark Law only applies to referrals by a "physician." The Stark Law does not define this term. The Stark Regulations, however, provide that, in general, a "physician" is "a doctor of medicine or osteopathy, a doctor of dental surgery or dental medicine, a doctor of podiatric medicine, a doctor of optometry, or a chiropractor."[1] More specifically, the term "physician" has the meaning set forth in 42 United

States Code (USC) §1395x(r) (defining "physician" for purposes of the Medicare program more generally). That is, a "physician" is:

- "a doctor of medicine or osteopathy legally authorized to practice medicine and surgery by the state" in which he or she "performs such function or action,"

- "a doctor of dental surgery or of dental medicine who is legally authorized to practice dentistry by the state in which" he or she "performs such function and who is acting within the scope of his or her license when" he or she "performs such functions,"

- "a doctor of podiatric medicine," but only "with respect to functions" that he or she "is legally authorized to perform as such by the state in which" he or she "performs them,"

- "a doctor of optometry," but only "with respect to the provision of items or services" that he or she "is legally authorized to perform as a doctor of optometry by the state in which" he or she "performs them," or

- "a chiropractor who is licensed as such by the state (or in a state which does not license chiropractors as such, is legally authorized to perform the services of a chiropractor in the jurisdiction in which" he or she "performs such services)," and who meets certain other criteria.[2]

II. 'Immediate family member'

The Stark Law only prohibits referrals by a physician to an entity if the physician or one of his or her "immediate family members" (IFM) has a financial relationship with the DHS entity. The Stark Law does not define the term IFM. The Stark Regulations, however, define this term broadly to include a physician's "husband or wife; birth or adoptive parent, child, or sibling; stepparent, stepchild, stepbrother, or stepsister; father-in-law, mother-in-law, son-in-law, daughter-in-law, brother-in-law, or sister-in-law; grandparent or grandchild; and spouse of a grandparent or grandchild."[3] Cousins, aunts, and uncles are not included in this definition.

Example 2.1

A physician has a granddaughter whose husband is an accountant. A hospital hires the accountant as an independent contractor.

Commentary: One of the physician's IFMs (i.e., the husband of the physician's granddaughter) has a financial relationship with the hospital (in the form of a direct compensation arrangement) and, as a result, the physician may not refer Medicare patients to the hospital for inpatient or outpatient hospital services, unless an exception applies.

Given the breadth of this definition, to ensure compliance with the Stark Law, DHS entities are strongly encouraged to develop policies and procedures designed to identify and track direct and indirect financial relationships both (1) with physicians who refer Medicare patients to the entity and (2) with the IFMs of such physicians. DHS entities have adopted a variety of procedures to accomplish this objective. Some hospitals, for example, require physicians who apply for staff privileges to complete a questionnaire designed to determine whether the physician has an IFM who has a financial relationship with the hospital. Other hospitals use this questionnaire and also require each staff physician to certify that the information contained in the questionnaire is accurate.

III. 'Does not violate the anti-kickback statute'

A. Background of the anti-kickback statute

The federal healthcare program anti-kickback statute is an older cousin of the Stark Law. The anti-kickback statute is a broad criminal statute that prohibits one person from "knowingly and willfully" giving (or offering to give) "remuneration" to another if the payment is intended to "induce" the recipient to (1) "refer" an individual to a person for the furnishing of any item or service for which payment may be made, in whole or in part, under a federal healthcare program (i.e., a "covered item or service"); (2) "purchase," "order," or "lease" any covered item or service; (3) "arrange for" the purchase, order, or lease of any covered item or service; or (4) "recommend" the purchase, order, or lease of any covered item or service.[4] The anti-kickback statute also prohibits the solicitation or receipt of remuneration for any of these purposes.[5]

"Remuneration" includes anything of value.[6] The term "inducement" has been interpreted to cover any act that is intended to influence a person's reason or judgment.[7] Some courts have held that as long as "one purpose" of the payment at issue is to induce referrals, the anti-kickback statute is implicated.[8] Under this one-purpose rule, an arrangement may implicate the anti-kickback statute (1) even if inducing referrals is not the primary purpose of the payment and (2) even where there are other, legitimate reasons for the arrangement. Courts also have recognized, however, that a party may hope or expect that a particular arrangement will result in referrals without necessarily triggering the one-purpose rule.[9]

Because the anti-kickback statute is so broad it covers a variety of common and non-abusive arrangements. Recognizing this overbreadth, Congress and the Office of Inspector General (OIG)—the lead enforcement agency with respect to the anti-kickback statute--have established a large number of statutory exceptions and regulatory safe harbors (collectively, "safe harbors"). An arrangement that fits squarely into a safe harbor is immune from prosecution under the anti-kickback statute. The safe harbors tend to be very narrow, and the OIG takes the position that immunity is afforded only to those arrangements that "precisely meet" all of the conditions of a safe harbor. Material or substantial compliance is insufficient. Moreover, safe harbors do not exist for every type of arrangement that does (or may) implicate the anti-kickback statute.

Importantly, however, the fact that a particular arrangement does not fit within a safe harbor does not mean that the arrangement implicates (or violates) the anti-kickback statute. In other words, although there are certain types of remuneration that necessarily implicate the anti-kickback statute and, therefore, must be safe harbored in order to ensure immunity from prosecution, most remuneration that flows between and among healthcare entities does not fall into this category.

For example, most hospitals have a variety of arrangements pursuant to which they provide remuneration to physicians who are in a position to refer patients to the hospital. When a hospital hires a physician to serve as a medical director, for example, the hospital normally compensates the physician for his or her services. This compensation is, of course, "remuneration." Just as plainly, however, this remuneration does not necessarily implicate the anti-kickback statute. Indeed, such remuneration will implicate the anti-kickback statute only if it is intended not only to compensate the physician for his or her services, but also to induce the physician to refer patients to the hospital. If the compensation is not intended to induce patient referrals, then—whether the arrangement is safe harbored or not—the arrangement will not implicate the anti-kickback statute.

Furthermore, the OIG recognizes that there are many arrangements that do implicate the anti-kickback statute and are not covered by a safe harbor, but that nevertheless do not implicate any of the law's principal policy objectives and, as such, do not pose a material risk of program abuse or warrant the imposition of sanctions. In a nutshell, the statute's principal policy objectives are to (1) prevent the overuse of healthcare items and services and any concomitant increase in federal healthcare program costs, (2) promote patient freedom of choice, and (3) promote market competition.

Because the anti-kickback statute is so broad and the protection offered by its safe harbors so limited, Congress created, and the OIG has implemented, an "advisory opinion" program. Pursuant to this program, individuals and organizations may submit proposed (but not hypothetical) arrangements to the OIG and request, in effect, a "case-specific" safe harbor. As of October 1, 2005, the OIG had issued more than 130 advisory opinions. In the majority of cases covered by these opinions, the requestor's proposed arrangement arguably implicated the anti-kickback statute but could not be safe harbored. More often than not, however, the OIG concluded that the arrangement (1) did not implicate the statute's principal policy objectives, (2) did not pose a material risk of program abuse, and (3) as such, would not be subject to sanctions.

B. Incorporation of the anti-kickback statute into the Stark Law

As the above description suggests, the anti-kickback statute is similar in many respects to the Stark Law—both in terms of its overarching policy objectives and general prohibitions. By the same token, there are material differences between the two authorities, including the following:

- The anti-kickback statute is a criminal statute, whereas the Stark Law provides for civil and administrative sanctions.

- The anti-kickback statute has a "state of mind" (or scienter) requirement (i.e., in order to be convicted, a defendant must have acted "knowingly and willfully"). The Stark Law is largely a "strict liability" statute (i.e., the Stark Law's referral and billing prohibitions may be violated even if the physician, provider, or supplier did not intend to violate them).

- The anti-kickback statute covers all federal healthcare programs (with the exception of the Federal Employee Health Benefits Program); the Stark Law's referral and billing prohibitions apply only to Medicare.

- The anti-kickback statute may be implicated by any type of arrangement involving any type of healthcare or non-healthcare organization; the Stark Law focuses on physicians (and their IFMs) and their financial relationships with certain types of entities (e.g., hospitals) that furnish certain types of services (i.e., DHS).

In light of these differences, the Centers for Medicare and Medicaid Services (CMS) historically took the position that the Stark Law and the anti-kickback statute, "while similar in that they address possible abuses of Medicare, are different in scope and application and, therefore, need to be distinguished."[10] In 1992, for example, CMS noted that although some of the terms used in the Stark Law, such as "fair market value" (FMV) are similar to those contained in the anti-kickback statute, "the two sets of rules are independent of each other and have different ramifications."[11] As a result, CMS cautioned that providers and physicians "need to examine ownership, compensation, and practice arrangements within the scope and objectives of each separate rule."[12] Similarly, in 1995, CMS emphasized that the Stark Law and anti-kickback statute "are intended to serve different purposes,"[13] and because of the distinctions between the two laws, "the provisions of the regulations implementing these laws will not exactly correspond."[14]

The OIG historically has taken the same position. In 1991, for example, the OIG stated that the Stark Law, "although in many respects aimed at the same problems" as the anti-kickback statute, "requires different elements of proof and has different remedies" than the anti-kickback statute.[15] Indeed, the OIG concluded, there is a "clear expression of legislative intent to keep enforcement under the [anti-kickback statute] separate from enforcement under [the Stark Law]" and, as such, it would be "inappropriate to adjust [the anti-kickback statute's] safe harbor provisions to take into account any exception or prohibition under [the Stark Law]."[16]

Notwithstanding these historic sentiments, in 2001, CMS began appending an anti-kickback statute compliance requirement to several of the Stark Law's exceptions. For example, one of the requirements of the FMV compensation exception is that the arrangement at issue "does not violate the anti-kickback statute" (or "any federal or state law or regulation governing billing or claims submission").[17] (We will refer to this as the "anti-kickback statute" requirement.)

The anti-kickback statute requirement also is included in the in-office ancillary services exception,[18] the academic medical center exception,[19] the ambulatory surgery center implants exception,[20] the dialysis-related drugs exception,[21] the preventive screening exception,[22] the eyeglasses and contact lenses exception,[23] the intra-family referrals exception,[24] the physician recruitment exception,[25] the charitable donations exception,[26] the compensation under $300 per year exception,[27] the medical staff incidental benefits exception,[28] the risk-sharing arrangements exception,[29] the indirect compensation arrangements exception,[30] the professional courtesy exception,[31] the physician retention exception,[32] and the community-wide health information systems exception.[33] Thus, the "strict liability" Stark Law has to some degree been infused with an intent-based analysis overlay through CMS rulemaking.

In 2001, CMS responded to commenters' objections to the inclusion of the anti-kickback statute requirement in Stark Law exceptions. "We recognize that [the Stark Law and anti-kickback statute] are different statutes and compliance with one does not depend on compliance with the other in most situations."[34] Nevertheless, CMS continued, pursuant to the Stark Law, the agency may only create exceptions to protect financial relationships if the excepted relationships will "not pose a risk of program or patient abuse."[35] Thus, CMS stated, the Stark Law

> sets a *minimum* standard for acceptable financial relationships; many relationships that may not merit blanket prohibition under [the Stark Law] can, in some circumstances and given necessary intent, violate the anti-kickback statute. If the requirement that a financial relationship comply with the anti-kickback statute were dropped, unscrupulous physicians and entities could potentially protect intentional unlawful and abusive conduct by complying with the minimal requirements of a regulatory exception created [by CMS].[36]

"As a practical matter," CMS concluded, "the statutory language authorizing exceptions leaves us two choices":

(1) we can limit the exceptions to those situations that pose no risk of fraud or abuse—a very stringent standard that few, if any, of the proposed regulatory exceptions meet; or (2) we can protect arrangements that, in most situations, would not pose a risk, and rely on the anti-kickback statute or other fraud and abuse laws to address any residual risk. Given the commenters' expressed preference for flexibility, we have chosen the latter alternative. Moreover, since the parties should be in compliance with the anti-kickback statute, the additional regulatory burden is minimal.[37]

C. Definition of 'does not violate anti-kickback statute'

Before 2004, CMS had not defined the phrase "does not violate the anti-kickback law." In the Stark II, Phase II Regulations, CMS defined the phrase, clarifying that an arrangement "does not violate the anti-kickback law" if any one of three conditions is met. First, an arrangement "does not violate the anti-kickback law" if it meets any of the regulatory safe harbors created by the OIG and codified at 42 Code of Federal Regulations (CFR) §1001.952.[38]

Example 2.2

A physician and hospital enter into a one-year personal services agreement, pursuant to which the physician agrees to serve full-time as the medical director of the hospital's cardiology department for a flat annual fee of $250,000. The arrangement meets all of the requirements of the anti-kickback statute's "personal services and management contracts" safe harbor, 42 CFR §1001.952(d). The hospital and physician seek to protect the arrangement under the Stark Law's FMV exception, which includes a requirement that the arrangement "does not violate the anti-kickback law."

Commentary: Because the arrangement qualifies for protection under an anti-kickback statute safe harbor, the arrangement "does not violate the anti-kickback law" and, as such, may qualify for protection under the Stark Law's FMV exception (provided that the other requirements of the exception are met).

Second, an arrangement "does not violate the anti-kickback law" if the arrangement "has been specifically approved by the OIG in a favorable advisory opinion issued to a party to the particular arrangement (e.g., the DHS entity) with respect to the particular arrangement (and not a similar arrangement)," provided "that the arrangement is conducted in accordance with the facts certified by the requesting party and the opinion is otherwise issued in accordance with" the relevant OIG regulations.[39] The Stark Regulations define a "favorable advisory opinion" as one in which the OIG opines (1) that the arrangement at issue "does not implicate the [anti-kickback statute], does not constitute prohibited remuneration, or fits in a safe harbor," or (2) the parties to the arrangement "will not be subject to any OIG sanctions arising under" the anti-kickback statute in connection "with the party's specific arrangement."[40]

Example 2.3

This includes the same facts as Example 2.2, except (1) the agreement provides for payment on a per-hour basis and, as such, cannot qualify for protection under the anti-kickback statute's personal services and management contracts safe harbor, which requires that the aggregate compensation to be paid under the agreement be set for the advance, 42 CFR §1001.952(d)(5), and (2) the physician and hospital seek and obtain a favorable advisory opinion from the OIG.

Commentary: Because the arrangement has been approved by the OIG in a favorable advisory opinion, the arrangement "does not violate the anti-kickback law" and, as such, may qualify for protection under the Stark Law's FMV exception (provided the other requirements of the exception are met).

Finally, and perhaps most importantly, an arrangement "does not violate the anti-kickback law" if the arrangement "does not violate the anti-kickback law."[41] Although obviously circular, this condition often will be the easiest for physicians and DHS entities to satisfy. As discussed above, the anti-kickback statute's safe harbors are narrow and, as such, many arrangements that implicate the Stark Law—because there is a financial relationship between the referring physician and DHS entity—will not fit into any anti-kickback statute safe harbor. Moreover, although the OIG's anti-kickback statute advisory opinion process is years ahead of CMS's Stark Law advisory opinion process (as discussed in Chapter 12), given the time and expense associated with obtaining an anti-kickback statute advisory opinion from the OIG (at the time of this writing, delays range from 12 to 24 months), this option rarely will be viable for physicians and DHS entities seeking to ensure that their financial relationships meet a Stark Law exception.

Thus, in many (and perhaps most) cases where a physician and DHS entity are trying to ensure that their arrangement fits into a particular Stark Law exception, and that exception includes the anti-kick-back statute requirement, the condition that will have to be satisfied is the condition that the arrangement "does not violate the anti-kickback law." Fortunately, in the majority of cases, this condition can be satisfied. As noted above, with respect to patient referrals, the anti-kickback statute is violated only if one person, acting with the requisite state of mind (i.e., "knowingly and willfully"), offers something of value (i.e., "remuneration") to another and that remuneration is specifically intended to "induce" the recipient to "refer" federal healthcare program patients (or business) to the payer (or another individual or entity). If the remuneration at issue is not intended to serve as such an inducement, then the arrangement will not violate the anti-kickback statute.

Example 2.4

This includes the same facts as Example 2.3, except the physician and hospital do not seek an advisory opinion from the OIG.

Commentary: Unless the arrangement is intended to induce the physician to refer federal healthcare program patients to the hospital, the arrangement should not violate the anti-kickback statute and, as such, may qualify for protection under the Stark Law's FMV exception (provided the other requirements of the exception are met).

Example 2.5

A physician who contracts with a tax-exempt hospital to staff its emergency department makes a $500 charitable contribution to the hospital. The contribution does not qualify for an anti-kickback statute safe harbor, and the parties do not submit the arrangement to the OIG for an advisory opinion. The physician and hospital are seeking to protect the financial relationship created by the physician's donation under the Stark Law's charitable donations exception, which includes the anti-kickback statute requirement.

Commentary: Unless the arrangement is intended to induce the hospital to refer federal healthcare program patients to the physician, it should not violate the anti-kickback statute and, as such, may qualify for protection under the Stark Law's charitable contributions exception (provided that the other requirements of the exception are met).

Example 2.6

As of December 30, 2004, a hospital had not provided anything of value to any of its 100 staff physicians. On December 31, 2004, the hospital holds a holiday dinner party for these physicians. The total cost of the party is $10,000, or $100 per physician. This remuneration from the hospital to each physician does not qualify for an anti-kickback statute safe harbor, and the parties do not submit the arrangement to the OIG for an advisory opinion. The hospital and physicians are seeking to protect the financial relationship created by the holiday party under the Stark Law's compensation under $300 per year exception, which includes the anti-kickback statute requirement.

Commentary: Unless the arrangement was intended to induce the physicians to refer federal healthcare program patients (or business) to the hospital, it should not violate the anti-kickback statute and, as such, may qualify for protection under the compensation under $300 per year exception (provided that the other requirements of the exception are met).

IV. 'Fair market value,' 'set in advance,' 'volume or value,' and 'other business generated' standards

As discussed in Chapter I, two closely related presumptions underlie the Stark Law. The first presumption is that where a physician has a financial relationship with a provider of DHS, the physician has a financial incentive to order healthcare items or services from that provider. The second presumption is that where a physician has a financial incentive to order healthcare items or services from a particular provider, the physician will, in fact, do so, even if the items and services at issue are not medically necessary.

These two presumptions manifest themselves in the Stark Law's basic (and sweeping) referral prohibition: A physician may not refer a Medicare patient to a DHS entity with which the physician (or an immediate family member) has a financial relationship unless an exception applies, even if there are no indications that the arrangement at issue is intended to, or will, induce the physician to refer Medicare patients to the entity for DHS that are not medically necessary.

These two presumptions are rebuttable, of course. How? By fitting the financial relationship or DHS at issue into a Stark Law exception. These exceptions, in turn, are designed to ensure, to the greatest extent possible, that the financial relationship at issue will not induce the physician to refer patients to the DHS provider (or reward the physician for doing so). In the case of financial relationships that take the form of compensation arrangements, the exceptions at issue accomplish this goal through a variety of conditions and limitations. Four of the most common conditions—set forth in the so-called "FMV," "set in advance," "volume or value," and "other business generated" standards—are discussed below.

A. 'Fair market value' standard

One of the most common conditions included in Stark Law compensation arrangement exceptions is that the compensation that flows between the referring physician and the DHS entity be consistent with "fair market value." For example, this standard is included in the FMV compensation exception,[42] the employment exception,[43] the personal services exception,[44] the space rental exception,[45] the equipment rental exception,[46] the payments by a physician exception,[47] the isolated transactions exception,[48] and the group practice arrangements with hospitals exception.[49] In addition, one all-purpose exception (the academic medical center exception[50]), the indirect compensation arrangements exception,[51] and three "special compensation rules" (discussed below) incorporate the FMV standard.

The Stark Law defines "fair market value" as

> the value in arms length transactions, consistent with the general market value, and, with respect to rentals or leases, the value of rental property for general commercial purposes (not taking into account its intended use) and, in the case of a lease of space, not adjusted to reflect the additional value the prospective lessee or lessor would attribute to the proximity or convenience to the lessor where the lessor is a potential source of patient referrals to the lessee."[52]

The Stark Regulations expand upon this definition in several respects. Although not a model of clarity, the Stark Regulations generally divide the definition of FMV into three subparts, discussing the definition as it applies to (1) payments for "assets," (2) payments for "services," and (3) "rental" payments.

1. Assets

With respect to "assets," the Stark Regulations provide that the FMV of an asset is the value of the asset "in arm's-length transactions, consistent with the general market value."[53] The Regulations define the "general market value" of an asset, in turn, as "the price that [the] asset would bring" (on the date it is acquired) "as the result of *bona fide* bargaining between well-informed buyers and sellers who are not otherwise in a position to generate business" for each other.[54] The Regulations further provide that "usually," the "fair market price" of an asset "is the price at which *bona fide* sales have been consummated for assets of like type, quality, and quantity in a particular market at the time of acquisition," where the price "has not been determined in any manner that takes into account the volume or value of anticipated or actual referrals."[55]

Example 2.7

Between January and June 2004, a vendor of power mattresses in the Washington, DC metropolitan area sold 1,000 mattresses to 10 different nursing homes and other non-hospital providers, for an average price of $500 each. The vendor is owned in part by a physician who is a member of the medical staff at a hospital in Washington. The hospital and vendor enter into an agreement in July 2004, pursuant to which the hospital agrees to purchase 100 mattresses from the vendor for $1,000 each.

Commentary: It does not appear that the hospital is paying FMV for the mattresses because the amount paid by the hospital ($1,000) is twice that at which sales have been consummated for assets of like type, quality, and quantity in a particular market (i.e., the Washington, DC metropolitan area) at the time of acquisition (i.e., 2004).

---

2. Services

With respect to "services," the Stark Regulations provide that the "fair market value" of a service means the value of the service "in arm's-length transactions, consistent with the general market value."[56] The Regulations define the "general market value" of a service, in turn, as the "compensation that would be included in a service agreement as the result of *bona fide* bargaining between well-informed parties to the agreement who are not otherwise in a position to generate business for the other party . . . at the time of the service agreement."[57] The Regulations further provide that "usually," the "fair market price" of a service is the "compensation that has been included in *bona fide* service agreements with comparable terms at the time of the agreement," where the "compensation has not been determined in any manner that takes into account the volume or value of anticipated or actual referrals."[58]

Example 2.8

In January 2004, there were 10 hospitals (Hospitals 1–10) in Smith County. Each hospital had 250 beds, an organ transplant center, a physician serving on a part-time basis (20 hours per week) as the medical director of the hospital's transplant department, and each hospital paid its medical director between $200,000 and $225,000 per year. In February 2004, the medical director for Hospital 10 retired, prompting Hospital 10 to begin negotiating with a local physician to fill the position under the same terms as the prior medical director—except with an annual compensation of $400,000.

Commentary: It does not appear that Hospital 10 would be paying FMV for the medical director services because the amount at issue ($400,000) is nearly twice as much as that included in *bona fide* service agreements with comparable terms at the time of the agreement.

With respect to hourly payments made to physicians for services, the Regulations create two "safe harbors" based on the methodology used to determine the hourly payment. First, the Regulations provide that "an hourly payment for a physician's personal services" (i.e., "services performed by the physician personally and not by employees, contractors, or others") "shall be considered to be fair market value if the "hourly rate is less than or equal to the average hourly rate for emergency room physician services in the relevant physician market, provided there are at least three hospitals providing emergency room (ER) services in the market."[59]

Example 2.9

There are three hospitals (Hospitals 1–3) in Jones County. On average, the three hospitals pay $100 per hour for ER physician services. Hospital 1 hires a physician to serve as the medical director of its cancer center.

Commentary: Provided Hospital 1 pays the physician $100 or less per hour, this compensation will be consistent with FMV for Stark Law purposes.

Note that, as a practical matter, the requirements of this FMV safe harbor—tied to the average hourly rate of three hospital ERs in a relevant physician market—may be difficult to meet because competing hospitals may not share this information. Moreover, in non-urban areas, there may not be three hospitals in the relevant physician market.

Second, the Stark Regulations provide that an hourly payment for a physician's personal services "shall be considered to be FMV" if the "hourly rate is determined by averaging the 50th percentile national compensation level for physicians with the same physician specialty (or, if the specialty is not identified in the survey, for general practice) in at least four of [six designated] surveys and dividing by 2,000 hours."[60]

Example 2.10

The 50th percentile national compensation levels for radiation oncologists in the six surveys identified in the Stark Regulations are $200,000, $200,000, $200,000, $210,000, $210,000, and $210,000, respectively. A hospital hires a radiation oncologist as an independent contractor on an hourly basis to furnish clinical services in the hospital's cancer department.

Commentary: Provided the hospital pays the physician no more than $103.75 per hour—that is, $207,500 (the average of $200,000 + $210,000 + $210,000 + $210,000) divided by 2,000—the compensation will be consistent with FMV for Stark Law purposes.

Even if the hourly amount that a DHS entity pays a physician for his or her personal services does not fit into either of the FMV safe harbors described above, this does not mean that the amount cannot meet the Stark Law's FMV standard. As CMS noted in the preamble to the 2004 Stark II, Phase II Regulations:

> compliance with these safe harbor methodologies is entirely voluntary; DHS entities may continue to establish fair market value through other methods. DHS entities that choose to use either of the two "safe harbor" methodologies will be assured that their compensation rates will be deemed fair market value for purposes of [the Stark Law] ... DHS entities

using other methodologies to determine fair market value will continue to bear the risk that their rates may not be considered fair market value.[61]

3. Rentals

With respect to "rentals" the Stark Regulations provide that the FMV of space or equipment generally means the value of the "rental property for general commercial purposes (not taking into account its intended use)."[62] The Regulations further provide that, in the case of space, the rental value "may not be adjusted to reflect the additional value the prospective lessee or lessor would attribute to the proximity or convenience to the lessor when the lessor is a potential source of patient referrals to the lessee."[63]

In 2001, CMS addressed complaints that this definition was "problematic for appraising a medical office building because it requires the appraiser to compare the property to the broad category of properties that are 'used for general commercial purposes.'"[64] According to commenters, the latter category could include "properties that are highly dissimilar in character and value."[65] For example, "the appraisal for medical office property could include retail or industrial rates. Such an approach conflicts with the fundamental principle that appraisals should be based on comparing properties with similar attributes."[66] In response, CMS offered the following clarification:

> We believe that a rental property meets the requirement that a payment reflect the
> "value of property for general commercial purposes, not taking into account its intended
> use" when the payment takes into account any costs that were incurred by the lessor in
> developing or upgrading the property or maintaining the property or its improvements,
> regardless of why the improvements were added. That is, the rental payment can reflect
> the value of any similar commercial property with improvements or amenities of a similar
> value, regardless of why the property was improved.[67]

CMS modified the Stark Regulations accordingly, making it clear that, for purposes of the definition of FMV, a "rental payment does not take into account intended use if it takes into account costs incurred by the lessor in developing or upgrading the property or maintaining the property or its improvements."[68] CMS also clarified in 2001 that the FMV definition "allows rental payments that reflect the fair market value of the area in which the property is located, even if a lease is for medical property in a 'medical community.'"[69] To qualify, however, such payments

> should not reflect any *additional* value, such as an amount that is above that paid by other medical practitioners in the same building or in the same or in a similar location, just because the lessor is a potential source of referrals to the lessee. That is, the rental payments should be roughly equivalent to those charged to similarly situated parties in arrangements in which referrals are not an issue.[70]

According to CMS, "rental payments would specifically take into account the intended use of the property if the lessee paid inflated amounts solely to enhance his or her medical practice."[71]

> For example, rental payments by a physical therapist would not be fair market value . . . if the physical therapist agreed to pay an inflated rate that was not justified by improvements or other amenities and was higher than the rate paid by other, similarly situated medical practitioners in the same building just because the building was occupied by several orthopedic practices.[72]

Finally, CMS addressed in 2001 the one-directional aspect of the FMV definition as it applies to space rentals. As noted above, the Stark Regulations (like the Stark Law) provide that, in the case of space, the rental value may not be adjusted to reflect the additional value the prospective lessee or lessor would attribute to the proximity or convenience to the lessor "when the *lessor* is a potential source of patient referrals to the *lessee*." CMS noted that the Stark Law's definition of "referral" (Chapter 4) "focuses only on actions and requests for services that are initiated by physicians; it does not include any requests for services initiated by entities or other providers or suppliers, nor does the referral prohibition itself apply to anything but physician referrals."[73] Thus, CMS concluded,

> we believe that it is fair to interpret the limitation in the fair market value definition as confined to situations in which a physician is the lessor and a potential source of referrals to an entity lessee. That limitation does not appear to us to apply when an entity, such as a hospital, is the lessor that rents space to physicians, even if the hospital is in a position to

refer to the physicians. As a result, we believe a hospital should factor in the value of proximity when charging rent to lessee physicians.[74]

Example 2.11

A physician specializing in internal medicine owns a medical office building that is across the street from a hospital. The hospital is seeking to lease space in the building.

Commentary: Because the lessor (i.e., the physician) is a potential source of patient "referrals" to the lessee (i.e., the hospital), the rent charged by the physician cannot be adjusted (e.g., increased) to reflect the additional value that might be attributed by the parties to the hospital's proximity to the physician.

Example 2.12

A hospital owns a medical office building that is across the street from the hospital. A physician specializing in internal medicine is seeking to lease space in the building.

Commentary: Because the lessor (i.e., the hospital) is not a potential source of patient "referrals" to the lessee (i.e., the physician), the rent charged by the hospital not only can be adjusted (e.g., increased) to reflect the additional value that might be attributed by the parties to the physician's proximity to the hospital, the rent *should* be adjusted to reflect any such additional value.

B. 'Set in advance' standard

Another common condition included in the Stark Law's exceptions for compensation arrangements is that the compensation flowing between the referring physician and the DHS entity be "set in advance." This standard is included in the FMV exception,[75] the personal services exception[76] the space rental exception,[77] and the equipment rental exception.[78] In addition, one all-purpose exception—the academic medical center exception[79]—includes the "set in advance" standard.

In most cases, determining whether the compensation at issue is "set in advance" is relatively straightforward.

Example 2.13

A hospital and physician enter into a one-year personal services agreement pursuant to which the physician agrees to serve as the medical director of the hospital's cardiology department on a part-time basis (i.e., 20 hours per week), in exchange for which the hospital agrees to pay the physician $100,000.

Commentary: The compensation to be paid by the hospital to the physician is "set in advance."

In other cases, whether compensation is "set in advance" may be less clear.

Example 2.14

This includes the same facts as Example 2.13, except that instead of paying the physician $100,000, the hospital will pay the physician $100 per hour. Thus, if the physician works 900 hours during the year, she will be paid $90,000; if she works 1,000 hours, she will be paid $100,000; and if she works 1,100 hours, she will be paid $110,000.

Commentary: Although the hourly rate the hospital will pay the physician is "set in advance," is the "compensation" under the arrangement—which will vary, at least in the aggregate, depending on how many hours the physician actually works—"set in advance"?

CMS has addressed the question in Example 2.14 (and several related questions) in the form of a "special rule on compensation." This rule provides that compensation will be considered set in advance if the "aggregate compensation" or a "time-based or per unit of service based (whether per use or per service) amount," is "set in an agreement between the parties before the furnishing of the items or services for which the compensation is to be paid."[80]

Example 2.15

This example includes the same facts as Example 2.14.

Commentary: The compensation is "set in advance" because the $100 per hour rate is a "time-based" amount that has been "set in an agreement between the parties" before the furnishing of the services for which the compensation is to be paid.

Example 2.16

A hospital enters into a one-year personal services agreement with a physician, pursuant to which the physician agrees to provide non-invasive vascular ultrasound studies for hospital inpatients for $150 per study.

Commentary: The compensation is "set in advance" because the $150 fee is a "per unit of service based" amount that has been "set in an agreement between the parties" before the furnishing of the services for which the compensation is to be paid.

Example 2.17

A physician owns a magnetic resonance imaging (MRI) machine. The physician enters into a one-year rental agreement with a hospital, pursuant to which the physician agrees to lease the MRI machine to the hospital on a per-use (or "per click") basis. More specifically, the hospital will be charged $250 each time it uses the MRI machine on behalf of a hospital patient.

Commentary: The compensation is "set in advance" because the $250 rental charge is a "per unit of service based" amount that has been "set in an agreement between the parties" before the furnishing of the services for which the compensation is to be paid.

The set in advance special rule on compensation also provides that compensation will be considered set in advance if a "specific formula for calculating the compensation" is "set in an agreement between the parties before the furnishing of the items or services for which the compensation is to be paid."[81] In order to qualify for protection, however, this "formula" (1) "must be set forth in sufficient detail so that it can be objectively verified" and (2) "may not be changed or modified during the course of the agreement in any manner that reflects the volume or value of referrals or other business generated by the referring physician."[82]

This "specific formula" provision is of recent vintage. The 1998 Proposed Stark II Regulations did not include such a provision. This caused commenters to question whether payments to a physician based on a percentage of gross revenues, collections, or expenses would satisfy the set in advance standard.[83] CMS responded to these comments in the 2001 Stark II, Phase I Regulations, taking the position that such "arrangements do not meet the requirement that compensation be fixed"—presumably meaning "set"—"in advance."[84]

Later that same year, however, CMS issued an interim final rule indicating that it was reconsidering its position and delaying the effective date of the "set in advance" standard as it related to percentage compensation arrangements.[85] In 2004, CMS announced that, upon reconsideration, percentage-based payments could meet the "set in advance" requirement, reasoning as follows:

> Many commenters urged us to abandon our position that percentage compensation arrangements based on fluctuating or indeterminate measures . . . are not "set in advance" . . . This was of particular concern to academic medical centers and hospitals, which argued that percentage compensation is commonplace in their physician compensation arrangements. Upon further consideration, we are persuaded that our original position was overly restrictive . . . [W]e are modifying the "set in advance" definition . . . to clarify that the formula for calculating percentage compensation must be established with specificity prospectively, must be objectively verifiable, and may not be changed over the course of the agreement between the parties based on the volume or value of referrals or other business generated by the referring physician.[86]

> **Example 2.18**
>
> A hospital that has a cancer center employs a radiation oncologist pursuant to a written agreement to furnish professional services and serve as the medical director of the center. The hospital agrees to pay the oncologist $200,000 per year, plus a bonus equal to 5% of the amount that the hospital collects from Medicare for professional services that are ordered and personally furnished by the oncologist.
>
> **Commentary:** A specific formula for calculating the compensation (i.e., 5% of collections for professional services that are ordered and personally furnished by the oncologist) is set forth in an agreement between the parties before the furnishing of the services for which the compensation is to be paid and the formula is set forth in sufficient detail so it can be objectively verified. Thus, assuming that this formula is not modified during the course of the agreement in any manner that reflects the volume or value of referrals or other business generated by the oncologist, the bonus should meet the "set in advance" standard.

C. 'Volume or value' standard

In addition to including a FMV and/or set in advance standard, many Stark Law exceptions include what is commonly referred to as the "volume or value" standard. The most common formulation of this standard is that the compensation at issue cannot be determined in a manner that "takes into account" the "volume or value" of any "referrals." For example, the space rental exception provides that rental charges cannot be determined in a manner that "takes into account" the "volume or value" of any "referrals."[87] Similarly, the personal services exception provides that the compensation at issue cannot be determined in a manner that "takes into account" the "volume or value" of any "referrals."[88] There are several slight variations on this theme. For example:

- the professional courtesy exception provides that the courtesy at issue must be offered to all physicians on the entity's medical staff "without regard" to the volume or value of referrals,[89]

- the physician retention exception provides that the amount of the compensation at issue cannot be "altered" during the term of the arrangement in any manner that takes into account the volume or value of referrals,[90]

- the community-wide health information systems exception provides that the information technology at issue cannot be "provided" to the physician in any manner that takes into account the volume or value of referrals,[91]

- the remuneration unrelated to DHS exception provides that remuneration "relates" to the furnishing of DHS if it takes into account the volume or value of referrals,[92] and

- the charitable donations exception provides that the donation at issue cannot be "solicited" or "made" in any manner that takes into account the volume or value of referralsl.[93]

In addition to these variations, in some cases, the phrase "directly or indirectly" finds its way into the exception. For example, the employment exception generally provides that the amount paid by the employer cannot be determined in a manner that "takes into account (directly or indirectly)" the volume or value of referrals.[94]

Several important Stark Law definitions also include a "volume or value" requirement. For example, the definition of "indirect compensation arrangement," which is discussed in Chapter 5, provides that, in order for an arrangement to constitute an "indirect compensation arrangement," the relevant individual or entity must receive "aggregate compensation" that "varies with" or "otherwise reflects" the "volume or value" of "referrals."[95] In addition, as discussed above, the definition of FMV provides that, in most cases, FMV is the price at which sales have been consummated for assets of like type, quality, and quantity in a particular market at the time of acquisition, or the compensation that has been included in *bona fide* service agreements with comparable terms at the time of the agreement, where the price or compensation has not been determined in any manner that "takes into account" the "volume or value" of "anticipated or actual referrals."

Finally, all four "special rules on compensation" include a "volume or value" reference of some kind. As discussed above, the "set in advance" special rule provides that compensation will be considered "set in advance" if there is a specific "formula" for calculating the compensation and this formula is not changed or modified during the course of the agreement in any manner that "reflects" the "volume or value" of "referrals." The three other special rules on compensation (i.e., the "other business generated," "volume or value," and "physician compensation" special rules, which are discussed below, include similar provisions.

1. Basic standard

In most cases, the issue is whether the compensation in question does or does not "take into account" the "volume or value" of "referrals." As an initial matter, CMS has made it clear that the term "referrals" means referrals to an entity for the furnishing of DHS that are covered by Medicare.[96] (We will refer to these as "DHS referrals.") As a result, where compensation is based on the volume or value of referrals (1) that do not involve Medicare beneficiaries or (2) that involve Medicare beneficiaries but do not involve DHS, the volume or value standard will not be implicated.

Example 2.19

This includes the same facts as Example 2.13 (i.e., a hospital and physician enter into a one-year personal services agreement pursuant to which the physician agrees to serve as the medical director of the hospital's cardiology department on a part-time basis), except in addition to paying the physician a flat fee of $100,000, the hospital also agrees to pay the physician a $100 bonus for each non-Medicare patient the physician admits to the hospital.

Commentary: The $100 bonus does not take into account the "volume or value" of "referrals" for Stark Law purposes, because it does not involve Medicare beneficiaries.

Example 2.20

This includes the same facts as Example 2.19, except instead of agreeing to pay the physician $100 for each non-Medicare patient who the physician refers to the hospital for inpatient hospital services, the hospital agrees to pay the physician a $100 bonus for each Medicare patient who the physician refers to a hospice that is owned by the hospital.

Commentary: The $100 bonus does not take into account the "volume or value" of "referrals" for Stark Law purposes because hospice services are not DHS.

The "volume or value" standard also is subject to the limitations that CMS has placed on the term "referral." For example, as discussed in Chapter 4, a physician generally will be deemed to have made a "referral" any time he or she orders, requests, or establishes a plan of care that includes or involves DHS covered by Medicare. There are exceptions to this rule, however. For example, the Stark Regulations provide that "referrals" do not include any DHS "personally performed or provided by the referring physician."[97] This exception (as well as the other exceptions discussed in Chapter 4) apply to the "volume or value" standard.

Example 2.21

A hospital that has a cancer center employs a radiation oncologist to serve as the center's medical director. The hospital agrees to pay the oncologist $200,000 per year, plus a bonus equal to 10% of the amount that the hospital collects from Medicare for professional services that are ordered and personally furnished by the oncologist.

Commentary: Although the services at issue are Medicare-covered DHS, because "referrals" do not include personally furnished services, the bonus does not take into account the "volume or value" of "referrals" for Stark Law purposes.

Assuming that there is a nexus between the compensation at issue and DHS referrals—as defined and limited by CMS—the next question is this: Under what circumstances will compensation be deemed to "take into account" the "volume or value" of such referrals? In most cases, this question is easily answered.

Example 2.22

A clinical laboratory offers a physician $10 for each Medicare patient the physician refers to the laboratory for the furnishing of clinical laboratory services.

Commentary: The compensation "takes into account" the "volume" of DHS referrals.

> **Example 2.23**
>
> A durable medical equipment (DME) supplier hires a physician as a consultant. The supplier pays the physician $50 for each Medicare patient the physician refers to the supplier for DME.
>
> **Commentary:** The compensation "takes into account" the "volume" of DHS referrals.

Under some circumstances, explored below, it is less clear whether the compensation at issue "takes into account" the "volume or value" of DHS referrals.

2. Required referrals

One issue that has arisen is whether compensation that is paid by an employer to an employee, for example, takes into account the "volume or value" of DHS referrals if a condition of the employment is that the employee refer all patients (requiring services that may be furnished by the employer) to the employer.

> **Example 2.24**
>
> A hospital employs a primary care physician and pays him a flat annual salary of $150,000, which is consistent with FMV. As a condition of employment, the physician is required to refer all of his patients that need inpatient or outpatient hospital services to the hospital, his employer.
>
> **Commentary:** Although the compensation at issue is FMV and set in advance, does it—by virtue of the referral requirement—"take into account" the "volume or value" of DHS referrals?

CMS's position on this issue has changed over the years. In the preamble to the 1998 Stark II Proposed Regulations, CMS stated that if an entity's payments to a physician—regardless of how calculated—were "predicated, either expressly or otherwise, on the physician making referrals to a particular provider," the arrangement would violate the "volume or value" standard.[98] For example, a hospital might include as a condition of a physician's employment the requirement that the physician only refer within the hospital's own network of ancillary services providers . . . We believe that in these situations, a physician's compensation reflects the volume or value of his or her referrals in the sense that the physician will receive no future compensation if he or she fails to refer as required.[99]

In response to a variety of comments—including complaints that CMS's proposed interpretation was inconsistent with the common law duty of loyalty owed by an employee to his or her employer[100]—CMS reversed its position in the 2001 Stark II, Phase I Regulations, stating that it would not "consider the volume or value standard implicated by otherwise acceptable compensation arrangements for physician services solely because the arrangement requires the physician to refer to a particular provider as a condition of payment."[101]

In the 2004 Stark II, Phase II Regulations, however, CMS—this time reacting to complaints that its interpretation was "overly broad and could permit required referrals beyond those that are reasonable and appropriate"[102]—revisited and tightened its interpretation of the volume or value standard. Specifically, under the Stark II, Phase II Regulations, a physician's compensation from "a *bona fide* employer or under a managed care or other contract" may be "conditioned on the physician's referrals to a particular provider, practitioner, or supplier," provided eight requirements—the "conditioned compensation requirements" for purposes of this chapter—are met.[103] These requirements are as follows:

1. The compensation at issue must be "set in advance for the term of the agreement."

2. The compensation must be "consistent with fair market value for services performed (that is, the payment does not take into account the volume or value of anticipated or required referrals)."

3. The compensation must "otherwise comply with an applicable exception."

4. The "requirement to make referrals to a particular provider, practitioner, or supplier" must be "set forth in a written agreement signed by the parties."

5. The "requirement to make referrals to a particular provider, practitioner, or supplier" must not apply if (1) "the patient expresses a preference for a different provider, practitioner, or supplier," (2) "the patient's insurer determines the provider, practitioner, or supplier," or (3) "the referral is not in the patient's best medical interests in the physician's judgment."

6. The required referrals must "relate solely to the physician's services covered by the scope of the employment or the contract." (Thus, for example, an entity that employs a physician on a part-time basis to provide services to the entity cannot condition the employment on "referrals of the physician's private practice business" to the entity.[104])

7. The referral requirement must be "reasonably necessary to effectuate the legitimate business purposes of the compensation relationship."

8. In "no event may the physician be required to make referrals that relate to services that are not provided by the physician under the scope of his or her employment or contract."

In most respects, these requirements are straightforward and will allow providers and suppliers to condition a physician's compensation on his or her referrals without running afoul of the "volume or value" standard. In a few cases, however, the conditioned compensation requirements make little sense. For example, it is circular to take the position that conditioning referrals on compensation will not violate the "volume or value" standard provided the compensation "does not take into account the volume or value of anticipated or required referrals." Nor is it clear why compliance with a Stark Law exception is a requirement for complying with the "volume or value" standard. That is, if a Stark Law exception already has a "volume or value" standard, then this requirement is redundant and unnecessary, and if the Stark Law exception does not have a "volume of value" standard, then CMS's interpretation of that standard is (or at least should be) irrelevant to meeting the exception's requirements.

3. Expected or assumed referrals

There are many types of arrangements that do not "condition" compensation to a physician on his or her referrals to a particular provider, practitioner, or supplier, but these arrangements do assume that such referrals will occur in the ordinary course of business or are otherwise predicated on such referrals.

Example 2.25

A hospital hires a physician as an independent contractor to provide full-time on-call coverage in the hospital's ER. The arrangement calls for the hospital to pay the physician a flat, annual amount of $150,000, which is consistent with FMV. Although the arrangement is not "conditioned" on the physician making DHS referrals to the hospital, both the hospital and physician expect and assume that, in the ordinary course of furnishing on-call coverage services, the physician will have occasion to refer patients (including Medicare patients) to the hospital for hospital services.

Commentary: Does the compensation from the hospital to the physician take into account the "volume or value" of DHS referrals?

Example 2.26

A hospital hires a radiation oncologist as an independent contractor to staff the hospital's radiation oncology department. The arrangement calls for the hospital to pay the oncologist a flat, annual fee of $200,000, which is consistent with FMV. Although the arrangement is not "conditioned" on the oncologist making DHS referrals to the hospital, both the hospital and oncologist expect and assume that, in the ordinary course of furnishing radiation oncology services, the physician will have occasion to refer patients (including Medicare patients) to the hospital for inpatient and outpatient hospital services.

Commentary: Does the compensation from the hospital to the oncologist take into account the "volume or value" of DHS referrals?

> ### Example 2.27
>
> A hospital and physician enter into a one-year personal services agreement, pursuant to which the physician agrees to serve as the medical director of the hospital's cardiology department on a part-time basis (i.e., 20 hours per week), in exchange for which the hospital agrees to pay the physician $100,000. The agreement provides that the physician will principally be responsible for providing administrative and management services, but will be available to furnish clinical services to hospital patients on an as-needed basis. Although the arrangement is not "conditioned" on the physician making DHS referrals to the hospital, both the hospital and the physician expect and assume that, in the ordinary course of furnishing medical director services, the physician will have occasion to furnish some clinical services and, in doing so, to refer some patients (including Medicare patients) to the hospital for inpatient and outpatient hospital services.
>
> **Commentary:** Does the compensation from the hospital to the physician take into account the "volume or value" of DHS referrals?

CMS has not directly addressed this issue of "expected" referrals. On the one hand, it could be argued that where a DHS entity is paying a physician a flat amount that will not go up or down based on either the "volume" or "value" of his or her DHS referrals (i.e., whether the physician makes 15 or 100 DHS referrals, his or her compensation will be the same), the "volume or value" standard is not implicated.

On the other hand, if the test were that simple and straightforward, it would apply with equal force to the type of conditioned compensation arrangements discussed above. For example, where a hospital employs a physician, pays him a flat annual salary, and "conditions" the physician's employment on a requirement that he make referrals to a particular provider, practitioner, or supplier, this arrangement implicates the "volume or value" requirement, even though the hospital will be paying the physician a flat amount that will not go up or down based on either the "volume" or "value" of his or her DHS referrals.

Put somewhat differently, CMS has taken the position that the "volume or value" standard may be implicated even where the aggregate compensation to be paid to the physician over the term of the agreement is set in advance and will not go up or down based on the specific "volume" or "value" of DHS referrals by the physician to the DHS entity. Having taken this position—at least with respect to arrangements that are "conditioned" on the physician making DHS referrals to the DHS entity—CMS should clarify how far its interpretation of the "volume or value" standard extends.

Until CMS provides such a clarification, providers, suppliers, and practitioners ought to be able to rely on the plain wording of the "volume or value" standard. In other words, except in cases where a physician's compensation is specifically "conditioned" on the physician's "referrals to a particular provider, practitioner, or supplier"—in which case, CMS has indicated that the standard will be violated unless the parties meet the eight requirements discussed above—providers, suppliers, and practitioners ought to be able to assume that if the aggregate compensation to be paid to the physician over the term of the arrangement is set in advance and FMV, then the compensation does not "take into account" the "volume or value" of DHS "referrals" simply because the parties assume that the physicians will make referrals to the DHS entity. The authors believe this reading is consistent with the language of the Stark Law and the practical realities of non-abusive physician arrangements.

4. Per unit compensation

Ironically, payments that fluctuate based on the volume or value of DHS referrals may be easier to fit within the "volume or value" standard than payments—like those described above—that do not fluctuate in this manner. This has not always been the case, however. In the preamble to the 1998 Proposed Stark II Regulations, CMS stated that compensation in the form of time-based or unit of service-based payments to a physician would not comply with the "volume or value" standard if the DHS at issue were furnished to patients who were referred by the physician.[105]

Example 2.28

A physician owns an MRI machine. Effective January 1, 1999, the physician entered into a one-year equipment rental agreement with a hospital. Pursuant to the agreement, the physician charged the hospital $250 each time it used the MRI machine on behalf of a hospital inpatient or outpatient.

Commentary: In 1999, CMS would have taken the position that the compensation from the hospital to the physician took into account the "volume or value" of the physician's DHS referrals to the hospital. Indeed, there was a one-to-one correlation: Each time the physician referred a Medicare patient to the hospital for an MRI scan, the hospital paid the physician $250.

In response to complaints that CMS's position was contrary to the Stark Law's legislative history, CMS reversed its position in the 2001 Stark II, Phase I Regulations. More specifically, CMS created a "volume or value" special rule on compensation, which provides as follows:

> Unit-based compensation (including time-based or per unit of service-based compensation) will be deemed not to take into account "the volume or value of referrals" if the compensation is fair market value for services or items actually provided and does not vary during the course of the compensation agreement in any manner that takes into account referrals of DHS.[106]

Example 2.29

This includes the same facts as Example 2.28.

Commentary: Pursuant to the Stark II, Phase I Regulations, as long as the $250 per scan payments are consistent with FMV, these payments will not "take into account" the "volume or value" of the physician's DHS referrals to the hospital for Stark Law purposes.

One commenter asked CMS whether a unit-based payment methodology would pass muster if the compensation methodology provided for the payment amount to decrease as volume increased.[107] In response, CMS stated that it would have to review such payment methodologies on a case-by-case basis.[108] CMS explained that if the decrease in payment amounts was a function of a decline in costs (e.g., amortization of costs associated with leased equipment), as opposed to an increase in volume, then the decreased payment methodology might accurately reflect FMV and, as such, not implicate the volume or value standard.[109] It is unclear whether CMS would offer the same flexibility with respect to volume or market-share discounts and rebates. For example, it is uncertain whether an arrangement that provides for a $1 discount on every $20 widget that the purchaser buys in excess of 1,000 widgets would trigger the "volume or value" standard because the unit price has the potential to vary (from $20 to $19) during the course of the arrangement, and this variance is volume driven.

5. 'Directly' v. 'indirectly'

As noted above, a handful of Stark Law exceptions include the term "directly or indirectly" (i.e., they provide that the compensation at issue must not be determined in a manner that takes into account "directly or indirectly" the volume or value of referrals). The employment exception, for example, provides that the amount paid by the employer cannot be determined in a manner that "takes into account (directly or indirectly)" the volume or value of referrals. In the preamble to the 1998 Stark II Proposed Regulations, CMS indicated that it "regards these provisions as essentially equivalent, since we believe not accounting for referrals can be interpreted as not accounting for them in any way."[110] Thus, it would appear that CMS takes the position that the "volume or value" standard will be interpreted in the same way, regardless of whether the provision at issue includes the phrase "directly or indirectly."

D. 'Other business generated' standard

Finally, in addition to including FMV, set in advance, and volume or value standards, many Stark Law exceptions include what is commonly referred to as the "other business generated" standard. The most common formulation of this standard is that the compensation at issue cannot be determined in a manner that "takes into account" "other business generated" by the referring physician (or between the parties). For example, the space rental exception provides that the rental charges at issue cannot be "determined" in a manner that "takes into account" "other business generated" between the parties.[111] There are some slight variations on this theme, such as the following:

- The medical staff incidental benefits exception provides that the compensation at issue must be provided to all members of the medical staff "without regard" to other business generated between the parties.[112]

- The charitable donations exception provides that the donation at issue cannot be "solicited" or "made" in any manner that takes into account other business generated between the physician and the entity.[113]

- The physician retention exception provides that the amount and terms of the retention payment cannot be "altered" in any manner that takes into account other business generated by the physician.[114]

As in the case of the "volume or value" standard, the term "directly or indirectly" sometimes finds its way into the "other business generated" standard. For example, the isolated transactions exception provides that the payment at issue cannot be determined in a manner that "takes into account (directly or indirectly)" "other business generated between the parties."[115] Also, like the "volume or value" standard, the "other business generated" standard is included in several definitions,[116] and in the "set in advance" special rule on compensation.

1. Basic standard

Where the "other business generated" standard is included in an exception, rule, or definition, a threshold question is: Other than what? Although CMS's guidance with respect to this issue has not been a model of clarity, the agency offered the following in the preamble to the 2001 Stark II, Phase I Regulations:

> Based on our review of the legislative history, we believe that the Congress intended the [other business generated standard] to be a limitation on the compensation or payment formula parallel to the statutory and regulatory prohibition on taking into account referrals of DHS business. Simply stated, in the provision in which the phrase appears, affected payments cannot be based or adjusted in any way on referrals of DHS or any other business referred by the physician, including other federal and private pay business.[117]

Example 2.30

A hospital and physician are negotiating a contract pursuant to which the physician will furnish consulting services to the hospital on an hourly basis. The hospital offers the physician $200 per hour. The physician indicates that if the hospital will increase the offer to $250 per hour, the physician will refer all of his non-Medicare patients requiring inpatient and outpatient services to the hospital. The hospital accepts the physician's proposal.

Commentary: The compensation at issue (i.e., the $250 per hour payment) takes into account "other business generated" by the physician for the hospital and, as such, does not satisfy the Stark Law's "other business generated" standard.

---

2. Personally furnished services

As discussed above, because the Stark Regulations provide that referrals do not include any DHS "personally performed or provided by the referring physician," compensation that is tied to such services will not violate the volume or value standard (which is tied to referrals). CMS has clarified that compensation that takes into account personally furnished services also will not violate the "other business generated" standard.[118]

Example 2.31

This includes similar facts to Example 2.18 (i.e., a hospital has a cancer center and employs a medical oncologist to serve as the center's medical director; and the hospital agrees to pay the oncologist $200,000 per year, plus a bonus equal to 5% of the amount that the hospital collects from Medicare for professional services that are ordered and personally furnished by the oncologist).

Commentary: Although the services at issue are Medicare-covered DHS, because they are personally furnished services, the bonus does not take into account "other business generated" by the physician for the hospital and, as such, satisfies the Stark Law's "other business generated" standard.

CMS also has clarified that although the "other business generated" standard will not be implicated by services that are personally furnished by the referring physician, "any corresponding technical component of a service that is billed by the DHS entity" is considered "other business generated for the entity."[119]

Example 2.32

This includes the same facts as Example 2.31, except the hospital also agrees to pay the physician a bonus equal to 1% of the amount that the hospital collects from Medicare for the technical component of any services that are ordered by the oncologist.

Commentary: The bonus does take into account "other business generated" by the physician for the hospital and, as such, does not satisfy the Stark Law's "other business generated" standard.

---

3. Per unit compensation

Finally, the Stark Regulations have an "other business generated" special rule on compensation, which provides as follows.

> Unit-based compensation (including time-based or per unit of service-based compensation) will be deemed to not take into account "other business generated between the parties" so long as the compensation is fair market value for items and services actually provided and does not vary during the course of the compensation arrangement in any manner that takes into account referrals or other business generated by the referring physician, including private pay healthcare business (except for services personally performed by the referring physician, which will not be considered "other business generated" by the referring physician).

Example 2.33

A hospital and physician are negotiating a contract pursuant to which the physician will furnish consulting services to the hospital on an hourly basis. The hospital offers the physician $200 per hour.

Commentary: The compensation at issue (i.e., the $200 per hour payment) will not take into account "other business generated" by the physician for the hospital provided (1) $200 per hour constitutes FMV for the consulting services at issue and (2) the parties do not change this rate in any manner that takes into account referrals or other business generated by the referring physician (except for services personally performed by the physician).

Notes

1. 42 CFR §411.351.

2. 42 USC §1395x(r).

3. 42 CFR §411.351.

4. 42 USC §1320a-7b(b)(2).

5. 42 USC §1320a-7b(b)(1). Where the anti-kickback statute has been violated, the government may proceed criminally or civilly. If the government proceeds criminally, a violation of the law is a felony punishable by up to five years' imprisonment and a fine of up to $25,000. Id. §§1320a-7b(b)(1)-(2). If the government proceeds civilly, it may impose a civil monetary penalty of $50,000 per violation and an assessment of not more than three times the total amount of "remuneration" involved, and it may exclude the defendant from participating in federal healthcare programs. Id. §§1320a-7a(a)(7), 1320a-7(b)(7).

6. 56 *Federal Register* (*FR*) 35952, 35958 (July 29, 1991). Unlike the Stark Law, the anti-kickback statute does not have an exception for de minimis amounts and remuneration means anything of value, no matter how small.

7. Hanlester Network v. Shalala, 51 F.3d 1390, 1398 (9th Cir. 1995).

8. See, e.g., United States v. Greber, 760 F.2d 68 (3rd Cir. 1985), cert. denied, 474 U.S. 988 (1985). United States v. Davis, 132 F. 2d 1092 (5th circuit 1998); United States v. Katz, 871 F. 2d 105 (9th Cir. 1989).

9. Hanlester Network v. Shalala, 51 F.3d 1390, 1398 (9th Cir. 1995); United States v. McClatchey, 217 F.3d 823, 834.

10. Stark I Regulations (Preamble), 60 *FR* 41914, 41927 (1995).

11. Stark I Proposed Regulations (Preamble), 57 *FR* 8588, 8595 (1992).

12. Stark I Proposed Regulations (Preamble), 57 *FR* 8588, 8595 (1992).

13. Stark I Regulations (Preamble), 60 *FR* 41914, 41960 (1995).

14. Stark I Regulations (Preamble), 60 *FR* 41914, 41960 (1995). Although the failure of the U.S. Department of Health and Human Services to "harmonize" these similar but distinct laws frustrates providers and many legal counsel, the government is unlikely to change this approach absent a legislative change.

15. 56 *FR* 35952 (1991).

16. 56 *FR* 35952 (1991).

17. 42 CFR §411.357(l)(5).

18. 42 CFR §411.355(b)(4)(v).

19. 42 CFR §411.355(e)(1)(iv).

20. 42 CFR §411.355(f)(3).

21. 42 CFR §411.355(g)(2).

22. 42 CFR §411.355(h)(2).

23. 42 CFR §411.355(i)(2).

24. 42 CFR §411.355(j)(1)(iv).

25. 42 CFR §411.357(e)(4)(vii) and (e)(5).

26. 42 CFR §411.357(j)(3).

27. 42 CFR §411.357(k)(1)(iii).

28. 42 CFR §411.357(m)(7).

29. 42 CFR §411.357(n).

30. 42 CFR §411.357(p)(3).

31. 42 CFR §411.357(s)(6).

32. 42 CFR §411.357(t)(1)(viii).

33. 42 CFR §411.357(u)(3). This requirement also is included in the temporary noncompliance exception to the Stark Law's billing prohibition. 42 CFR §411.353(f)(1)(iii).

34. Stark II, Phase I Regulations (Preamble), 66 *FR* 856, 863 (2001).

35. Stark II, Phase I Regulations (Preamble), 66 *FR* 856, 863 (2001).

36. Stark II, Phase I Regulations (Preamble), 66 *FR* 856, 863 (2001).

37. Stark II, Phase I Regulations (Preamble), 66 *FR* 856, 863 (2001).

38. 42 CFR §411.351.

39. 42 CFR §411.351.

40. 42 CFR §411.351.

41. 42 CFR §411.351.

42. 42 CFR §411.357(l)(3).

43. 42 USC §1395nn(e)(2)(B)(i); 42 CFR §411.357(c)(2)(i).

44. 42 USC §1395nn(e)(3)(A)(v); 42 CFR §411.357(d)(1)(v).

45. 42 USC §1395nn(e)(1)(A)(iv); 42 CFR §411.357(a)(4).

46. 42 USC §1395nn(e)(1)(B)(iv); 42 CFR §411.357(b)(4).

47. 42 USC §1395nn(e)(8)(B); 42 CFR §411.357(i)(2).

48. 42 CFR §411.357(f)(1)(i).

49. 42 USC §1395nn(e)(7)(A)(v); 42 CFR §411.357(h)(5).

50. 42 CFR §411.355(e)(l)(ii).

51. 42 CFR §411.357(p)(1).

52. 42 USC§1395 nn(h)(3). This is the same definition of FMV that appears in the safe harbor regulations to the anti-kickback statute.

53. 42 CFR §411.351.

54. 42 CFR §411.351.

55. 42 CFR §411.351.

56. 42 CFR §411.351.

57. 42 CFR §411.351.

58. 42 CFR §411.351.

59. 42 CFR §411.351.

60. 42 CFR §411.351. The six surveys are (1) the "Physician Compensation and Productivity Survey" (Sullivan, Cotter & Associates, Inc.), (2) the "Physicians Compensation Survey" (Hay Group), (3) the "Hospital and Healthcare Compensation Services, Physician Salary Survey Report," (4) the "Physician Compensation and Productivity Survey" (Medical Group Management Association), (5) the "Hospital and Healthcare Management Compensation Report" (ECS Watson Wyatt), and (6) the "Integrated Health Networks Compensation Survey" (William M. Mercer). 42 CFR §411.351.

61. Stark II, Phase II Regulations (Preamble), 69 FR 16054, 16092 (2004).

62. 42 CFR §411.351.

63. 42 CFR §411.351.

64. Stark II, Phase I Regulations (Preamble), 66 FR 856, 945 (2001).

65. Stark II, Phase I Regulations (Preamble), 66 FR 856, 945 (2001).

66. Stark II, Phase I Regulations (Preamble), 66 FR 856, 945 (2001).

67. Stark II, Phase I Regulations (Preamble), 66 FR 856, 945 (2001).

68. 42 CFR §411.351.

69. Stark II, Phase I Regulations (Preamble), 66 FR 856, 945 (2001).

70. Stark II, Phase I Regulations (Preamble), 66 FR 856, 945 (2001).

71. Stark II, Phase I Regulations (Preamble), 66 *FR* 856, 945 (2001).

72. Stark II, Phase I Regulations (Preamble), 66 *FR* 856, 945 (2001).

73. Stark II, Phase I Regulations (Preamble), 66 *FR* 856, 945 (2001).

74. Stark II, Phase I Regulations (Preamble), 66 *FR* 856, 945 (2001).

75. 42 CFR §411.357(l)(3).

76. 42 USC §1395nn(e)(3)(A)(v); 42 CFR §411.357(d)(1)(v).

77. 42 USC §1395nn(e)(1)(A)(iv); 42 CFR §411.357(a)(4).

78. 42 USC §1395nn(e)(1)(B)(iv); 42 CFR §411.357(b)(4).

79. 42 CFR §411.357(e)(1)(ii).

80. 42 CFR §411.354(d)(1).

81. 42 CFR §411.354(d)(1).

82. 42 CFR §411.354(d)(1).

83. Stark II, Phase I Regulations (Preamble), 66 *FR* 856, 877 (2001).

84. Stark II, Phase I Regulations (Preamble), 66 *FR* 856, 878 (2001).

85. 66 *FR* 60154, 60155 (2001).

86. Stark II, Phase II Regulations (Preamble), 69 *FR* 16054, 16068 (2004).

87. 42 USC §1395nn(e)(1)(A)(iv); 42 CFR §411.357(a)(5).

88. 42 USC §1395nn(e)(3)(A)(v); 42 CFR §411.357(d)(1)(v).

89. 42 CFR §411.357(s)(1).

90. 42 CFR §411.357(t)(1)(vi).

91. 42 CFR §411.357(u)(1).

92. 42 CFR §411.357(g)(3).

93. 42 CFR §411.357(j)(2).

94. 42 USC §1395nn(e)(2)(B)(ii); 42 CFR §411.357(c)(2)(ii).

95. 42 CFR §411.354(c)(2)(ii).

96. Stark II Proposed Regulations (Preamble), 63 *FR* 1659, 1690-91, 1714 (1998).

97. 42 CFR §411.351.

98. Stark II Proposed Regulations (Preamble), 63 *FR* 1659, 1700 (1998).

99. Stark II Proposed Regulations (Preamble), 63 *FR* 1659, 1700 (1998).

100. Stark II, Phase I Regulations (Preamble), 66 *FR* 856, 878 (2001).

101. Stark II, Phase I Regulations (Preamble), 66 *FR* 856, 877 (2001).

102. Stark II, Phase II Regulations (Preamble), 69 *FR* 16054, 16069 (2004).

103. 42 CFR §411.354(d)(4).

104. Stark II, Phase II Regulations (Preamble), 69 *FR* 16054, 16069-70 (2004).

105. 63 *FR* 1659, 1690-91, 1714 (1998).

106. 42 CFR §411.354(d)(2).

107. Stark II Phase II Regulations (Preamble), 69 *FR 16056,* 16069, (2004)

108. Stark II Phase II Regulations (Preamble), 69 *FR 16056,* 16069, (2004)

109. Stark II Phase II Regulations (Preamble), 69 *FR 16056,* 16069, (2004)

110. Stark II Proposed Regulations (Preamble), 63 *FR* 1659, 1700 (1998)

111. 42 USC §1395nn(e)(1)(A)(iv); 42 CFR §411.357(a)(5).

112. 42 CFR §411.357(m)(1).

113. 42 CFR §411.357(j)(2).

114. 42 CFR §411.357(t)(1)(vi).

115. 42 USC §1395nn(e)(6)(A); 42 CFR §411.357(f)(1)(ii).

116. For example, the definition of "indirect compensation arrangement" provides that "[a]n indirect compensation arrangement exists if ... [t]he ... aggregate compensation ... varies with, or otherwise reflects ... other business generated by the referring physician for the entity furnishing the DHS ... and ... [t]he entity furnishing DHS has actual knowledge of, or acts in reckless disregard or deliberate ignorance of, the fact that the referring physician (or immediate family member) receives aggregate compensation that varies with, or otherwise reflects ... other business generated by the referring physician for the entity furnishing the DHS." 42 CFR §354(c)(2)(ii)-(iii).

117. Stark II, Phase I Regulations (Preamble), 66 *FR* 856, 877 (2001).

118. Stark II, Phase II Regulations (Preamble), 69 *FR* 16054, 16067 (2004); 42 CFR §411.354(d)(3).

119. Stark II, Phase II Regulations (Preamble), 69 *FR* 16054, 16067-68 (2004).

Chapter 3

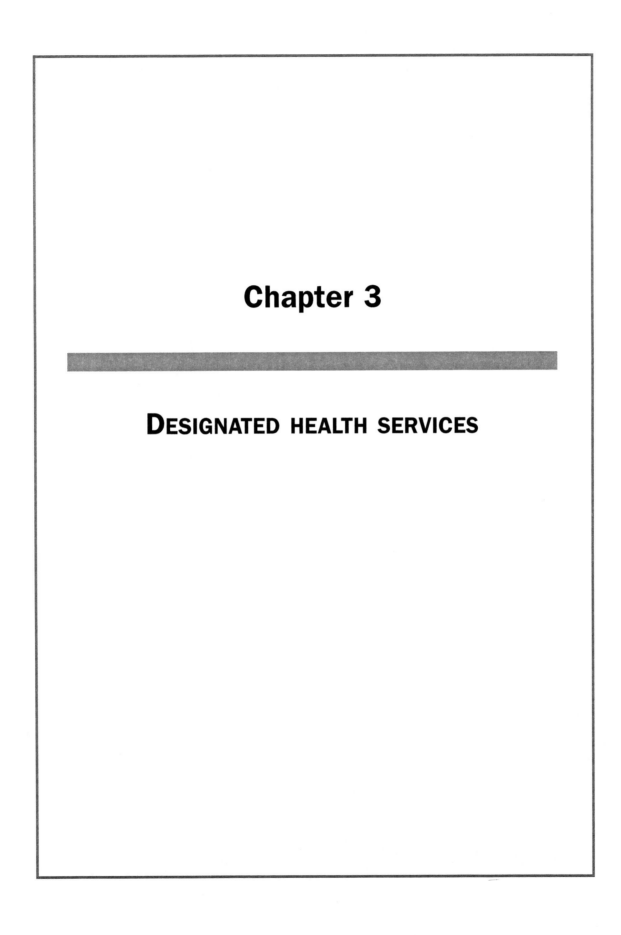

DESIGNATED HEALTH SERVICES

Chapter 3

DESIGNATED HEALTH SERVICES

As discussed in Chapter 1, determining whether an arrangement violates the Stark Law is a three-step process. The first step requires answering the following question: Does the arrangement involve a "physician" making a "referral" "to" an "entity" for the "furnishing" of "designated health services" (DHS) covered by Medicare? We define "physician" in Chapter 2, and discuss the terms "referral," "to," "entity," and "furnishing" in Chapter 4. This chapter addresses the following question: What are DHS? This question is important, of course, because if the services at issue are not DHS, then the Stark Law will not be implicated (and, therefore, cannot be violated).

Example 3.1

A physician owns a freestanding imaging center. Throughout 2004, the physician sends Medicare beneficiaries to that center for nuclear imaging scans.

Commentary: These referrals do not (and cannot) violate the Stark Law's referral prohibition, because in 2004, nuclear medicine procedures were not DHS.

On the other hand, if the services are DHS, then the arrangement may implicate and potentially violate the Stark Law, provided that the other elements of the referral prohibition are present. These other elements are discussed in Chapters 4 and 5.

> **Example 3.2**
>
> This example includes the same facts as Example 3.1, except the physician refers the Medicare beneficiaries to the imaging center for magnetic resonance imaging (MRI) scans.
>
> **Commentary:** This referral may implicate the Stark Law's referral prohibition (provided that the other elements of the referral prohibition are present) because, as discussed below, MRI scans are DHS.

I. Categories of DHS

Under the Stark Law, there are 11 categories of DHS: clinical laboratory services; physical therapy services; occupational therapy services; radiology services, including MRIs, computerized axial tomography (CAT) scans, and ultrasound services; radiation therapy services and supplies; durable medical equipment (DME) and supplies; parenteral and enteral nutrients, equipment, and supplies; prosthetics, orthotics, and prosthetic devices and supplies; home health services; outpatient prescription drugs; and inpatient and outpatient hospital services.[1]

Although the Stark Law itself does not define any of these DHS categories, the Centers for Medicare & Medicaid Services (CMS) has defined each of them in the Stark Regulations. Indeed, with respect to the first five DHS categories (clinical laboratory, physical therapy, occupational therapy, radiology, and radiation therapy services), CMS has indicated by current procedural terminology (CPT) code and healthcare common procedure coding system (HCPCS) code the precise items and services that constitute DHS.

These codes are set forth in CMS's "List of CPT/HCPCS Codes Used to Describe Certain Designated Health Services Under the Physician Referral Provisions (Section 1877 of the Social Security Act)" (the "CMS List"). The CMS List is published annually as part of CMS's physician fee schedule and is posted on CMS's Web site.[2]

CMS has concluded that the six remaining categories of DHS—DME and supplies; parenteral and enteral nutrients, equipment, and supplies; prosthetics, orthotics, and prosthetic devices and supplies;

home health services; outpatient prescription drugs; and inpatient and outpatient hospital services—are "not amenable to definition through codes."[3] Thus, the Stark Regulations provide more general definitions and guidance with respect to these categories (in some cases, simply by cross-referencing existing, non-Stark, statutory and regulatory definitions of identical or similar terms).

Sections A through L below address each category of DHS. Although the Stark Law treats "inpatient and outpatient hospital services" as a single DHS category, we discuss these services separately in Sections K and L, respectively. This chapter also addresses two more generally applicable issues: the technical/professional component distinction (for purposes of the DHS rules) and the applicability of the DHS rules to composite/bundled Medicare payments.

One note of caution: In most cases, determining whether a service constitutes DHS is fairly straightforward, either because the service at issue is included on the CMS List or because the service falls squarely into one of the other categories (e.g., inpatient hospital services). In some cases, however, determining whether an item or service is DHS requires more careful analysis, which may include reviewing not only the relevant provisions of the Stark Law and Stark Regulations, but also a variety of other laws, regulations, and related authorities. Although the discussion of DHS in this chapter cross-references and, in some cases, summarizes many of these non-Stark authorities, it does not analyze them in detail. As such, if an organization has any question about whether an item or service is DHS, we recommend that the organization consult all potentially relevant primary and secondary authorities (including, of course, the relevant provisions of the Stark Law and Stark Regulations).

A. Clinical laboratory services

The Stark Regulations include both a general and a specific definition of "clinical laboratory services." In general, such services include "the biological, microbiological, serological, chemical, immunohematological, hematological, biophysical, cytological, pathological, or other examination of materials derived from the human body for the purpose of providing information for the diagnosis, prevention, or treatment of any disease or impairment of, or the assessment of the health of, human beings," including "procedures to determine, measure, or otherwise describe the presence or absence of various substances or organisms in the body."[4]

CMS has clarified that irrespective of this general definition, for Stark Law purposes, "clinical laboratory services" include only those services specifically identified as such on the CMS List.[5] Some examples of clinical laboratory services from the CMS List (effective January 1, 2005) are set forth in Table 3.1.

Table 3.1 — CMS List—Clinical laboratory services (examples)

Code	Description
CPT code 80051	Electrolyte panel
CPT code 80061	Lipid panel
CPT code 80069	Renal function panel
CPT code 80076	Hepatic function panel
CPT code 82947	Glucose
CPT code 86803	Hepatitis C antibody
CPT code 84295	Sodium

B. Physical therapy services

Once again, the Stark Regulations include both a general and a specific definition of "physical therapy services." In general, this category includes those services described in the relevant section of the Social Security Act, codified at 42 United States Code (USC) §1395x(p) (defining "outpatient physical therapy services" for purposes of the Medicare program), provided the services include the following:

• assessments, function tests, and measurements of strength, balance, endurance, range of motion, and activities of daily living;

• therapeutic exercises, massage, and use of physical medicine modalities, assistive devices, and adaptive equipment;

- establishment of a maintenance therapy program for an individual whose restoration potential has been reached; or

- speech-language pathology services that are for the diagnosis and treatment of speech, language, and cognitive disorders that include swallowing and other oral-motor dysfunctions.[6]

Once again, CMS has clarified that this general definition notwithstanding, only those services specifically identified as "physical therapy services" on the CMS List fall into this category for Stark Law purposes.[7] Some examples of physical therapy services from the CMS List effective (January 1, 2005) are set forth in Table 3.2.

Table 3.2   **CMS List—Physical therapy services (examples)**

Code	Description
CPT code 97001	Physical therapy evaluation
CPT code 97002	Physical therapy reevaluation
CPT code 97110	Therapeutic procedure, one or more areas, each 15 minutes; therapeutic exercises to develop strength, endurance, range of motion, and flexibility
CPT code 97113	Therapeutic procedure, one or more areas, each 15 minutes; aquatic therapy with therapeutic exercises
CPT code 92507	Treatment of speech, language, voice, communication, and/or auditory processing disorder (includes aural rehabilitation), individual
CPT code 92607	Evaluation for prescription for speech-generating augmentative and alternative communication device, face-to-face with the patient; first hour
CPT code 92609	Therapeutic services for the use of speech-generating device, including programming and modification

C. Occupational therapy services

The Stark Regulations also have a general and a specific definition of "occupational therapy services." In general, this category includes those services described in the relevant section of the Social Security Act, codified at 42 USC §1395x(g) (defining "outpatient occupational therapy services" for purposes of the Medicare program), provided the services include the following:

- teaching of compensatory techniques to permit an individual with a physical or cognitive impairment or limitation to engage in daily activities;

- evaluation of an individual's level of independent functioning;

- selection and teaching of task-oriented therapeutic activities to restore sensory-integrative function; or

- assessment of an individual's vocational potential, except when the assessment is related solely to vocational rehabilitation.[8]

Again, CMS has clarified that, this general definition notwithstanding, only those services specifically identified as "occupational therapy services" on the CMS List fall into this category.[9] Some examples of occupational therapy services from the CMS List (effective January 1, 2005) are set forth in Table 3.3.

D. Radiology services including MRIs, computerized axial tomography scans, and ultrasound devices

The Stark Regulations, which refer to this category as "radiology and certain other imaging services," have general and specific definitions for this DHS category. In general, this category includes the "professional and technical components of any diagnostic test or procedure using x-rays, ultrasound, or other imaging services, CAT, or MRIs" as described in 42 USC §1395x(s)(3) (defining certain "medical and other health services" for purposes of the Medicare program) and 42 Code of Federal Regulations (CFR) §§410.32 and 410.34 (same). However, the definition specifically excludes the following:

Table 3.3 | **CMS List—Occupational therapy services (examples)**

Code	Description
CPT code 97003	Occupational therapy evaluation
CPT code 97004	Occupational therapy reevaluation
CPT code 97532	Development of cognitive skills to improve attention, memory, problem solving, (includes compensatory training), direct (one-on-one) patient contact by the provider, each 15 minutes
CPT code 97533	Sensory integrative techniques to enhance sensory processing and promote adaptive responses to environmental demands, direct (one-on-one) patient contact by the provider, each 15 minutes
CPT code 97535	Self-care/home management training (e.g., activities of daily living and compensatory training, meal preparation, safety procedures, and instructions in the use of assistive technology devices/adaptive equipment), direct (one-on-one) patient contact by the provider, each 15 minutes
CPT code 97537	Community/work reintegration training (e.g., shopping, transportation, money management, avocational activities and/or work environment/modification analysis, work task analysis, use of assistive technology devices/adaptive equipment), direct (one-on-one) patient contact by provider, each 15 minutes

- x-ray, fluoroscopy, or ultrasound procedures that require the insertion of a needle, catheter, tube, or probe through the skin or into a body orifice;

- radiology procedures that are integral to the performance of a nonradiological medical procedure and performed (1) during the nonradiological medical procedure; or (2) immediately following the nonradiological medical procedure when necessary to confirm placement of an item placed during the nonradiological medical procedure; and

- diagnostic nuclear medicine procedures.[10]

Note, however, that in August 2005, CMS issued a proposed rule that, if adopted by the agency, would include diagnostic nuclear medicine procedures as "radiology and certain other imaging services" for Stark Law purposes.[11]

Example 3.3

In July 2005, two patients (A and B) present to a cardiologist with chest pains and shortness of breath. The cardiologist orders a stress echocardiogram for Patient A and a positron emission tomography (PET) scan for Patient B.

Commentary: The cardiologist has ordered DHS for Patient A (because echocardiography is an ultrasound procedure)[12] but has not ordered DHS for Patient B (because as of July 2005, a PET scan, which is a diagnostic nuclear medicine procedure, was not DHS).[13]

CMS has clarified that, this general definition notwithstanding, only those services specifically identified as "radiology or other imaging services" on the CMS List fall into this category for purposes of the Stark Law.[14] Some examples of radiology and other imaging services from the CMS List (effective January 1, 2005) are set forth in Table 3.4.

Table 3.4   CMS List—Radiology and other imaging services (examples)

Code	Description
CPT code 70100	Radiologic examination, mandible; partial, less than four views
CPT code 70250	Radiologic examination, skull; less than four views
CPT code 70360	Radiologic examination; neck, soft tissue
CPT code 70450	Computed tomography, head or brain; without contrast material
CPT code 70496	Computed tomographic angiography, head, without contrast material(s), followed by contrast material(s) and further sections, including image post-processing
CPT code 71550	Magnetic resonance (e.g., proton) imaging, chest (e.g., for evaluation of hilar and mediastinal lymphadenopathy); without contrast material(s)
CPT code 72141	Magnetic resonance (e.g., proton) imaging, spinal canal and contents, cervical; without contrast material

E. Radiation therapy services and supplies

The Stark Regulations have a general and a specific definition for "radiation therapy services and supplies." In general, this category includes radiation therapy services and supplies as described in 42 USC §1395x(s)(4) (defining certain medical and other health services for purposes of the Medicare program) and 42 CFR §410.35 (same), excluding nuclear medicine procedures.[15] (Note, however, that in August 2005, CMS issued a proposed rule that, if adopted by the agency, would include therapeutic nuclear medicine procedures as "radiation therapy services and supplies" for Stark Law purposes.)[16] Despite requests, CMS has declined to exclude prostate brachytherapy items and services from this category of DHS.[17]

CMS has clarified that, this general definition notwithstanding, only those services specifically identified as "radiation therapy services and supplies" on the CMS List fall into this category.[18] Some examples of radiation therapy services and supplies from the CMS List (effective January 1, 2005) are set forth in Table 3.5.

Table 3.5	CMS List—Radiation therapy services and supplies (examples)

Code	Description
CPT code 77261	Therapeutic radiology treatment planning; simple
CPT code 77280	Therapeutic radiology simulation-aided field setting; simple
CPT code 77301	Intensity modulated radiotherapy plan, including dose-volume histograms for target and critical structure partial tolerance specifications
CPT code 77326	Brachytherapy isodose plan; simple (calculation made from single plane, 1–4 sources/ribbon application, remote afterloading brachytherapy, 1–8 sources)
CPT code 77336	Continuing medical physics consultation, including assessment of treatment parameters, quality assurance of dose delivery, and review of patient treatment documentation in support of the radiation oncologist, reported per week of therapy
CPT code 77401	Radiation treatment delivery, superficial and/or ortho voltage
CPT code 77781	Remote afterloading high intensity brachytherapy; 1–4 source positions or catheters

F. Durable medical equipment and supplies

The Stark Regulations provide that DME and supplies has the meaning set forth by statute 42 USC §1395x(n) and regulation, 42 CFR §414.202.[19]

- By statute, DME generally includes rented or purchased iron lungs, oxygen tents, hospital beds, and (under certain circumstances) wheelchairs used in the patient's home (including certain institutional settings), as well as blood-testing strips and blood glucose monitors for individuals with diabetes.[20]

- By regulation, DME also includes any equipment furnished by a supplier or a home health agency that (1) can withstand repeated use, (2) is primarily and customarily used to serve a medical purpose, (3) generally is not useful to an individual in the absence of an illness or injury, and (4) is appropriate for use in the home.[21]

Examples of DME include nebulizers, walkers, and crutches.[22] Excluded from this category are home dialysis equipment and supplies.[23] In general, CMS advises that the easiest way to determine whether an item or service falls into the DME category is to consult the DME prosthetics, orthotics, and supplies (DMEPOS) fee schedule, which identifies such items by HCPCS code.[24]

G. Prosthetics, orthotics, and prosthetic devices and supplies

The Stark Regulations define "prosthetics, orthotics, and prosthetic devices and supplies" to include the following (along with all HCPCS Level 2 Codes for these services that are covered by Medicare):

- "prosthetics," meaning artificial legs, arms, and eyes.

- "orthotics," meaning leg, arm, back, and neck braces.

- "prosthetic devices," meaning devices (other than dental devices) that replace all or part of an internal body organ (including colostomy bags) and one pair of conventional eyeglasses or contact lenses furnished subsequent to each cataract surgery with insertion of an intraocular lens.

- "prosthetic supplies," meaning supplies that are necessary for the effective use of a prosthetic device (including supplies directly related to colostomy care).[25]

These definitions ordinarily include the services necessary to design, measure, fit, and align the device
at issue and instruct patients in its proper use.[26] As with DME, CMS advises that the easiest way to
determine whether an item or service falls into the prosthetics, orthotics, and supplies category is to
consult the DMEPOS fee schedule.[27]

H. Parenteral and enteral nutrients, equipment, and supplies

The Stark Regulations define "parenteral" and "enteral" nutrients, equipment, and supplies separately.

- Parenteral nutrients, equipment, and supplies include those items and supplies needed to provide nutriment to a patient with permanent, severe pathology of the ali-
mentary tract that does not allow absorption of sufficient nutrients to maintain
strength commensurate with the patient's general condition, as described in Section
65-10 of the Medicare Coverage Issues Manual (CMS Pub. 6), as amended or
replaced from time to time.[28]

   (*Note:* The Medicare Coverage Issues Manual, Section 65-10, has been replaced by the
   Medicare National Coverage Determinations Manual (CMS Pub. 100-3), Section 180.2.)

- Enteral nutrients, equipment, and supplies include those items and supplies needed
to provide enteral nutrition to a patient with a functioning gastrointestinal tract who,
due to pathology or nonfunction of the structures that normally permit food to
reach the digestive tract, cannot maintain weight and strength commensurate with
his or her general condition, as described in section 65-10 of the Medicare
Coverages Issues Manual (CMS Pub. 6), as amended or replaced from time to
time.[29]

   (*Note:* The Medicare Coverage Issues Manual, Section 65-10, has been replaced by the
   Medicare National Coverage Determinations Manual (CMS Pub. 100-3), Section 180.2.)

Both categories include all HCPCS Level 2 Codes for the services at issue.[30]

I. Home health services

The Stark Regulations provide that "home health services" has the meaning given by statute, 42 USC §1395x(m), and regulation, 42 CFR Part 409, Subpart E, both of which define home health services for purposes of the Medicare program.[31] In general, "home health services" include items and services furnished to a home-bound individual by a home health agency (or by others under arrangement with the agency) under a plan of care established and periodically reviewed by a physician, where such items and services are provided on a visiting basis in the individual's home, including (among other things) part-time or intermittent nursing care under the supervision of a registered nurse, physical or occupational therapy, speech-language pathology services, medical social services under direction of a physician, and certain medical supplies and DME.[32]

J. Outpatient prescription drugs

The Stark Regulations define "outpatient prescription drugs" as "all prescription drugs covered by Medicare Part B."[33] This category includes prescription drugs dispensed by pharmacies, as well as those mixed and administered in a physician's office.[34] At present, there is no definitive list of CPT and HCPCS codes that constitute "outpatient prescription drugs" for purposes of the Stark Law. Moreover, CMS notes in the preamble to the Stark II, Phase II Regulations that, effective January 1, 2006, many additional drugs will be covered under Medicare Part D and, as a result, the agency will revisit the definition of "outpatient prescription drugs" in a future rulemaking.[35]

K. Inpatient hospital services

The Stark Regulations provide that the term "inpatient hospital services" generally is defined by statute, 42 USC §§§1395x(b), 1395x(c), and 1395x(mm)(2), and regulation, 42 CFR §§409.10(a) and 409.10(b).[36] More specifically, "inpatient hospital services" include certain items and services furnished—either directly by the hospital or under arrangements made by the hospital with others—to an inpatient of a hospital, an inpatient of a psychiatric hospital, or an inpatient of a critical access hospital. These services include bed and board, nursing services and other related services, use of hospital facilities, medical social services, drugs, biologicals, supplies, appliances and equipment, certain other diagnostic or therapeutic services, medical or surgical services provided by certain interns or residents-in-training, and transportation services, including transport by ambulance.[37]

The Stark Regulations provide that "inpatient hospital services" generally do not include emergency inpatient services provided by a hospital located outside of the United States, emergency inpatient services provided by a non-participating hospital within the United States, or dialysis furnished by a hospital that is not certified to provide end-stage renal disease services.[38] In addition, "inpatient hospital services" do not include "professional services performed by physicians, physician assistants, nurse practitioners, clinical nurse specialists, certified nurse midwives, certified registered nurse anesthetists, and qualified psychologists if Medicare reimburses the services independently and not as part of the inpatient hospital service (even if the hospital bills the services under an assignment or reassignment)."[39]

Example 3.4

A surgeon removes the inflamed appendix of a Medicare beneficiary in a hospital operating room.

Commentary: The items and services furnished to the beneficiary at the hospital (from the point of admission through discharge), with the exception of the professional services of the surgeon, constitute "inpatient hospital services," which will be covered by the relevant diagnosis-related group payment under Medicare Part A and, as such, are considered DHS. The professional services of the surgeon constitute "physician services," which will be covered by the relevant physician fee schedule payment under Medicare Part B and, as such, are not DHS.

L. Outpatient hospital services

The Stark Regulations provide that the term "outpatient hospital services" generally is defined by statute, 42 USC §§1395x(s)(2)(B)(C), 1395x(f), and 1395x(mm)(3).[40] More specifically, "outpatient hospital services" include certain items and services furnished—either directly by the hospital or under arrangements made by the hospital with others—to an outpatient of a hospital, an outpatient of a psychiatric hospital, or an outpatient of a critical access hospital. These services include hospital services (including drugs and biologicals that are not usually self-administered by the patient) incident to physician services, partial hospitalization services incident to physician services, and diagnostic services.[41]

Example 3.5

A Medicare beneficiary presents to his primary care physician with a swollen knee. The physician sends the patient to a hospital's outpatient diagnostic imaging clinic for an MRI.

Commentary: The MRI constitutes DHS for two reasons: It is an imaging service and it is an outpatient hospital service.

Example 3.6

A physician sends a Medicare beneficiary to a hospital's diagnostic catheterization laboratory.

Commentary: Although diagnostic cardiac catheterizations are not DHS in the form of radiology or other imaging services,[42] the procedure nevertheless constitutes DHS in the form of an outpatient hospital service.

The Stark Regulations provide that "outpatient hospital services" (like inpatient hospital services) generally do *not* include either emergency services furnished by non-participating hospitals or "professional services performed by physicians, physician assistants, nurse practitioners, clinical nurse specialists, certified nurse midwives, certified registered nurse anesthetists, and qualified psychologists if Medicare reimburses the services independently and not as part of the outpatient hospital service (even if they are billed by a hospital under an assignment or reassignment)."[43]

Note also that despite receiving hundreds of comments requesting that lithotripsy be excluded from the definition of outpatient (and inpatient) hospital services, in 2001, CMS determined, in the context of promulgating the Stark II, Phase I Regulations, that there was no reason for lithotripsy to be treated any differently than other hospital services.[44] In *American Lithotripsy Society v. Thompson*, however, the U.S. District Court for the District of Columbia held that lithotripsy was not DHS within the meaning of the Stark Law.[45] In the preamble to the 2004 Stark II, Phase II Regulations, CMS declined to revise the regulatory definition but concluded that "in light of the unique legislative history" regarding the application of the Stark Law to lithotripsy, it will not consider lithotripsy an "inpatient or outpatient service for purposes of [the Stark Law]."[46]

II. General DHS issues

A. Professional v. technical component

To the extent that a particular DHS includes both a technical and a professional component, both are DHS for purposes of the Stark Law. Although some commenters have taken the position that "Congress did not intend for professional services to come within the physician self-referral law prohibition and that [CMS] exceeded [its] authority to promulgate regulations by including them," CMS disagrees.[47]

According to CMS, "it was not the intent of the [Stark Law] to exclude all professional services from the list of DHS. Many of the DHS, such as radiology and radiation therapy, have substantial physician service components. If the Congress intended to exclude them, we would expect the [Stark Law] to specifically do so."[48] Indeed, CMS notes, "there are some DHS that consist only of a professional component (for example, some radiation therapy services) or are primarily professional in nature, and these would not otherwise be subject to the law if we carved out all professional components."[49]

Example 3.7

This example includes the same facts as Example 3.5 (i.e., a physician sends a patient to the hospital's outpatient diagnostic imaging clinic for an MRI), except that once the MRI scan is completed, the images are forwarded to a hospital-based radiologist, who reads the MRI images and sends her interpretation to the physician.

Commentary: The radiologist's professional services are not outpatient hospital services. They are DHS, however, because the professional components of radiology and imaging services are DHS (as long as the CPT code at issue is included on the CMS List).

B. Composite payments

In 1998, CMS took the position that it would consider a service to be DHS even if it were "billed as something else" or "subsumed within another service category by being bundled with other services for billing purposes."[50] Several commenters "complained that this interpretation would result in an expansion of the DHS beyond the services specifically listed" in the Stark Law and observed that "when the Congress intended to cover specific Medicare services (including composite rate services, such as hospital or home health services), it did so expressly."[51]

CMS ultimately agreed and has modified the definition of DHS in the Stark Regulations to provide that "DHS do not include services that are reimbursed by Medicare as part of a composite rate (for example, ambulatory surgical center services or skilled nursing facility (SNF) Part A payments), except to the extent [such] services … are themselves payable through a composite rate (for example, all services provided as home health services or inpatient and outpatient hospital services are DHS)."[52]

Example 3.8

A physician refers a Medicare beneficiary to an ambulatory surgery center (ASC) for outpatient orthopedic surgery. While at the ASC for the surgery, the ASC furnishes clinical laboratory services to the beneficiary.

Commentary: As long as the clinical laboratory services are not separately reimbursable by Medicare, but rather are covered by the composite rate payment that the provider receives from Medicare for the full "bundle" of ASC services, the physician has not made a referral to the ASC for the furnishing of DHS.

Example 3.9

A physician refers a Medicare beneficiary to a home health agency (HHA). The HHA furnishes clinical laboratory services to the beneficiary.

Commentary: The physician has made a referral to the HHA for the furnishing of DHS. It is not because the clinical laboratory services are not covered by the composite rate payment that the agency receives from Medicare for the full "bundle" of home health services—they probably are. Rather, it is because home health services, unlike hospice services or ASC services, are themselves DHS.

CMS's position with respect to services that are covered through a composite payment should not be confused with services, such as SNF services, which are subject to consolidated billing requirements. Although SNF services are not DHS, SNF patients regularly receive services from SNFs (either directly or under arrangements with another entity) that fall into a DHS category (e.g., physical or occupational therapy). Such services may be DHS if they are reimbursed separately under Medicare Part B and not as part of a composite, per diem payment under Medicare Part A.

Example 3.10

A physician admits two Medicare beneficiaries (A and B) to a SNF. Both patients receive physical therapy at the SNF. Patient A has not exhausted her Medicare Part A SNF benefit (which is covered by a composite payment). However, Patient B has exhausted her Part A SNF benefit and, as a result, Medicare Part B covers the physical therapy (under a non-composite payment methodology).

Commentary: Patient A did not receive DHS from the SNF, but Patient B did.

Notes

1. 42 USC §1395nn(h)(6).

2. www.cms.gov/medlearn/refphys.asp.

3. Stark II, Phase II Regulations (Preamble), 69 *Federal Register* (*FR*) 16054, 16100 (2004).

4. 42 CFR §411.351.

5. 42 CFR §411.351.

6. 42 CFR §411.351.

7. 42 CFR §411.351.

8. 42 CFR §411.351.

9. 42 CFR §411.351.

10. 42 CFR §411.351.

11. 70 *FR* 45764, 45854-56 (2005).

12. Stark II, Phase I Regulations (Preamble), 66 *FR* 856, 928 (2001).

13. Stark II, Phase II Regulations (Preamble), 69 *FR* 16054, 16104 (2004).

14. 42 CFR §411.351.

15. 42 CFR §411.351.

16. 70 *FR* 45764, 45854-56 (2005).

17. Stark II, Phase I Regulations (Preamble), 66 *FR* 856, 931 (2001); Stark II, Phase II Regulations (Preamble), 69 *FR* 16054, 16105 (2004).

18. 42 CFR §411.351.

19. 42 CFR §411.351.

20. 42 USC §1395x(n).

21. 42 CFR §414.202.

22. Stark II Proposed Regulations (Preamble), 63 *FR* 1659, 1677 (1998); Stark II, Phase I Regulations (Preamble), 66 *FR* 856, 932 (2001).

23. Stark II, Phase II Regulations (Preamble), 69 *FR* 16054, 16105 (2004).

24. Stark II, Phase II Regulations (Preamble), 69 *FR* 16054, 16100. The current DMEPOS fee schedule may be found at *www.cms.hhs.gov/providers/pufdownload/#dme*.

25. 42 CFR §411.351.

26. Stark II, Phase I Regulations (Preamble), 66 *FR* 856, 935 (2001).

27. Stark II, Phase II Regulations (Preamble), 69 *FR* 16054, 16100 (2004).

28. 42 CFR §411.351. The Medicare Coverage Issues Manual is available on CMS's Web site, *www.cms.hhs.gov/manuals/pm_trans/R165CIM.pdf*.

29. 42 CFR §411.351.

30. 42 CFR §411.351; Stark II, Phase I Regulations (Preamble), 66 *FR* 856, 933 (2001).

31. 42 CFR §411.351.

32. 42 USC §1395x(m).

33. 42 CFR §411.351.

34. Stark II, Phase II Regulations (Preamble), 69 *FR* 16054, 16106 (2004).

35. Stark II, Phase II Regulations (Preamble), 69 *FR* 16054, 16106 (2004).

36. 42 CFR §411.351.

37. 42 CFR §409.10(a).

38. 42 CFR §411.351.

39. 42 CFR §411.351.

40. 42 CFR §411.351.

41. 42 USC §§§1395x(s)(2)(B)-(C), 1395x(f), and 1395x(mm)(3).

42. Stark II, Phase I Regulations (Preamble), 66 *FR* 856, 929 (2001).

43. 42 CFR §411.351.

44. Stark II, Phase I Regulations (Preamble), 66 *FR* 856, 940 (2001).

45. 215 F. Supp. 2d. 23 (D.D.C. 2002).

46. Stark II, Phase II Regulations (Preamble), 69 *FR* 16054, 16106 (2004).

47. Stark II, Phase I Regulations (Preamble), 66 *FR* 856, 924 (2001).

48. Stark II, Phase I Regulations (Preamble), 66 *FR* 856, 924 (2001). The professional services performed by clinical pathologists also are, in large part, DHS.

49. Stark II, Phase I Regulations (Preamble), 66 *FR* 856, 924 (2001).

50. Stark II, Phase I Regulations (Preamble), 66 *FR* 856, 923 (2001).

51. Stark II, Phase I Regulations (Preamble), 66 *FR* 856, 923 (2001).

52. 42 CFR §411.351.

Chapter 4

REFERRALS

Chapter 4

4

REFERRALS

As discussed in Chapter 1, determining whether an arrangement violates the Stark Law is a three-step process. The first step requires answering the following question: Does the arrangement involve a "physician" "referring" patients "to" an "entity" for the "furnishing" of "designated health services" (DHS) covered by Medicare? We define "physician" in Chapter 2 and discuss DHS in Chapter 3. In this chapter, we address the remaining elements of the step one inquiry (i.e., what are the circumstances under which a physician will be deemed to have made a "referral" "to" an "entity" for the "furnishing" of DHS?).

I. 'Referral'

The Stark Law has a two-part definition of the term "referral." First, "referral" is defined as a "request by a physician for [an] item or service" for which payment may be made under Medicare Part B, including (1) the "request by a physician for a consultation with another physician" and (2) "any test or procedure ordered by, or to be performed by (or under the supervision of) that other physician."[1] Second, the Stark Law provides that a "referral" means "the request or establishment of a plan of care by a physician [that] includes the provision of [DHS]."[2]

The Stark Regulations expand upon this statutory definition. First, the Stark Regulations provide that the term "referral" means the following:

[t]he request by a physician for, or ordering of, or the certifying or recertifying of the need for, any [DHS] for which payment may be made under Medicare Part B, including a request for a consultation with another physician and any test or procedure ordered by or to be performed by (or under the supervision of) that other physician. . .[3]

Second, the Stark Regulations provide that the term "referral" also means the following:

[a] request by a physician that includes the provision of any [DHS] for which payment may be made under Medicare, the establishment of a plan of care by a physician that includes the provision of such a [DHS], or the certifying or recertifying of the need for such a [DHS] …[4]

In addition, the Stark Regulations clarify that a "referral" may "be in any form, including, but not limited to, written, oral, or electronic."[5]

Although confusing in certain respects and redundant, the Stark Law and the Stark Regulations do make at least two things clear: (1) the definition of "referral" for Stark Law purposes is very broad and (2) in general, a physician will be deemed to have made a "referral" any time he or she orders, requests, or establishes a plan of care that includes or involves DHS covered by Medicare.

Example 4.1

A physician examines a Medicare beneficiary and determines that she needs an outpatient prescription drug that is covered by Medicare Part B (and, therefore, constitutes DHS). Accordingly, the physician fills out a prescription for the drug.

Commentary: The physician—simply by filling out the prescription—has made a "referral" for Stark Law purposes because she has ordered DHS covered by Medicare Part B. Of course, this referral will not implicate the Stark Law unless the remaining elements of the referral prohibition are present. Specifically, the physician must make this referral "to" an "entity" for the "furnishing" of the drug and the physician or one of his or her immediate family members must have a "financial relationship" with that entity.

Example 4.2

A Medicare beneficiary presents to her primary care physician with acute lower back pain, prompting the physician to write an order for six sessions of physical therapy.

Commentary: The physician—simply by completing the order—has made a "referral" for Stark Law purposes.

Example 4.3

During an office visit, a Medicare beneficiary complains to his primary care physician about chest pain. The physician asks his nurse to perform an electrocardiogram (EKG) on the patient. The physician also sends the patient to a cardiologist for a cardiology consultation, and the cardiologist schedules the patient for a diagnostic catheterization at a community hospital.

Commentary: The primary care physician arguably has made three separate "referrals": (1) the request for the EKG, (2) the request for a cardiology consultation, and (3) the request for the diagnostic catheterization.

The Stark Law and Regulations are less clear about whether more than one physician may be held accountable for the "referral" of the *same* DHS. Thus, the question arises of whether in Example 4.3 the request for the diagnostic catheterization constitutes a "referral" not only by the primary care physician (who requested the cardiology consultation in the first instance), but also by the cardiologist. Although not free from doubt, a literal reading of the definition of "referral" suggests that the answer may be "yes."

A related question arises when multiple services are requested by more than one physician but the services are reimbursed under a single composite payment.

> **Example 4.4**
>
> This example includes the same facts as Example 4.3, except that immediately following the diagnostic catheterization, the patient is admitted to the hospital as an inpatient by the cardiologist and is operated on by a cardiovascular surgeon, with the assistance of an anesthesiologist.
>
> **Commentary:** It would appear that a "referral" to the hospital for inpatient services would be attributed to the cardiologist, not to the primary care physician. A literal reading of the Stark Law and Regulations, however, suggests that the cardiovascular surgeon and anesthesiologist also may have made "referrals."

A. Exceptions

There are two narrow exceptions to the definition of "referral," one covering orders/requests by certain consulting specialists and the other covering self-referrals. Each of these exceptions is discussed below.

1. Consultation exception

The Stark Law provides a specialty-specific exception, which we will refer to as the "consultation exception," to the general rule regarding referrals discussed above. Under this exception, the following do not give rise to a "referral" for Stark Law purposes:

- a request by a pathologist for clinical diagnostic laboratory tests and pathological examination services if these services are "furnished by (or under the supervision of)" the pathologist pursuant to a consultation requested by another physician,[6]

- a request by a radiologist for diagnostic radiology services if these services are "furnished by (or under the supervision of)" the radiologist pursuant to a consultation requested by another physician,[7] and

- a request by a radiation oncologist for radiation therapy if the services at issue are "furnished by (or under the supervision of)" the radiation oncologist pursuant to a consultation requested by another physician.[8]

Example 4.5

A surgical oncologist removes a mass of tissue from a Medicare patient's breast and sends the specimen to a clinical pathologist (who is part of a group practice) for analysis. The pathologist requests that the pathology lab prepare the biopsy slides and then dictates a pathology report for the surgeon, which confirms that the growth is cancerous.

Commentary: Although the pathologist has ordered DHS (i.e., the preparation of the biopsy slides), this order will not give rise to a "referral" by the pathologist for Stark Law purposes, provided that each of the requirements of the consultation exception is met.

The Stark Regulations track—but also expand upon and clarify—these statutory provisions, providing that a "referral" does not include a request (1) by a pathologist for clinical diagnostic laboratory tests and pathological examination services, (2) by a radiologist for diagnostic radiology services, and (3) by a radiation oncologist for radiation therapy, if both of the following are true:

- the request results from a consultation initiated by another physician (whether the request for a consultation was made to a particular physician or to an entity with which the physician is affiliated), and

- the tests or services are furnished (1) by or under the supervision of the pathologist, radiologist, or radiation oncologist, or (2) under the supervision of a pathologist, radiologist, or radiation oncologist, respectively, in the same group practice as the pathologist, radiologist, or radiation oncologist.[9]

Example 4.6

This example includes the same facts as Example 4.5, except the surgical oncologist asks the pathologist's group practice (and not the pathologist specifically) for a consultation.

Commentary: Although the pathologist has ordered DHS (i.e., the biopsy slides), this order will not constitute a "referral" by the pathologist for Stark Law purposes due to the more protective consultation exception in the Stark Regulations, which covers consultations made both "to a particular physician or to an entity with which the physician is affiliated."

Example 4.7

This example includes the same facts as Example 4.5, except the pathologist who ordered the slides (the "ordering pathologist") does not supervise the technician who prepares the slides. Instead, another pathologist in the ordering pathologist's group practice provides such supervision.

Commentary: The ordering pathologist's request will not constitute a "referral" for Stark Law purposes pursuant to the consultation exception in the Stark Regulations (which covers relevant DHS if it is supervised by a "pathologist, radiologist, or radiation oncologist, respectively, in the same group practice as the [ordering] pathologist, radiologist, or radiation oncologist").[10]

---

a. Consultation

Under both the Stark Law and Stark Regulations, a pre-condition to the applicability of the consultation exception is that the "request" for DHS by the pathologist/radiologist/radiation oncologist (i.e., the "specialist") must result from a "consultation" request by another physician (i.e., the "requesting physician"). Although the Stark Law does not define "consultation," the Stark Regulations provide that a "consultation" means "a professional service furnished to a patient by a physician" if three conditions are satisfied:

- the specialist's "opinion or advice regarding evaluation or management of a specific medical problem" is requested by the requesting physician,[11]

- the "request and need for the consultation" is "documented in the patient's medical record,"[12] and

- after the consultation is provided by the specialist, the specialist prepares "a written report of his or her findings" and provides it to the requesting physician.[13]

Example 4.8

This example includes the same facts as Example 4.5, except the pathologist, after ordering and examining the specimen, contacts the surgical oncologist by phone but does not prepare a written report of her findings.

Commentary: The pathologist's order of DHS *will* constitute a "referral" by the pathologist for Stark Law purposes.

With respect to radiation therapy services, commenters pointed out that radiation oncology treatments frequently extend over prolonged periods of time, effectively rendering the radiation oncologist the sole supervisor of the patient's care.[14] In response, the Centers for Medicare & Medicaid Services (CMS) modified the Stark Regulations to provide that "a course of radiation treatments over a period of time will be considered to be pursuant to a consultation, provided the radiation oncologist communicates with the [requesting] physician on a regular basis about the patient's course of treatment and progress."[15] CMS, however, has not provided any guidance concerning either the type or the frequency of such communications.

b. Primary physician v. consulting specialist

It is important to remember that when a radiologist (for example) orders a diagnostic radiology procedure pursuant to the consultation exception, this order will not constitute a "referral" by the specialist, but it *will* constitute a "referral" by the requesting physician. Indeed, as noted above, the definition of "referral" in both the Stark Law and Stark Regulations expressly covers both a physician's request for a consultation by another physician and any test or procedure ordered by the second (i.e., consulting) physician.

> ### Example 4.9
>
> The surgical oncologist in Example 4.5 requests that a radiation oncologist provide a consultation with respect to the surgeon's patient, who is a Medicare beneficiary diagnosed with breast cancer. Pursuant to this consultation, the radiation oncologist recommends that the patient undergo a course of radiation therapy. The radiation oncologist orders such services from the cancer center at the local community hospital.
>
> **Commentary:** This order of radiation therapy services will not constitute a "referral" by the radiation oncologist (provided the conditions of the consultation exception are met), but it *will* constitute a "referral" by the surgical oncologist.

Consistent with this limitation, CMS has cautioned that a physician "may not make [a] referral to [a] consultant if he or she knows or has reason to suspect that the consultant will order DHS from an entity with which the referring physician has a direct or indirect financial relationship to which no exception applies."[16]

c. Covered DHS v. non-covered DHS

Finally, the consultation exception does not apply to all DHS ordered by pathologists, radiologists, or radiation oncologists. Rather, the exception is specifically limited to "clinical diagnostic laboratory tests and pathological examination services" ordered by a pathologist, "diagnostic radiology services" ordered by a radiologist, and "radiation therapy" ordered by a radiation oncologist.

> ### Example 4.10
>
> This example includes the same facts as Example 4.9, except that, in addition to radiation therapy, the radiation oncologist also orders clinical laboratory services.
>
> **Commentary:** Although the order of radiation therapy services will not constitute a "referral" by the radiation oncologist, the order of clinical laboratory services will constitute such a "referral."

In the preamble to the 2004 Stark II, Phase II Regulations, CMS acknowledged that the consultation exception "would fail its intended purpose" with respect to radiation oncology consultations if the exception was not expanded to cover—and protect—non-radiation ancillary services (such as computed tomography (CT) scans, magnetic resonance imaging, and other imaging services) that are "necessary and integral" to the radiation therapy.[17] Although CMS stated in this 2004 preamble that it had "modified the regulations accordingly," the Stark Regulations themselves do not, in fact, reflect this change.[18] The authors believe that this omission was inadvertent, and commenters have asked CMS to correct it.

Example 4.11

A radiation oncologist implants radioactive seeds into the prostate of a Medicare patient. Several weeks after the procedure, the radiation oncologist sends the patient to an independent diagnostic testing facility (IDTF) to obtain a CT scan for postoperative dosimetry purposes.

Commentary: The current Stark Regulations provide that the oncologist has made a "referral" for Stark Law purposes (although, again, CMS has suggested that it intended to revise the regulations to exclude this referral under the consultation exception).

Along these lines, providers, suppliers, and practitioners should be careful to avoid a common Stark Law pitfall: glossing over the fact that the consultation exception covers a radiologist's request for *diagnostic* radiology but not *interventional* radiology. Although many interventional radiology procedures do not constitute DHS in the form of "radiology and certain other imaging services," as discussed in Chapter 3, thereby reducing the need to rely on the consultation exception in certain settings when interventional radiology services are furnished in a hospital—and, as such, constitute inpatient or outpatient hospital services—such services will constitute DHS and cannot be protected by the consultation exception.

2. Self-referrals

The Stark Regulations provide a second exception to the general rule discussed above regarding referrals. Pursuant to this exception, which we will call the "self-referral" exception, "referrals" do not include any DHS "personally performed or provided by the referring physician."[19] The regulations emphasize, however, that DHS "is not personally performed or provided by the referring physician if it is performed or provided by any other person, including, but not limited to, the referring physician's employees, independent contractors, or group practice members."[20] Thus, "incident to" services do not qualify for the self-referral exception.[21]

Example 4.12

A physician is a member of a group that is organized as a professional corporation. The physician sees a Medicare beneficiary who presents with an acute allergic reaction. The physician prepares an antigen and furnishes it to the patient.

Commentary: The physician has not made a "referral" for purposes of the Stark Law and, as such, the physician's conduct does not (and cannot) violate the Stark Law.

Example 4.13

This example includes the same facts as Example 4.12 except that, instead of personally furnishing the antigen, the physician asks a certified nurse who is employed by the group to furnish it.

Commentary: The physician has made a "referral" for purposes of the Stark Law—to the group—and this referral may implicate the Stark Law.

B. 'Imputed' referrals

CMS has taken the position that, under some circumstances, where one individual makes a "referral" (i.e., the individual orders, requests, or establishes a plan of care that includes DHS covered by Medicare), this "referral" may be "imputed" to *another* individual. CMS set forth its policy rationale for this position in the preamble to the 2001 Stark II, Phase I Regulations. A commenter suggested that DHS referrals by nonphysician personnel, such as a nurse practitioner or physician assistant, should not be imputed to a physician as long as the "nonphysician is authorized and licensed to prescribe treatment on his or her own and can make independent decisions regarding referrals."[22]

In response, CMS stated that, in general, "the question of whether a referral by a nurse practitioner or a physician assistant should be imputed to an employer physician will depend on the facts and circumstances of the referral."[23] The critical inquiry, in CMS's view, is whether the physician "controls" or "influences" the nonphysician's referral.[24] According to CMS,

[t]he Congress and HHS have recognized that many nurse practitioners and physician assistants are independent providers authorized and licensed to prescribe treatment and make independent decisions regarding referrals. However, these practitioners do not always act independently of their employers . . . In short, we are concerned that physicians could attempt to circumvent [the Stark Law] by funneling referrals through nonphysician practitioners.[25]

CMS's position (and concern) has manifested itself in the Stark Regulations' definition of "referring physician," which means either a physician who makes a "referral," "directs another person or entity to make a referral," or "controls referrals made by another person or entity."[26] CMS has provided virtually no guidance, however, concerning the "facts and circumstances" under which a physician will be deemed to have "directed" or "controlled" the referrals of another.

II. 'To'

Assuming a physician has made a "referral," the next question is whether he or she has made a referral "to" an entity for the furnishing of DHS. In most cases, this question is easily answered. For example, if a physician determines that a Medicare patient needs a blood test and sends the patient (or the patient's blood specimen) to a particular clinical laboratory for testing the physician has referred the patient "to" the laboratory at issue. In other cases, however, the answer to this question is less clear.

Example 4.14

A physician determines that a Medicare beneficiary needs a blood test. The physician prepares an order for the test and provides it to the patient. Two days later, the patient takes the order to a diagnostic clinical laboratory—one of three in the community—that performs the blood test pursuant to the physician's order.

Commentary: Under what circumstances, if any, will the physician be deemed to have made a referral "to" the clinical laboratory that furnished the blood test?

Example 4.15

A physician diagnoses a Medicare beneficiary and determines that the patient needs skilled nursing and physical therapy (PT) services. The physician refers the patient to a skilled nursing facility (SNF) and orders PT services. The SNF has a contract with a PT company and, pursuant to that contract, the PT company furnishes the PT services ordered by the physician to the patient.

Commentary: Under what circumstances, if any, will the physician be deemed to have made a referral "to" the PT company that furnished the DHS?

A. The 'steering' issue

In the preamble to the 1998 Proposed Stark II Regulations, CMS stated that it would "presume" that a physician had made a referral "to" an entity whenever any of his or her Medicare patients received DHS from an entity with which the physician had a financial relationship.[27] Pursuant to this curious logic, whether the physician in Example 4.14 referred the patient "to" the clinical laboratory would depend on whether the physician had a financial relationship with the laboratory.

CMS did provide, however, that physicians could "rebut [this] presumption by establishing that they mentioned no specific provider or supplier or that the patient was directly referred by some other independent individual or through an unrelated entity."[28] Thus, in Example 4.14, even if the physician had a financial relationship with the laboratory, if he could establish that he did not mention the laboratory to the patient, then he would not be deemed to have referred the patient "to" the laboratory.

In the preamble to its 2001 Stark II, Phase I Regulations, CMS did not indicate clearly whether it had adopted the rebuttable presumption that the agency proposed in 1998. The preamble suggests, however, that (at a minimum) there needs to be some element of patient "direction or steering" before a physician can be said to have referred a patient "to" an entity.[29] For example, CMS stated "when a physician provides an order or prescription for a DHS to a patient that ostensibly can be filled by any of a number of entities and then suggests or informs the patient that the order can be serviced by a particular entity, there would be a referral 'to' that entity."[30] By the same token, logic and fairness suggest that a physician should be able to negate the existence of such a referral by establishing that no such "suggestion" or "information" was made or given.

CMS revisited this issue (albeit, only in part, and much less directly) in the 2004 Stark II, Phase II Regulations. In response to a suggestion that the Stark Regulations should "protect any physician who provides patients with accurate information about all appropriate DHS entities and discloses his or her financial relationships with any of those DHS entities," CMS stated that the Stark Law

> embodies a congressional determination to discourage physicians from having financial relationships with DHS entities to which they refer Medicare patients ... Although disclosure of financial interests to patients informs patients of the potential conflict of interest, we do not believe, nor does the statute contemplate, that such disclosure adequately protects against improper referrals or overutilization. If DHS entities and physicians insist on entering into financial relationships, they can protect themselves by structuring the relationships to fit in one of the exceptions. The commenter's proposed exception would swallow the statute and inhibit enforcement.[31]

Thus, it would appear that CMS's current position with respect to this issue is as reflected in the following hypothetical: Assume (1) that a physician sees a Medicare beneficiary, (2) the physician concludes that the patient needs a blood test, (3) the test can be furnished by several different entities (Lab A, Lab B, or Lab C), (4) the physician has an ownership interest in Lab A, and (5) the blood test ultimately is furnished by Lab A.

- If the physician provides an order for the test to the patient and does not mention Lab A, Lab B, or Lab C, then the physician has *not* made a referral "to" Lab A.

- If the physician provides an order for the test to the patient and notes that the services could be furnished by Lab A, Lab B, or Lab C, but does not direct or steer the patient—in any way—to Lab A, then the physician has *not* made a referral "to" Lab A.

- If the physician provides an order for the test to the patient, notes that the services could be furnished by Lab A, Lab B, or Lab C, and discloses that he has an ownership interest in Lab A, then—presumably on the grounds that simply by mentioning the fact that he has an ownership interest in Lab A, the physician has "steered" the patient to Lab A—the physician *has* made a referral "to" Lab A.

Finally, it is unclear whether in the first two scenarios above, the physician or the government (or a whistleblower) would have the burden of establishing the absence or presence of patient steering. This is important because if a referral is to be "presumed," as suggested in the 1998 Stark II Proposed Regulations, then, as a practical matter, this presumption may prove difficult to rebut, particularly if a pattern emerges reflecting that a higher percentage of the ordering physician's patients selected Lab A.

B. The 'knowledge' issue

CMS has taken the position that, in some cases, where a physician orders DHS (i.e., the physician makes a "referral"), but a third party (other than the patient) decides which entity will furnish the DHS, the physician nevertheless will be deemed to have made a referral "to" that furnishing entity. The issue arises in Example 4.15: A physician refers a patient to a SNF, the referral includes a request for PT services, the SNF has a contract with a particular PT company, and that company furnishes the services at issue. The question is whether the physician can be said to have referred the patient "to" the PT company for the furnishing of DHS (i.e., the physical therapy services). According to CMS,

> a physician can make a referral of DHS "to an entity" even though the referral is first directed or routed through another person or entity, provided the physician has reason to know the identity of the actual provider of the service. In the SNF/PT provider example . . . if the physician referring the patient to the SNF [1] knows that the PT company . . . will furnish DHS to the patient or [2] could reasonably be expected to know that the PT company will actually furnish DHS to the patient, the referral is a referral "to the entity . . ."[32]

III. 'Entity'

Only referrals by a physician to an "entity" implicate the Stark Law. The Stark Law does not define the term "entity." The Stark Regulations, however, define the term to mean any of the following:

- A physician's sole practice
- A practice of multiple physicians

- Any other person
- A sole proprietorship
- A public or private agency or trust
- A corporation
- A partnership
- A limited liability company
- A foundation
- A not-for-profit corporation
- An unincorporated association[33]

After setting forth this general definition, the Stark Regulations then go on to discuss several "inclusions" and "exclusions" from the definition of the term "entity." First, the regulations provide that an "entity" does not include "the referring physician himself or herself, but does include his or her medical practice."[34] This provision is probably unnecessary. Even if a referring physician could be an "entity," the definition of "referral" (discussed above) specifically excludes any DHS that are "personally performed or provided by the referring physician."[35] Moreover, a referring physician's "medical practice" is already covered by the general definition of "entity" set forth above.

Next, the Stark Regulations provide that the term "entity" includes a health plan, managed care organization (MCO), provider-sponsored organization (PSO), or independent practice association (IPA) that employs a supplier or operates a facility that could accept reassignment from a supplier pursuant to 42 Code of Federal Regulations (CFR) §424.80(b)(1)-(2), with respect to any DHS provided by that supplier.[36] This provision also is probably unnecessary (and arguably misplaced). In virtually all cases, the MCO, PSO, or IPA at issue will be a corporation, limited liability company, etc., and, as such, will constitute an "entity" under the general definition of the term. This provision really relates to the circumstances under which an MCO will be deemed the entity that is "furnishing" DHS. That topic is covered in the next section.

Finally, the Stark Regulations provide that the definition of "entity" does "not include a physician's practice when it bills Medicare for a diagnostic test in accordance with [42 CFR §414.50], physician billing for purchased diagnostic tests, and section 3060.4 of the Medicare Carriers Manual (purchased diagnostic tests), as amended or replaced from time to time."[37] Again, this provision conflates two separate Stark Law elements: "entity" and "furnishing." As discussed below, in most cases, an entity will be the "furnishing" entity if it receives payment from Medicare for the DHS at issue. Instead of providing an exception to this rule where the entity at issue is a physician practice and the DHS at issue are diagnostic tests that have been purchased by the practice, CMS has created an exception to the definition of "entity."

IV. 'Furnishing'

Assuming that a physician has made a referral to an entity, the next question is whether that entity is, in fact, "furnishing" the DHS in question. Although the identity of the "furnishing" entity often is obvious, there are many common arrangements that involve multiple entities, raising the question (at least historically) of whether the analysis was focused on the correct entity. The ensuing uncertainty, which was exacerbated by the Stark Law's failure to define the term "furnishing," prompted CMS, in the 2001 Stark II, Phase I Regulations, to develop a definition of the term. Pursuant to the regulations, an entity will be considered to be "furnishing" DHS in three situations.

First, an entity will be considered to be "furnishing" DHS if it is the entity to which CMS makes payment for the DHS "directly."

Example 4.16

A physician determines that a Medicare beneficiary needs surgery, which is furnished in a hospital on an inpatient basis. Medicare reimburses the hospital directly for its services.

Commentary: The hospital is the entity that "furnished" the DHS at issue (i.e., the inpatient hospital services).

Second, an entity will be considered to be "furnishing" DHS if it is the entity to which CMS makes payment for the DHS "upon assignment on the patient's behalf."

Example 4.17

A physician determines that a Medicare beneficiary needs an x-ray. The physician orders the x-ray, which the patient obtains at an imaging center (operating as an IDTF) that is unaffiliated with the physician. The patient "assigns" his claim for reimbursement to the imaging center, the imaging center furnishes the x-ray and submits the assigned claim to Medicare Part B for reimbursement, and Medicare reimburses the imaging center.

Commentary: The imaging center is the entity that "furnished" the DHS at issue (i.e., the radiology services).

Third, except as discussed below, an entity will be considered to be "furnishing" DHS if it is the entity "to which the right to payment for the DHS" "has been reassigned" pursuant to the regulatory reassignment exceptions for employers,[38] facilities,[39] and healthcare delivery systems.[40]

Example 4.18

An oncology practice group that is organized as a professional corporation employs a radiation oncologist. The oncologist determines that a Medicare beneficiary needs radiation therapy services. The professional component of these services is furnished by the oncologist. With respect to these professional radiation therapy services, the patient "assigns" her claim for reimbursement to the oncologist, and the oncologist, in turn, "reassigns" the claim to his employer (i.e., the practice group). The practice group submits the reassigned claim to Medicare for reimbursement, and Medicare reimburses the group.

Commentary: The practice group is the entity that "furnished" the DHS (i.e., the radiation therapy services).

The exception to the reassignment rule above is as follows: If the entity to which the right to payment for the DHS has been reassigned is a "health plan"[41] or an MCO, PSO, or IPA that contracts with a health plan to provide services to plan enrollees (collectively, an "MCO"), then the MCO will *not* be considered to be "furnishing" DHS unless the MCO either employs the supplier that furnished the DHS or operates a facility that could accept reassignment from the supplier with respect to DHS furnished by the supplier.

Example 4.19

A Medicare beneficiary is enrolled through his employer in a commercial health plan. The health plan has network provider agreements with various retail pharmacies. One of these pharmacies fills a prescription for the enrollee. The prescription is for a drug covered by Medicare Part B. The enrollee "assigns" his claim for reimbursement to the pharmacy, and the pharmacy (pursuant to its contract with the health plan) "reassigns" the claim to the health plan. The health plan submits the reassigned claim to Medicare for reimbursement, and Medicare reimburses the plan.

Commentary: The pharmacy—and not the health plan—is the entity that "furnished" the DHS (i.e., the outpatient prescription drug).

Example 4.20

A Medicare beneficiary is enrolled through his employer in a commercial health plan. The health plan employs a radiation oncologist. The oncologist furnishes professional radiation therapy services to the patient. The patient "assigns" his claim for reimbursement to the oncologist, who "reassigns" the claim to his employer (i.e., the health plan). The health plan submits the reassigned claim to Medicare for reimbursement, and Medicare reimburses the plan.

Commentary: The health plan is the entity that "furnished" the DHS (i.e., the radiation therapy services).

Notes

1. 42 United States Code (USC) §1395nn(h)(5)(A). In the preamble to the 1998 Proposed Stark II Regulations, CMS clarified that the portions of the Stark Law definition relating to Medicare Part B do not cover requests for all Medicare Part B items and services, but only those Part B items and services that constitute DHS. Proposed Stark II Regulations (Preamble), 63 *Federal Register (FR)* 1659, 1690 (1998).
2. 42 USC §1395nn(h)(5)(B).
3. 42 CFR §411.351.
4. 42 CFR §411.351.

5. 42 CFR §411.351.

6. 42 USC §1395nn(h)(5)(C).

7. 42 USC §1395nn(h)(5)(C).

8. 42 USC §1395nn(h)(5)(C).

9. 42 CFR §411.351.

10. 42 CFR §411.351.

11. 42 CFR §411.351. It would appear that the request for the consultation may be made in writing, electronically, or orally. Id.

12. 42 CFR §411.351.

13. 42 CFR § 411.351. In the preamble to the Stark I Proposed Regulations, CMS took the position that in addition to a written report, a "consultation" must include "the history and examination of the patient." Stark I Proposed Regulations (Preamble), 57 *FR* 8588, 8595 (1992). Commenters complained, however, that the physician specialists covered by the consultation exception often do not take patient histories or perform physical examinations. Stark II, Phase I Regulations (Preamble), 66 *FR* 856, 875 (2001). In response to these comments, CMS clarified "that a consultation does not necessarily include either taking the history of a patient or performing a physical examination." Id.

14. Stark II, Phase I Regulations (Preamble), 66 *FR* 856, 874 (2001).

15. 42 CFR §411.351.

16. Stark II, Phase I Regulations (Preamble), 66 *FR* 856, 874.

17. Stark II, Phase II Regulations (Preamble), 69 *FR* 10654, 16065 (2004).

18. Stark II, Phase II Regulations (Preamble), 69 *FR* 16054, 16065 (2004).

19. 42 CFR §411.351.

20. 42 CFR §411.351.

21. Stark II, Phase II Regulations (Preamble), 69 *FR* 16056, 16063 (2004).

22. Stark II, Phase I Regulations (Preamble), 66 *FR* 856, 872 (2001).

23. Stark II, Phase I Regulations (Preamble), 66 *FR* 856, 872 (2001).

24. Stark II, Phase I Regulations (Preamble), 66 *FR* 856, 872 (2001).

25. Stark II, Phase I Regulations (Preamble), 66 *FR* 856, 872. See also id. at 901 ("If a nonphysician practitioner is referring a physician's patients at the physician's suggestion or in lieu of the treating physician, we would impute the referrals to the physician. Simply stated, physicians may not delegate their own referrals to avoid the referral prohibition. On the other hand, we would not impute the

referrals if the nurse practitioner or the physician assistant is independently treating the patients and initiates the referrals on his or her own. We think the determination will depend on the specific facts and circumstances.")

26. 42 CFR §411.351. See also 42 CFR §411.353(a) ("a referral made by a physician's group practice, its members, or its staff may be imputed to the physician, if the physician directs the group practice, its members, or its staff to make the referral or if the physician controls referrals made by his or her group practice, its members, or its staff").

27. Stark II Proposed Regulations (Preamble), 63 *FR* 1659, 1711 (1998).

28. Stark II Proposed Regulations (Preamble), 63 *FR* 1659, 1711 (1998).

29. Stark II, Phase I Regulations (Preamble), 66 *FR* 856, 873 (2001).

30. Stark II, Phase I Regulations (Preamble), 66 *FR* 856, 873 (2001).

31. Stark II, Phase II Regulations (Preamble), 69 *FR* 16056, 16064 (2004).

32. Stark II, Phase I Regulations (Preamble), 66 *FR* 856, 873 (2001). Pursuant to consolidated billing, the SNF, rather than the PT company, would be considered to be the furnishing entity.

33. 42 CFR §411.351.

34. 42 CFR §411.351.

35. 42 CFR §411.351.

36. 42 CFR §411.351.

37. 42 CFR §411.351.

38. 42 CFR §§ 411.351 and 424.80(b)(1).

39. 42 CFR §§ 411.351 and 424.80(b)(2).

40. 42 CFR §§ 411.351 and 424.80(b)(3).

41. For purposes of this provision, "health plan" has the meaning set forth in 42 CFR §1001.952(l).

Chapter 5

FINANCIAL RELATIONSHIPS

Chapter 5

FINANCIAL RELATIONSHIPS

In the first four chapters of this book, we discuss the first step of the three-step process used to determine whether an arrangement may violate the Stark Law: Does the arrangement involve a "physician" making a "referral" "to" an "entity" for the "furnishing" of "designated health services" (DHS) covered by Medicare?

If the answer to this question is "yes," then the second step in the process—which is addressed in this chapter—requires determining whether the physician or one of the physician's immediate family members (IFM) has a "financial relationship" with the entity furnishing DHS.[1]

If a financial relationship does not exist, then the arrangement does not implicate (and cannot violate) the Stark Law. If a financial relationship does exist, then the arrangement does implicate the Law and one must proceed to step three, which requires determining whether the arrangement qualifies for protection under one or more Stark Law exceptions (covered in Chapters 6–10).

I. Overview

There are four basic types of financial relationships:

1. Direct ownership/investment interests
2. Indirect ownership/investment interests
3. Direct compensation arrangements
4. Indirect compensation arrangements

A. Ownership interests

The Stark Law's discussion of financial relationships is fairly limited. With respect to ownership and investment interests—to which we will refer collectively as "ownership interests"—the Stark Law provides the following guidelines:

- a physician/IFM has a financial relationship with an entity if the physician/IFM has "an ownership or investment interest" in the entity,[2]

- an ownership interest "may be through equity, debt, or other means,"[3] and

- an ownership interest "includes an interest in an entity that holds an ownership . . . interest in any entity providing the DHS."[4]

B. Compensation arrangements

With respect to compensation arrangements, the Stark Law is equally general, providing that a physician/IFM has a financial relationship with an entity if there is a "compensation arrangement" between the physician/IFM and the entity.[5] A "compensation arrangement" in turn, is "any arrangement" involving "any remuneration" between a physician/IFM and an entity.[6] Finally, somewhat circularly, "remuneration" means "any remuneration, directly or indirectly, overtly or covertly, in cash or in kind."[7]

C. Direct v. indirect financial relationships

The Stark Regulations include a lengthy discussion of financial relationships and several provisions for distinguishing between direct and indirect financial relationships. This distinction is critical because some Stark Law exceptions apply only to specific types of financial relationships.

For example, as its name implies, the "indirect compensation arrangements exception" (which is discussed in Chapter 9) applies only to indirect compensation arrangements. Similarly, the Centers for Medicare & Medicaid Services (CMS) has made it clear that even if an exception protects one or more links in the chain that makes up an indirect compensation arrangement, if (1) the indirect compensation arrangement as a whole is not covered by the indirect compensation arrangements exception or (2) the DHS at issue are not covered by an all-purpose exception, then referrals of DHS by the physician to the DHS entity at issue may violate the Stark Law's referral prohibition.

In general, the Stark Regulations provide that a direct financial relationship exists if "remuneration" passes "between" the physician/IFM and DHS entity "without any intervening persons or entities."[8] Thus, when remuneration passes between a physician/IFM and DHS entity and there are one or more "intervening persons or entities," the *only* type of financial relationship that may exist between the physician/IFM and entity is an "indirect" financial relationship. To determine whether an "indirect" ownership interest or compensation arrangement exists, one must apply the definitions of those terms, discussed below.

Finally, note that a financial relationship between a physician/IFM and a DHS entity may exist for Stark Law purposes even if the ownership interest or compensation arrangement at issue is wholly unrelated to DHS or to the provision of healthcare services more generally.[9]

Example 5.1

A physician's granddaughter is a caterer. A physical therapy (PT) company hires the granddaughter to cater its annual holiday party.

Commentary: One of the physician's IFMs (her granddaughter) has a "financial relationship" (a direct compensation arrangement) with the PT company and, unless an exception applies, the physician may not refer patients to the PT company for DHS covered by Medicare.

Example 5.2

A physician's son-in-law is a landscaper. A hospital hires him to maintain its grounds.

Commentary: One of the physician's IFMs (his son-in-law) has a "financial relationship" (a direct compensation arrangement) with the hospital, and unless an exception applies, the physician may not refer patients to the hospital for DHS covered by Medicare.

II. Direct ownership interests

The Stark Law provides that a physician/IFM has a financial relationship with an entity if he or she has "an ownership or investment interest" in the entity.[10] The Law further provides that an ownership interest "may be through equity, debt, or other means."[11]

The Stark Regulations clarify that a "direct" ownership interest exists only when no "intervening persons or entities" are between the physician/IFM and DHS entity. The Stark Regulations also expand upon the Stark Law's discussion of direct ownership interests in several respects, which are discussed below.

A. Inclusions v. exclusions

The Stark Regulations provide that—subject to certain exceptions and clarifications (discussed below)—an ownership interest may include (1) stock, (2) stock options, (3) partnership shares, (4) limited liability company (LLC) memberships, and (5) loans, bonds, and other financial instruments that are secured with an entity's property or revenue (or a portion of that property or revenue).[12]

CMS has clarified that a loan secured by a particular piece of a provider's equipment, for example, does not itself create an ownership interest in the provider.[13] Moreover, the Stark Regulations provide that an ownership interest does not include the following:

- stock options and convertible securities received as compensation, until the stock options are exercised or the convertible securities are converted to equity,

- an interest in a retirement plan,

- an unsecured loan subordinated to a credit facility, or

- an "under arrangement" contract between a hospital and an entity owned by one or more physicians (or a group of physicians) providing DHS "under arrangement" with the hospital.[14]

It should be emphasized that with the exception of an interest in a retirement plan, although these arrangements do not create an "ownership interest" in the entity at issue, they do (or may) create a "compensation arrangement" with that entity.[15]

Example 5.3

A physician serves as the medical director of a home health agency (HHA). Her compensation package includes both a salary and stock options that she may exercise on or after January 1, 2010.

Commentary: The physician does not have an "ownership interest" in the HHA and will not have such an interest until and unless she exercises the stock options on or after January 1, 2010. In the interim, however, the physician has a "compensation arrangement" with the HHA.

B. Parents and subsidiaries

The Stark Regulations also clarify that an ownership interest in a subsidiary company does not create an ownership interest in the parent company or in any other subsidiary of the parent company (unless the "subsidiary company itself has an ownership or investment interest in the parent or such other subsidiaries").[16]

Example 5.4

A hospital has a 100% ownership interest in an HHA and a 90% ownership interest in a clinical laboratory. A physician also has a 10% ownership interest in the laboratory.

Commentary: The physician has a direct ownership interest in the clinical laboratory but does not have a direct ownership interest in either the laboratory's sister subsidiary (the HHA) or its parent (the hospital).

C. Application of exceptions

Finally, the Stark Regulations clarify that "with respect to profit distributions, dividends, or interest payments on secured obligations," as long as the underlying ownership interest meets an ownership interest or all-purpose exception, the distributions/dividends/payments (i.e., the returns on the investment at issue) do not also have to fit within a compensation arrangement exception.

Example 5.5

In 2004, a physician purchases shares in a for-profit hospital and, as a result, has a direct ownership interest in the hospital. In 2005, the hospital declares a dividend and makes a cash distribution to all of its shareholders, including the physician.

Commentary: The distribution creates a direct compensation arrangement between the physician and the hospital. Provided that an ownership interest or all-purpose exception protects the underlying ownership interest, this exception also will protect the compensation arrangement resulting from the dividend.

III. Indirect ownership interests

Although the Stark Law does not use the term "indirect" ownership interest, it does provide that an "ownership or investment interest . . . includes an interest in an entity that holds an ownership or investment interest in any entity" providing the DHS.[18] The Stark Regulations clarify and expand upon this statutory language, providing that a physician has an indirect ownership interest in an entity if two conditions (discussed below) are satisfied. The Stark Regulations also address (1) whether "common control" arrangements may give rise to one or more indirect ownership interests and (2) how Stark Law exceptions apply to indirect ownership interests.

A. Condition one: Unbroken chain

The first condition of the indirect ownership interest definition is that, between the physician/IFM and DHS entity, there must be "an unbroken chain of any number (but no fewer than one) of persons or entities having ownership or investment interests."[19]

Example 5.6

A physician has a 1% ownership interest in an LLC. The LLC has ownership interests in several companies. For example, the LLC has a 1% ownership interest in a clinical laboratory.

Commentary: There is an "unbroken chain" of entities with ownership interest between the physician and the laboratory (i.e., the physician has an ownership interest in the LLC, and the LLC has an ownership interest in the laboratory). As such, the physician *may* have an indirect ownership interest in the laboratory, depending on whether the second condition of the indirect ownership interest definition (discussed below) is satisfied.

If any link in the chain of financial relationships between the physician/IFM and DHS entity is not an ownership interest, but instead is a compensation arrangement, the first condition will not be met and the physician/IFM cannot have an indirect ownership interest in the DHS entity. However, as discussed below, under such circumstances, the physician/IFM and DHS entity may have an indirect compensation arrangement.

Example 5.7

A physician has a 10% ownership interest in a management services company (MSC), the MSC has a personal services contract with a hospital, and the hospital owns a laboratory.

Commentary: Because one link in the chain of financial relationships between the physician and the laboratory—the personal services arrangement between the MSC and the hospital—is not an ownership interest, the physician does not have an indirect ownership interest in the laboratory. The physician may, however, have an indirect compensation arrangement with the laboratory.

B. Condition two: State of mind

The second condition of the indirect ownership interest definition is that the DHS entity either must have "actual knowledge of," or must act "in reckless disregard or deliberate ignorance of," the fact that the referring physician/IFM has an ownership interest "through any number of intermediary ownership or investment interests" in the DHS entity.[20]

> **Example 5.8**
>
> This example includes the same facts as Example 5.6 (i.e., the physician has a 1% interest in the LLC, which has a 1% interest in the clinical laboratory).
>
> **Commentary:** The second condition will be satisfied—and the physician will have an indirect ownership interest in the laboratory—if the laboratory knows that the physician has an ownership interest in the LLC or acts "in reckless disregard or deliberate ignorance of" this fact.

The Stark Regulations do not define the terms "reckless disregard" or "deliberate ignorance." In the preamble to the 2001 Stark II, Phase I Regulations, however, CMS stated that this "knowledge" element "generally imposes a duty of reasonable inquiry on providers."[21] CMS has emphasized, however, that

> given the impracticability of investigating every possible indirect financial relationship involving a referring physician, the knowledge element does not impose an affirmative obligation to inquire as to indirect financial relationships. A duty of reasonable inquiry does require, however, that providers in possession of facts that would lead a reasonable person to suspect the existence of an indirect financial relationship take reasonable steps to determine whether such a financial relationship exists . . . The reasonable steps to be taken will depend on the circumstances. [22]

CMS acknowledged that including a state-of-mind element in the definition of indirect ownership interest "may allow more claims to be paid than a requirement that would interpret the statute to impose an absolute duty to investigate (and may impose a higher evidentiary burden on the government in an enforcement action)."[23] According to CMS, however, "incorporating a knowledge element in the definition of indirect financial relationships more fairly balances the burden of compliance against the risk of abuse the statute was intended to prevent."[24]

> We iterate that for purposes of [the Stark Law,] the DHS entity has no affirmative duty to inquire or investigate whether an indirect financial relationship with a referring physician (or immediate family member) exists, absent some information that would put a reasonable person on alert, and that the duty that is imposed is one of reasonable inquiry in the circumstances.[25]

> ### Example 5.9
>
> This example includes the same facts as Example 5.6 (i.e., the physician has a 1% interest in the LLC, which has a 1% interest in the clinical laboratory). In addition, although lab personnel have never seen a list of all the individuals and entities that have ownership interests in the LLC, the LLC has informed the lab's management that some physicians in the lab's community have ownership interests in the LLC. In addition, several patients have informed laboratory personnel that the physician has stated that he owns several clinical laboratories in the community through other companies.
>
> **Commentary:** The laboratory arguably (1) is in possession of facts that would lead a reasonable person to suspect that the physician has an indirect ownership interest in the laboratory and (2) must take reasonable steps to determine whether such a financial relationship exists.

CMS indicated that a DHS entity may meet the "reasonable steps" standard by obtaining a good faith, written assurance from the referring physician that he or she does not have a direct or indirect ownership interest in the entity.[26] CMS hastened to add, however, that a written assurance will not be determinative, especially when the DHS entity possesses information that contradicts or discredits the written assurance.[27]

Finally, the Stark Regulations emphasize that an indirect ownership interest exists "even though the entity furnishing DHS does not know or acts in reckless disregard or deliberate ignorance of the precise composition of the unbroken chain or the specific terms of the ownership or investment interests that form the links in the chain."[28]

> ### Example 5.10
>
> This example includes the same facts as Example 5.9. In addition, the laboratory contacts the physician, who confirms that he has an ownership interest in the LLC.
>
> **Commentary:** This arrangement will meet the second condition of the indirect ownership interest definition even if the laboratory does not know the size of the physician's ownership interest in the LLC (e.g., 1%) or the specific terms of this interest.

C. Common ownership

The Stark Regulations clarify that "common ownership or investment in an entity does not, in and of itself, establish an indirect ownership or investment interest by one common owner or investor in another common owner or investor."[29] Similarly, the Regulations state that an indirect ownership interest requires an unbroken chain of ownership interests between the physician/IFM and the DHS entity "such that the [physician/IFM] has an indirect ownership or investment interest in the entity furnishing DHS."[30]

Example 5.11

This example includes the same facts as Example 5.4 (i.e., a hospital has a 90% ownership interest and a physician has a 10% ownership interest in a clinical laboratory).

Commentary: The physician does not have an indirect ownership interest in the hospital. First, the hospital's and physician's common ownership of the laboratory does not establish an indirect ownership interest by one common owner (the physician) in another common owner (the hospital). Second, the physician does not have an ownership interest "in" the hospital.

D. Exceptions

Finally, CMS has clarified that "if a referring physician's direct ownership or investment interest in a DHS entity would be protected" under an ownership interest or all-purpose exception, "then a similar indirect ownership or investment interest of the physician in that same DHS entity would be excepted."[31]

Example 5.12

A physician has an ownership interest in a company with an ownership interest in a hospital in Puerto Rico.

Commentary: Assuming that the physician has an indirect ownership interest in the hospital—which will turn on the "state-of-mind" condition—this interest may be protected by the Stark Law exception for ownership interests in hospitals located in Puerto Rico.[32]

Note: As noted above and discussed further in Chapter 9, this principle does not apply to indirect compensation arrangements.

IV. Direct compensation arrangements

The Stark Law provides that, subject to a few narrow exceptions, a "compensation arrangement" is "any arrangement" involving "any remuneration" between a physician/IFM and a DHS entity[33] and "remuneration" is "any remuneration, directly or indirectly, overtly or covertly, in cash or in kind." [34]

The Stark Regulations generally track the Stark Law in this regard, providing that a compensation arrangement is "any arrangement involving remuneration" between a physician/IFM and DHS entity,[35] and that (with a few narrow exceptions) "remuneration" means "any payment or other benefit made directly or indirectly, overtly or covertly, in cash or in kind."[36]

As discussed above, the Stark Regulations clarify that a compensation arrangement will be considered "direct" only if "remuneration passes between the referring physician (or a member of his or her family) and the entity furnishing DHS without any intervening persons or entities."[37] Thus, if a payment passes from a DHS entity to a third party (i.e., an "intervening person or entity"), and from that third party to the physician/IFM, the physician/IFM cannot have a direct compensation arrangement with the DHS entity. However, the physician/IFM and DHS entity may have an indirect compensation arrangement.

Historically, CMS took the position that a person or entity serving as the "agent" of a physician/IFM or entity would not qualify as an "intervening" person or entity in the context of determining whether a compensation arrangement was "direct" or "indirect." For example, the 2001 Stark II, Phase I Regulations provided that a "direct financial relationship" would exist if remuneration passed between the physician/IFM and DHS entity "without any intervening persons or entities (not including an agent of the physician, the [IFM], or the entity furnishing the DHS)."[38]

CMS appears to have changed its mind regarding the exclusion of "agents" as "intervening persons or entities" from the definition of "direct financial relationships." The 2004 Stark II, Phase II Regulations provide that a "direct financial relationship" exists if "remuneration passes between the referring

Example 5.13

A hospital asks a physician to serve as the medical director of one of its clinical departments in return for a monthly fee of $10,000. The physician is a shareholder in a three-physician practice group. The hospital, physician, and group agree that the hospital will transfer the $10,000 monthly fee to the group—acting as the physician's agent with respect to the payment—and the group, in turn, will transfer the $10,000 to the physician.

Commentary: It appears that under the 2001 Stark II, Phase I Regulations, CMS would have taken the position that, because the group was acting as the physician's agent, it did not qualify as an "intervening person or entity" for purposes of the "direct financial relationships" definition and, as such, that the hospital and physician would have had a "direct" compensation arrangement (and not, potentially, an "indirect" compensation arrangement).

physician (or an IFM) and the entity furnishing DHS without any intervening persons or entities."[39] The deletion of the "not including an agent" language from the definition of direct financial relationships appears to mean that if remuneration passes from a DHS entity to a physician/IFM through *any* intervening person or entity—including an agent—the physician/IFM and DHS entity cannot have a direct compensation arrangement. They may have an indirect compensation arrangement, but only if the arrangement meets the definition of such an arrangement.

Example 5.14

This example includes the same facts as Example 5.13.

Commentary: Under the Stark II, Phase II Regulations, it appears that although the group was acting as the physician's agent, it still qualifies as an "intervening person or entity" for purposes of the "direct financial relationship" definition and, as such, that the hospital and physician do not have a direct compensation arrangement (although they may have an indirect compensation arrangement).

Finally, it cannot be emphasized enough how broadly the Stark Law and Regulations define the term "compensation arrangement," especially when considering the related definition of "remuneration." As noted in the Introduction, it arguably is the case that (1) each and every physician has a direct compensation arrangement with each and every hospital to which the physician refers patients and (2) as a result, no physician may refer a Medicare patient to any such hospital for the furnishing of DHS without implicating—and, in the absence of an applicable exception, violating—the Stark Law.

As discussed above, a compensation arrangement is "*any* arrangement involving remuneration," and "remuneration" means "*any* payment or other benefit made . . . overtly or covertly, in cash or in kind." Thus, if a hospital provides a physician with anything of value, regardless of how small—notepads and coffee mugs are two examples that CMS has identified[40]—then the hospital and physician have a "financial relationship" in the form of a "direct compensation arrangement" and, in the absence of an exception, the physician may not refer Medicare patients to the hospital—and the hospital may not bill for DHS furnished to such patients—without violating the Stark Law.

V. Indirect compensation arrangements

Although the Stark Law does not use the term "indirect ownership interest," it provides that an ownership interest "includes an interest in an entity that holds an ownership or investment interest in any entity providing the DHS."[41] The Stark Law includes no similar provision with respect to compensation arrangements, however. In fact, the Stark Law simply provides that a "compensation arrangement" means an arrangement involving any remuneration "between" a physician/IFM and a DHS entity.

Arguably, when a hospital contracts with a practice group to provide medical director services to the hospital's cardiology department and the practice group compensates its employed physicians through a salary, there would be (1) an "arrangement" involving "remuneration" "between" the hospital and the practice group and (2) an "arrangement" involving "remuneration" "between" the practice group and each of its employed physicians. However, there would not be an "arrangement" involving "remuneration" "between" the hospital and any of the group's physicians.

It is true that the Stark Law defines the term "remuneration" to include "any remuneration, directly or indirectly, overtly or covertly, in cash or in kind."[42] But the fact that "remuneration" may be provided "indirectly" does not necessarily mean that, in the above hypothetical, for example, the two arrangements can be transformed into a single "compensation arrangement" "between" the hospital and each physician in the group.

It may simply mean that, when a hospital employs a particular physician at a salary of $10,000 per month, whether the hospital pays the physician $10,000 in cash each month (i.e., the remuneration is provided to the physician "directly") or the hospital deposits the $10,000 into the physician's bank account electronically (i.e., the remuneration is provided to the physician "indirectly"), there is a compensation arrangement "between" the physician and the hospital.

Alternatively, Congress may have intended the definition of "remuneration" to address obvious circumvention schemes. Assume, for example, that a hospital and physician agree that the hospital will pay the physician $100 for each referral for the furnishing of DHS covered by Medicare. Instead of paying the physician the money "directly," the hospital and physician agree that the hospital will pay the $100 per referral to one of the physician's friends who will, in turn, provide it to the physician. The Stark Law's definition of "remuneration" would support the existence of a "compensation arrangement" "between" the hospital and the physician, even if the hospital made referral payments to the physician "indirectly."

The above discussion is largely academic, however, because CMS has clearly stated its position that, for Stark Law purposes, "financial relationships" include both "direct" and "indirect" compensation arrangements. Indeed, as defined and interpreted by CMS, a physician/IFM may have an indirect compensation arrangement with a DHS entity even if there are many "intervening individuals or entities" between the physician/IFM and the DHS entity.

Specifically, the Stark Regulations provide that a physician/IFM and DHS entity will have an "indirect" compensation arrangement if three conditions are satisfied. Note that if *any* one of the three conditions is not satisfied, the physician/IFM and DHS entity will not have an indirect compensation arrangement and, as such, unless the physician/IFM and DHS entity have some other financial relationship, the physician may make referrals to the entity for the furnishing of DHS without violating the Stark Law's referral prohibition.

A. Condition one: Unbroken chain

In order for an "indirect compensation arrangement" to exist between a physician/IFM and a DHS entity, there must first be "an unbroken chain" of persons or entities that have financial relationships "between them (i.e., each link in the chain has either an ownership or investment interest or a compensation arrangement with the preceding link)."[43]

Example 5.15

A hospital contracts with (and pays) a physician practice group to furnish medical director services to the hospital. The practice group in turn has a paid employee, Physician A.

Commentary: There is an unbroken chain of financial relationships between the hospital and Physician A, consisting of the compensation arrangement between the hospital and the group (link one) and the compensation arrangement between the group and Physician A (link two). As such, the hospital may have an indirect compensation arrangement with Physician A, depending on whether the second and third conditions of the indirect compensation arrangement definition are satisfied.

Example 5.16

This example includes the same facts as Example 5.15, except the practice group also has a physician *owner*, Physician B.

Commentary: There is an unbroken chain of financial relationships between the hospital and Physician B, consisting of the compensation arrangement between the hospital and the group (link one) and Physician B's ownership interest in the group (link two). As such, the hospital may have an indirect compensation arrangement with Physician B, depending on whether the second and third conditions of the indirect compensation arrangement definition are satisfied.

Example 5.17

This includes the same facts as Example 5.15, except the practice group also has a physician, Physician C, who has an ownership interest in the practice group and is employed by (i.e., has a compensation arrangement with) the group.

Commentary: There are two separate and distinct "unbroken chains" of financial relationships between the hospital and Physician C, each of which must be analyzed separately for purposes of the indirect compensation arrangement definition. The first unbroken chain of financial relationships consists of the compensation arrangement between the hospital and the group (link one) and the compensation arrangement between the group and Physician C (in his capacity as an employee) (link two). The second unbroken chain of financial relationships consists of the compensation arrangement between the hospital and the group (link one), and Physician C's ownership interest in the group (link two). Either or both of these unbroken chains may give rise to an indirect compensation arrangement between the hospital and Physician C, depending on whether the second and third conditions of the indirect compensation arrangement definition are satisfied with respect to each.

Significantly, CMS takes the position that "[a] direct financial relationship can form a link in a chain of financial arrangements that creates an indirect compensation arrangement, even if the direct financial relationship qualifies for an exception."[44] Accordingly, even if each link in an "unbroken chain" of financial relationships is protected by a Stark Law exception, the physician/IFM and DHS entity will have an indirect compensation arrangement—which must meet the requirements of either the indirect compensation arrangements exception or an all-purpose exception—provided that the other two conditions of the indirect compensation arrangement definition are satisfied.[45]

Example 5.18

This includes the same facts as Example 5.15 (i.e., a hospital contracts with and pays a physician practice group to furnish medical director services to the hospital, and the practice group, in turn, has a paid physician employee, Physician A).

Commentary: Even if the compensation arrangement between the group and Physician A fits into the Stark Law's employment exception (or any other exception), there would still be an "unbroken chain" of financial relationships between Physician A and the hospital and, as such, the hospital may have an indirect compensation arrangement with Physician A, depending on whether the second and third conditions of the definition are satisfied.

It is somewhat less clear whether an "unbroken chain" exists for purposes of the indirect compensation arrangement definition if the remuneration at issue flows in opposite directions. A literal reading of the definition suggests that it does.

Example 5.19

A hospital hires (and pays) a clinical laboratory to furnish certain services to the hospital. The hospital also hires (and pays) a physician to furnish certain services to the hospital. Thus, the following represents the flow of payments:
physician ← hospital → laboratory.

Commentary: Although remuneration arguably is not "flowing" from the laboratory to the physician, for purposes of the indirect compensation arrangement definition, it appears that there is an unbroken chain of financial relationships "between" the physician and the laboratory and, as such, the physician and laboratory may have an indirect compensation arrangement, depending on whether the second and third conditions of the definition are satisfied.

B. Condition two: Volume or value

Assuming that there is an unbroken chain of financial relationships between a physician/IFM and DHS entity, determining whether the second condition of the indirect compensation arrangement definition is satisfied requires determining whether the physician/IFM has either of the following:

- a direct *compensation arrangement* in the chain of financial relationships at issue, in which case the "physician link test" applies, or

- a direct *ownership interest* in the chain of financial relationships at issue, in which case the "nonphysician link test" applies.

Example 5.20

A physician is employed by a clinical laboratory that has a services contract with a hospital.

Commentary: The physician has a direct compensation arrangement (with the laboratory) in the chain of financial relationships between the physician and the hospital and, as such, the physician link test applies.

> **Example 5.21**
>
> A physician has an ownership interest in a clinical laboratory that has a services contract with a hospital.
>
> **Commentary:** The physician has a direct ownership interest in the chain of financial relationships between the physician and the hospital and, as such, the "nonphysician link test" applies.

1. Physician link test

When the physician/IFM has a direct compensation arrangement in the chain of financial relationships at issue, the second condition of the indirect compensation arrangement definition will be satisfied if the physician/IFM receives "aggregate compensation" from the person/entity in the chain with which the physician/IFM has a direct compensation arrangement "that varies with, or otherwise reflects, the volume or value of referrals or other business generated by the referring physician for the entity furnishing the DHS," regardless of whether the "individual unit of compensation satisfies the special rules on unit-based compensation" (i.e., special compensation rules).[46]

> **Example 5.22**
>
> This example includes the same facts as Example 5.20 (i.e., a physician is employed by a clinical laboratory that has a services contract with a hospital).
>
> **Commentary:** The second condition of the indirect compensation arrangement definition will be satisfied if the *physician* receives aggregate compensation from the *laboratory* that varies with, or otherwise reflects, the volume or value of referrals or other business generated by the physician for the hospital. However, if the aggregate compensation that the laboratory pays to the physician does not vary with, or otherwise reflect, the volume or value of referrals or other business generated by the referring *physician* for the *hospital*, then (1) the second condition will not be satisfied, (2) the physician will not have an indirect compensation arrangement with the hospital, and (3) the physician may make referrals to the hospital for the furnishing of DHS without violating the Stark Law's referral prohibition.

Applying the physician link test is, of course, more complicated than Example 5.22 suggests because the test actually consists of four separate questions, each of which is considered regardless of the special compensation rules:

- **Vary with referrals.** Does the aggregate compensation paid to the physician "vary with" the "volume or value" of "referrals" by the referring physician to the DHS entity?

- **Otherwise reflect referrals.** Does the aggregate compensation paid to the physician "otherwise reflect" the "volume or value" of "referrals" by the referring physician for the DHS entity?

- **Vary with other business.** Does the aggregate compensation paid to the physician "vary with" any "other business generated by" the referring physician to the DHS entity?

- **Otherwise reflect other business.** Does the aggregate compensation paid to the physician "otherwise reflect" any "other business generated" by the referring physician to the DHS entity?

If the answer to any of these four questions is "yes," then the second condition of the indirect compensation arrangement definition is satisfied and, as such, the physician/IFM and DHS entity *may* have an indirect compensation arrangement, depending on whether the third condition is satisfied.

The various components of these four questions—i.e., the "volume or value" and "other business generated" standards and "otherwise reflects," and the special compensation rules—are discussed in Chapter 2. In addition, a discussion of these components as they relate to the definition of indirection compensation arrangements is set forth later in this chapter.

2. Nonphysician link test

When the physician/IFM has a direct ownership interest in the unbroken chain of financial relationships at issue, "the determination of whether the aggregate compensation varies with, or otherwise reflects, the volume or value of referrals or other business generated" by the physician/IFM for the DHS entity is measured by the *compensation* arrangement closest to the physician/IFM.[47]

> ### Example 5.23
>
> This example includes the same facts as Example 5.21 (i.e., a physician has an ownership interest in a clinical laboratory that has a services contract with a hospital).
>
> **Commentary:** The second condition of the indirect compensation arrangement definition will be satisfied if the *laboratory* receives aggregate compensation from the *hospital* that varies with, or otherwise reflects, the volume or value of referrals or other business generated by the *physician* for the *hospital*. However, if the aggregate compensation that the hospital pays to the laboratory does not vary with, or otherwise reflect, the volume or value of referrals or other business generated by the referring physician for the hospital, then (1) the second condition will not be satisfied, (2) the physician will not have an indirect compensation arrangement with the hospital, and (3) the physician may make referrals to the hospital for the furnishing of DHS without violating the Stark Law's referral prohibition.

Like the physician link test, the nonphysician link test can be broken down into the four questions listed above. Once again, if the answer to any of these questions is "yes," then the second condition of the indirect compensation arrangement definition is satisfied and, as such, the physician/IFM and DHS entity may have an indirect compensation arrangement, depending on whether the third condition of this definition is satisfied.

3. Aggregate compensation

As discussed in Chapter 2, the special compensation rules provide that certain time-based or unit-of-service (e.g., per procedure or per click) payments will not trigger the Stark Law's "volume or value" or "other business generated" standards.[48] For example, a hospital may pay a physician $100 each time he or she performs a particular medical procedure without having that per-procedure payment trigger the "volume or value" standard, provided that the $100 represents fair market value (FMV) for the procedure and does not vary during the course of the arrangement.[49]

According to CMS, the agency focused on "aggregate compensation" for purposes of the indirect compensation arrangement definition—and specifically prohibited parties from relying on the special compensation rules—to distinguish the indirect compensation arrangement *definition* from the indirect compensation arrangements *exception* (see Chapter 9 for more information about this exception).

Like the indirect compensation arrangement definition, the exception has three conditions, one of which is that the "compensation" received by the physician/IFM at issue "may not be determined in any manner that takes into account the value or volume of referrals or other business generated by the referring physician for the entity furnishing DHS." Because this exception focuses on "compensation" and not on "aggregate compensation," and because it does not preclude the application of the special compensation rules, a compensation methodology that may be permissible for purposes of the indirect compensation arrangement exception (e.g., the $100 per procedure payment by the hospital to the physician referenced above) may not be permissible for purposes of the indirect compensation arrangement definition. Several issues relating to CMS's effort to distinguish the indirect compensation arrangement definition and exception are worth noting.

4. Unit-of-service compensation; volume or value standard

In the preamble to the 2004 Stark II, Phase II Regulations, CMS stated that when considered in the "aggregate," time-based or unit-of-service compensation arrangements "always" trigger the "volume or value" standard, even if they meet the requirements of the special compensation rules.[50] That seems to be an overstatement, as the following example demonstrates.

Example 5.24

A physician has an ownership interest in a practice group. The group enters into a contract with a hospital pursuant to which the group agrees to mow the hospital's lawn each month for one year for $50 (which is FMV and will not vary during the term of the arrangement). On behalf of the group, the physician furnishes the services at issue.

Commentary: The first condition of the indirect compensation arrangement definition is satisfied because there is an unbroken chain of financial relationships between the physician and the hospital. With respect to the second condition, because the physician has a direct ownership interest in the chain of financial relationships at issue, the question is whether the "aggregate compensation" paid by the *hospital* to the *group* "varies with, or otherwise reflects, the volume or value of referrals or other business generated by" the *physician* for the *hospital*. CMS's comments notwithstanding, the answer appears to be "no." That is, whether viewed on a per-service basis ($50 per month) or on an aggregate basis ($600 per year), the group receives the same compensation regardless of whether the physician refers 10, 100, or 1,000 patients to the hospital.

---

5. 'Referrals' v. 'services'

CMS also stated in the preamble to the 2004 Stark II, Phase II Regulations that "time-based or unit-of-service based compensation will always vary with the volume or value of *services* when considered in the aggregate . . ."[51] Presumably, this was a misstatement. As noted above, in defining "indirect compensation arrangements," the Stark Regulations actually focus on whether the referring physician's "aggregate compensation varies with, or otherwise reflects, the volume or value of [his or her] *referrals*," not his or her "services."[52]

The importance of this distinction is reflected in Example 5.24. The aggregate amount of compensation flowing from the hospital to the group plainly will "vary" based on the "volume" of lawn mowing *services* the physician furnishes for the hospital (i.e., for each month the physician mows the hospital's lawn, the hospital pays the group $50). However, the aggregate amount of compensation flowing from the hospital to the group will not "vary" based on the "volume" of the physician's *referrals* to the hospital.

6. 'Varies with' v. 'otherwise reflects'

Significantly, CMS also takes the position that compensation in the form of a fixed fee (e.g., $100,000 per year) may satisfy the second condition of the indirect compensation arrangement definition.[53] Although by definition a "fixed" fee cannot "vary with" referrals or other business generated by a physician/IFM for the DHS entity, according to CMS, such a fee may be deemed to "take into account" (and, presumably, to "otherwise reflect") the volume or value of referrals if it "exceeds fair market value" or is "inflated."[54]

Perhaps a more interesting and difficult question—which CMS has not yet addressed—is whether a fixed fee that is consistent with FMV may nevertheless be deemed to "reflect" the volume or value of physician referrals and, therefore, satisfy the second condition of the definition of an indirect compensation arrangement.

> **Example 5.25**
>
> A physician is a shareholder in a practice group that contracts with a hospital to staff its emergency department (ED). Under the arrangement, the group bills for the professional services furnished by its physicians under the group's name and billing number, and the hospital pays the group a $10,000 per month subsidy.
>
> **Commentary:** There is an unbroken chain of financial relationships between the physician and the hospital. With respect to the second condition of the indirect compensation arrangement definition, because the physician has a direct ownership interest in the chain of financial relationships, the question is whether the "aggregate compensation" paid by the *hospital* to the *group* "varies with, or otherwise reflects, the volume or value of referrals or other business generated by" the physician for the hospital. Plainly, the monthly $10,000 subsidy payments from the hospital to the group do not "vary with" the physician's referrals to the hospital. However, would CMS take the position that the subsidy payments "otherwise reflect" the physician's referrals to the hospital because the purpose of the hospital-group contract is to ensure ED coverage, and such coverage will necessarily involve the physicians ordering DHS, such as laboratory and other diagnostic tests?

This might be an aggressive position for CMS to take. However, it is clear that the phrase "otherwise reflects" has a different—and potentially broader—meaning than the phrase "varies with."[55] Among other things, (1) if the two phrases were interchangeable, there would have been no reason for CMS to use both, (2) by definition, the term "reflects" is broader and more far-reaching than the term "varies," and (3) the use of the word "otherwise" before the word "reflects" suggests that the word "reflects" is intended to cover more than "varies" for purposes of the second condition of the indirect compensation arrangement definition.

As Example 5.25 suggests, the distinction between these two phrases may have practical ramifications. Another example, based on an arrangement that the Office of Inspector General (OIG) analyzed in a 2004 advisory opinion, further demonstrates the real-world implications of the "varies with" versus "otherwise reflects" distinction.[56]

> **Example 5.26**
>
> Two neurosurgeons who are shareholders of a practice group have privileges at a local hospital. The group informs the hospital that (1) its insurance carrier will no longer provide malpractice coverage to the two neurosurgeons; (2) another carrier has agreed to pick up the coverage, but at a much steeper premium; and (3) the two neurosurgeons intend to retire unless the hospital will compensate the group for the difference between the old and new premium amounts. The hospital agrees.
>
> **Commentary:** There is an unbroken chain of financial relationships between each physician and the hospital that consists of the physician's ownership interest in the group (link one) and the group's (premium support) compensation arrangement with the hospital (link two). With respect to the second condition of the indirect compensation arrangement definition, because each physician has a direct ownership interest in the chain of financial relationships at issue, the question is whether the "aggregate compensation" paid by the *hospital* to the *group* "varies with, or otherwise reflects, the volume or value of referrals or other business generated by" the *physician* for the *hospital*. The compensation at issue—in this case, the difference between the old and new premium amounts—is fixed and does not "vary with" either physician's referrals to the hospital. But would CMS take the position that the payment "otherwise reflects" the physician's referrals to the hospital because the malpractice insurance premium support will ensure that the physicians remain in practice in the hospital's community and, as such, remain in a position to refer patients to the hospital?

7. Joint ownership

As discussed earlier in this chapter, co-ownership of a company by a physician/IFM and DHS entity does not give rise to an indirect ownership interest by the physician/IFM in the DHS entity. Under some circumstances, however, the physician/IFM and DHS entity may have an indirect compensation arrangement with one another. According to CMS, this would be the case, for example, when (1) a hospital and physician jointly own a company that leases imaging equipment, (2) the hospital leases equipment for its imaging center from the company on a per-click basis, and (3) the physician refers Medicare patients to the hospital's imaging center. Under these circumstances, the physician may have an indirect compensation arrangement with the hospital because the aggregate compensation from the hospital to the leasing company varies with the volume of referrals by the physician to the hospital.[57]

C. Condition three: State of mind

The third condition for identifying indirect compensation arrangements is that the DHS entity must have "actual knowledge" or act "in reckless disregard or deliberate ignorance" of the fact that the physician/IFM "receives aggregate compensation that varies with, or otherwise reflects, the volume or value of referrals or other business generated by the referring physician for the entity furnishing the DHS."[58]

With respect to what constitutes "reckless disregard" or "deliberate indifference," the comments by CMS concerning the state-of-mind condition of the indirect ownership interest definition also apply here.

Although the third condition of the indirect compensation arrangement definition can (as written) apply when the financial relationship of the physician/IFM in the unbroken chain of financial relationships takes the form of a compensation arrangement, it does not apply (as written) when that financial relationship takes the form of an ownership interest. The reason is simple: In the latter case, the focus is on a compensation arrangement that does *not* involve the physician/IFM; however, the third condition focuses on whether the DHS entity is (or should be) aware that the referring physician/IFM receives aggregate compensation that varies with, or otherwise reflects, the volume or value of referrals or other business generated by the referring physician for the entity furnishing the DHS.

Presumably, this is a drafting error, and the provision should read to the following effect: The DHS entity must have actual knowledge or must act in reckless disregard or deliberate ignorance of the fact that the physician/IFM *or other relevant individual or entity* receives aggregate compensation that varies with, or otherwise reflects, the volume or value of referrals or other business generated by the referring physician for the entity furnishing the DHS. However, until CMS clarifies this, the third condition of the indirect compensation arrangement definition is bound to cause some confusion among providers, suppliers, and physicians.

Notes

1. According to CMS, "[t]he existence of a financial relationship between the referring physician (or an IFM) and the entity furnishing DHS is the factual predicate triggering the application of [the Stark Law]." Stark II, Phase II Regulations (Preamble), 69 *Federal Register (FR)* 16054, 16057 (2004).

2. 42 United States Code (USC) §1395nn(a)(2).

3. 42 USC §1395nn(a)(2).

4. 42 USC §1395nn(a)(2).

5. 42 USC §1395nn(a)(2).

6. 42 USC §1395nn(h)(1)(A). A compensation arrangement will not be created if the remuneration at issue consists solely of (1) "[t]he forgiveness of amounts owed for inaccurate tests or procedures, mistakenly performed tests or procedures, or the correction of minor billing errors," (2) "[t]he provision of items, devices, or supplies that are used solely to [a] collect, transport, process, or store specimens for the entity providing the item, device, or supply, or [b] order or communicate the results of tests or procedures for such entity," (3) "[a] payment made by an insurer or a self-insured plan to a physician to satisfy a claim, submitted on a fee for service basis, for the furnishing of health services by that physician to an individual who is covered by a policy with the insurer or by the self-insured plan, if [a] the health services are not furnished, and the payment is not made, pursuant to a contract or other arrangement between the insurer or the plan and the physician, [b] the payment is made to the physician on behalf of the covered individual and would otherwise be made directly to such individual, [c] the amount of the payment is set in advance, does not exceed FMV, and is not determined in a manner that takes into account directly or indirectly the volume or value of any referrals, and [d] the payment meets such other requirements as the secretary may impose by regulation as needed to protect against program or patient abuse." 42 USC §1395nn(h)(1)(C).

7. 42 USC §1395nn(h)(1)(B).

8. 42 Code of Federal Regulations (CFR) §411.354(a)(2).

9. Stark II, Phase II Regulations (Preamble), 69 *FR* 16054, 16057 (2004).

10. 42 USC §1395nn(a)(2).

11. 42 USC §1395nn(a)(2).

12. 42 CFR §411.354(b)(1). An unsecured loan may give rise to a compensation arrangement, but not an ownership interest.

13. Stark II, Phase II Regulations (Preamble), 69 *FR* 16054, 16063 (2004).

14. 42 CFR §§411.354(b)(3)(i)-(iv).

15. 42 CFR §§411.354(b)(3)(ii), (iii) and (iv).

16. 42 CFR §411.354(b)(2). Such an arrangement may give rise to an "indirect" financial relationship between and among the physician, the parent company, and the parent company's other subsidiaries.

17. 42 CFR §411.354(b)(4).

18. 42 USC §1395nn(a)(2).

19. 42 CFR §411.354(b)(5)(i)(A).

20. 42 CFR §411.354(b)(5)(i)(B).

21. Stark II, Phase I Regulations (Preamble), 66 *FR* 856, 865 (2001).

22. Stark II, Phase I Regulations (Preamble), 66 *FR* 856, 865 (2001).

23. Stark II, Phase I Regulations (Preamble), 66 *FR* 856, 865 (2001).

24. Stark II, Phase I Regulations (Preamble), 66 *FR* 856, 865 (2001).

25. Stark II, Phase I Regulations (Preamble), 66 *FR* 856, 865 (2001).

26. Stark II, Phase I Regulations (Preamble), 66 *FR* 856, 865 (2001).

27. Stark II, Phase I Regulations (Preamble), 66 *FR* 856, 865 (2001). Although the Stark Law is predicated on physician referrals, CMS has elected to focus on the state of mind of the furnishing entity and not on the state of mind of the physician. This may lead to some curious results. For example, it appears that it is possible that a physician with an indirect ownership interest in an entity may knowingly make a DHS referral to that entity, and this referral will not give rise to a violation of the Stark Law.

28. 42 CFR §411.354(b)(5)(ii).

29. 42 CFR §411.354(b)(5)(iii); Stark II, Phase II Regulations (Preamble), 69 *FR* 16054, 16061 (2004).

30. 42 CFR §411.354(b)(5)(iv).

31. Stark II, Phase II Regulations (Preamble), 69 *FR* 16054, 16062 (2004).

32. Stark II, Phase II Regulations (Preamble), 69 *FR* 16054, 16062 (2004).

33. 42 USC §1395nn(h)(1)(A); 42 USC §1395nn(h)(1)(C).

34. 42 USC §1395nn(h)(1)(B).

35. 42 CFR §411.354(c). The Stark Regulations clarify that a contract between a hospital and an entity providing DHS "under arrangements" to the hospital creates a compensation arrangement.

36. 42 CFR §411.351. Paralleling the Stark Law, the Stark Regulations provide that the following are not considered "remuneration": (1) the "forgiveness of amounts owed for inaccurate tests or procedures, mistakenly performed tests or procedures, or the correction of minor billing errors," (2) the "furnishing of items, devices, or supplies (not including surgical items, devices, or supplies) that are used solely to collect, transport, process, or store specimens for the entity furnishing the items, devices, or supplies or are used solely to order or communicate the results of tests or procedures for the entity," (3) a "payment made by an insurer or a self-insured plan (or a subcontractor of the insurer or plan) to a physician to satisfy a claim, submitted on a fee-for service basis, for the furnishing of health services by that physician to an individual who is covered by a policy with the insurer or by the self-insured plan," if (a) "[t]he health services are not furnished, and the payment is not made under a contract or other arrangement between the insurer or the plan (or a subcontractor of the insurer or plan) and the physician," (b) "[t]he payment is made to the physician on behalf of the covered individual and would otherwise be made directly to the individual," and (c)"[t]he amount of the payment is set in advance, does not exceed fair market value, and is not determined in a manner that takes into account directly or indirectly the volume or value of any referrals." 42 CFR §411.351. The Stark Regulations make clear, however, that although (1) "[a] compensation arrangement does not include the portion of any business arrangement that consists solely of the remuneration described [above]," any "other portion of the arrangement" may still constitute a compensation arrangement. 42 CFR §411.354(c)(1).

37. 42 CFR §411.354(a)(2).

38. Stark II, Phase I Regulations (Preamble), 66 *FR* 856, 958, setting forth 42 CFR §411.354(a)(2).

39. 42 CFR §411.354(a)(2).

40. Stark II Proposed Regulations (Preamble), 63 *FR* 1659, 1699 (1998).

41. 42 USC §1395nn(a)(2).

42. 42 USC §1395nn(h)(1)(B).

43. 42 CFR §411.354(c)(2)(i).

44. Stark II, Phase II Regulations (Preamble), 69 *FR* 16054, 16059 (2004).

45. Stark II, Phase II Regulations (Preamble), 69 *FR* 16054, 16059-16060 (2004).

46. 42 CFR §411.354(c)(2)(ii).

47. 42 CFR §411.354(c)(2)(ii). Although the nonphysician link test does not incorporate the phrase "regardless of whether the individual unit of compensation satisfies the special rules on unit-based compensation," CMS presumably intended that qualification to apply to both the physician link and nonphysician link tests.

48. 42 CFR §§411.354(d)(2)-(3).

49. 42 CFR §§411.354(d)(2)-(3).

50. Stark II, Phase II Regulations (Preamble), 69 *FR* 16054, 16058-16059 (2004).

51. Stark II, Phase II Regulations (Preamble), 69 *FR* 16054, 16058-16059 (2004).

52. 42 CFR §411.354(c)(2)(ii) (emphasis added).

53. Stark II, Phase II Regulations (Preamble), 69 *FR* 16054, 16059 (2004).

54. Stark II, Phase II Regulations (Preamble), 69 *FR* 16054, 16059 (2004).

55. Although the regulation uses the phrase "varies with, or otherwise reflects," the preamble to the Stark II, Phase II Regulations confusingly uses the phrase "takes into account." Stark II, Phase II Regulations (Preamble), 69 *FR* 16054, 16059 (2004).

56. OIG Advisory Opinion 04-19 (2004).

57. Stark II, Phase II Regulations (Preamble), 69 *FR* 16054, 16061 (2004).

58. 42 CFR §411.354(c)(2)(iii).

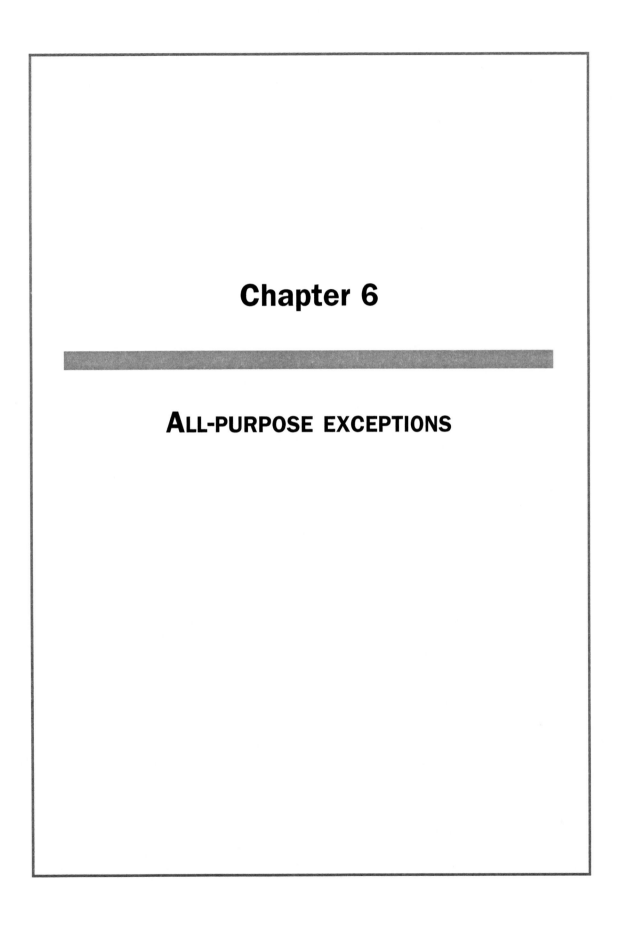

Chapter 6

ALL-PURPOSE EXCEPTIONS

Chapter 6

ALL-PURPOSE EXCEPTIONS

As its name implies, the Stark Law's "all-purpose" exceptions protect referrals by a physician to an entity for the furnishing of designated health services (DHS) regardless of whether the financial relationship at issue takes the form of a direct or indirect ownership interest or a direct or indirect compensation arrangement. This chapter discusses the nine exceptions that fall into the "all-purpose" category.

Congress created three of the all-purpose exceptions: the "in-office ancillary services" exception, the "physicians' services" exception, and the "pre-paid plans" exception. The Centers for Medicare & Medicaid Services (CMS) created the remaining all-purpose exceptions. Because the in-office ancillary services exception (in part) and the physicians' services exception (in its entirety) require the existence of a physician "group practice"—a term that CMS has painstakingly defined over the years—this definition is covered, first in Section I.A. Sections I.B. and I.C. address the specific requirements of the in-office ancillary services and physicians' services exceptions, respectively. Sections II–VIII cover the remaining all-purpose exceptions, which protect the following:

- DHS furnished in an academic medical center (Section II)
- DHS furnished to enrollees of certain types of pre-paid health plans (Section III)
- Certain implants furnished in ambulatory surgical centers (Section IV)
- Certain dialysis-related outpatient prescription drugs (Section V)
- Certain preventative screening tests, immunizations, and vaccines (Section VI)
- Eyeglasses and contact lenses furnished following certain types of surgery (Section VII)
- DHS furnished pursuant to certain intra-family referrals (Section VIII)

I. In-office ancillary services and physicians' services exceptions

A. 'Group practice'

Under both the Stark Law and Stark Regulations, physician practices must meet eight requirements to qualify as a "group practice."

1. Single legal entity

The Stark Law provides that, in order to qualify as a "group practice," a physician practice must be "legally organized as a partnership, professional corporation, foundation, not-for-profit corporation, faculty practice plan, or similar association."[1] The Stark Regulations expand upon (and clarify) this requirement in two principal respects.

First, the Stark Regulations provide that the physician practice must consist of a "single legal entity" that is formed "primarily for the purpose of being a physician group practice."[2] This single legal entity may take any organizational form recognized by the state in which the practice operates (e.g., a partnership, professional corporation or association, limited liability company, foundation, or similar entity). The Stark Regulations clarify that the "single legal entity" may be organized by any party or parties, healthcare facilities (where permitted by law), or professional corporations created by individual physicians.[3] Indeed, another group of physicians may own and organize the entity at issue, as long as that group does not function as a physician practice.[4]

Second, in a significant change from its earlier position, in the 2004 Stark II, Phase II Regulations, CMS stated that a physician practice operating in more than one state and composed of multiple legal entities will, nevertheless, be considered a "single legal entity" for purposes of the "group practice" definition, provided that (1) the states in which the practice operates are contiguous (although, if there are more than two states, each state need not be contiguous to all of the others); (2) the legal entities are identical with respect to ownership, governance, and operation; and (3) the organization of the practice in multiple entities is necessary to comply with state licensing laws.[5]

> ### Example 6.1
>
> A physician practice operates in Illinois, Wisconsin, and Indiana. To comply with state licensing laws, the practice operates as a separate legal entity in each state. In Illinois and Wisconsin, the practice operates as separate professional corporations owned by four physicians (Physicians A–D). In Indiana, the practice operates as a partnership composed of Physicians A–D and a fifth physician, Physician E.
>
> **Commentary:** The Indiana partnership may not be part of the "group practice" because its ownership is not identical to that of the Illinois and Wisconsin entities.

2. Members of the group

Assuming that a physician practice is organized as a "single legal entity," the next requirement of the "group practice" definition is that the practice must have at least two "members."[6] Although the Stark Law does not define the term, the Stark Regulations provide that a "member" of a practice includes (1) a physician with a direct or indirect ownership interest in the practice, (2) a full- or part-time physician-employee of the practice, (3) a locum tenens physician, or (4) a physician who provides on-call services for other members of the group practice.[7] The definition of "member" expressly excludes independent contractors and leased physicians, unless the leased physicians meet the definition of "employees" under the relevant Internal Revenue Service (IRS) rules.[8]

> ### Example 6.2
>
> A physician (Physician A) is the sole shareholder (and also an employee) of a professional corporation, Community Doctors. Three physicians furnish services to Community Doctors' patients: Physician A, Physician B (an independent contractor), and Physician C (also an independent contractor).
>
> **Commentary:** Community Doctors cannot qualify as a "group practice" because it has only one "member" (Physician A).

Example 6.3

This includes the same facts as Example 6.2, except Physician B is a part-time employee of Community Doctors and not an independent contractor.

Commentary: Community Doctors may qualify as a "group practice" (provided that the other requirements of the definition are met) because it has two "members" (Physician A and Physician B).

---

3. Full range of services (by members)

Assuming that a physician practice qualifies as a "single legal entity" and has at least two "members," the next requirement of the Stark Law's group practice definition is that each member must provide "substantially the full range of services" that he or she "routinely provides, including medical care, consultation, diagnosis, or treatment through the joint use of shared office space, facilities, equipment, and personnel."[9] We will refer to this as the "full range of services" requirement.

The Stark Regulations generally track this statutory requirement, but they replace the word "services" with the term "patient care services." More specifically, the Stark Regulations require that each member of the practice "furnish substantially the full range of patient care services that the physician routinely furnishes, including medical care, consultation, diagnosis, and treatment through the joint use of shared office space, facilities, equipment, and personnel."[10]

The Stark Regulations define "patient care services" as "any task(s) performed by a physician in the group practice that address the medical needs of specific patients or patients in general, regardless of whether they involve direct patient encounters or generally benefit a particular practice."[11] Such services may include, for example, "time spent by a physician consulting with other physicians or reviewing laboratory tests, or time spent training staff members, arranging for equipment, or performing administrative or management tasks."[12]

> **Example 6.4**
>
> A physician retires from his clinical practice but continues to furnish management and administrative services to his former practice (Group 1) on Monday through Thursday as an independent contractor. A second physician practice (Group 2) hires the physician as a part-time employee, also to provide management and administrative services. The physician performs his duties for Groups 1 and 2 from his home.
>
> **Commentary:** Although the physician furnishes substantially the full range of patient care services through Group 2, Group 2 cannot meet the full range of services requirement because the physician furnishes the services at his home and not "through the use of shared office space, facilities, equipment, and personnel." This fact does not affect Group 1 because (as an independent contractor) the physician is not a "member" of Group 1 and, as such, does not need to meet the full range of services requirement.

In 1998, CMS suggested that a physician who furnished one service to one practice one day a week and another service to a second practice on another day of the week could satisfy the full range of services requirement.[13] It appears that CMS has changed its position. In the preamble to the 2001 Stark II, Phase I Regulations, CMS stated that "the services for the group's patients should be comparable in scope to those provided outside of the group setting."[14] This statement, together with a literal reading of the term "full range of services," suggests that if a physician practices medicine as a solo practitioner Monday through Thursday and furnishes administrative and management services for a physician practice (as a part-time employee) on Fridays, the physician is not providing "substantially the full range of services [that he or she] routinely provides" through the physician practice and, as such, the physician practice cannot qualify as a "group practice" for purposes of the Stark Law.

4. Quantity of services (by member/group)

Next, the Stark Law provides that "substantially all of the services of the physicians who are members of the group" must "be provided through the group" and "billed under a billing number assigned to the group," and the "amounts so received" must be "treated as receipts of the group."[15] We will refer to this as the "substantially all services" requirement.

The Stark Regulations expand upon and clarify this statutory requirement in several respects. As an initial matter, the regulations provide that, subject to the exceptions discussed below, the "substantially all services" requirement will be met as long as "75% of the total patient care services of the group practice members"—in the aggregate—are "furnished through the group and billed under a billing number assigned to the group, and the amounts received [are] treated as receipts of the group."[16] Two examples offered by CMS in the preamble to the 1995 Stark I Regulations help illustrate the application of this requirement.

Example 6.5

A physician practice has 10 members who devote the following percentages of their time to furnishing patient care services through the practice: seven physicians at 100% (700%), two physicians at 50% (100%), and one physician at 10% (10%).

Commentary: The 10 physician members meet the substantially all services requirement because, in the aggregate, 81% of their time is spent providing patient care services though the practice. As such, the practice may qualify as a "group practice" for purposes of the Stark Law (provided that the other requirements of the "group practice" definition are met).[17]

Example 6.6

A physician practice has 10 members who devote the following percentages of their time to furnishing patient care services through the practice: Two physicians at 100% (200%), five physicians at 70% (350%), two physicians at 25% (50%), and one physician at 10% (10%).

Commentary: The 10 physician members do not meet the substantially all services requirement because, in the aggregate, only 61% of their time is spent providing patient care services though the practice. As such, the practice cannot qualify as a "group practice" for purposes of the Stark Law.[18]

The Stark Regulations provide that for purposes of the substantially all services requirement, patient care services must be measured based on either (1) the total time each member spends on patient care services, documented by any reasonable means (such as time cards or appointment schedules) or (2) any alternative measure that is "reasonable, fixed in advance of the performance of the services being measured, uniformly applied over time, verifiable, and documented."[19] It is important to remember that time spent by physicians on non-patient care activities (such as teaching or research) should not be included in calculating these percentages.

Example 6.7

A physician spends three days each week conducting research and two days furnishing patient care services to the patients of a physician practice.

Commentary: The physician provides 100% of his total patient care services through the practice.[20]

Note also that "patient care services" include activities that may not involve direct patient encounters, such as time spent by a physician consulting with other physicians, reviewing laboratory tests, training staff members, arranging for equipment, or performing administrative or management tasks.

Example 6.8

A physician works four days a week. The physician spends two days a week furnishing clinical services to the patients of a physician practice, one day training members of the practice's staff, and one day arranging for the purchase of healthcare items and services by the practice.

Commentary: The physician provides 100% of his total patient care services through the practice.

Finally, in response to concerns that the substantially all services requirement could be difficult (or impossible) to meet for many new (and some evolving) physician practices, the 2004 Stark II, Phase II Regulations created a 12-month "start up." This "start up" period is available to a new physician practice provided that it makes a reasonable, good faith effort to comply with the requirement as soon as practicable but no later than 12 months from the date of the practice's initial formation.[21] The start up period is available to an *existing* group practice, provided that it meets the following requirements:

- a physician is "relocating" his or her practice to become a member of the group practice,

- the addition of the new member will cause the group practice to fall out of compliance with the substantially all services requirement,

- during the 12-month period, the group practice would otherwise be in compliance with the substantially all services requirement, and

- the new member's ownership interest in, or employment arrangement with, the group practice is documented in writing at the commencement of his or her relationship with the group.[22]

5. Physician-patient encounters

Next, the Stark Law provides that to qualify as a "group practice" the "members" of the practice must "personally conduct no less than 75% of the physician-patient encounters of the . . . practice."[23] For purposes of this chapter, we will refer to this as the "physician-patient encounter" requirement. The Stark Regulations mirror this provision,[24] which was "designed to differentiate between legitimate group practices and those with 'member' owners or investors who are members in name, but who treat few, if any, patients."[25]

Two issues should be kept in mind with respect to the physician-patient encounter requirement. First, as discussed above, because independent contractors cannot qualify as "members" of a "group practice," the physician practices should not take into account the physician-patient encounters of independent contractors for purposes of meeting this requirement. Second, unlike the substantially all services requirement, the physician-patient encounter requirement is measured on a per capita basis (and not as a function of time).[26]

Example 6.9

A physician practice employs three physicians (Physician A, Physician B, and Physician C) and hires one physician (Physician D) as an independent contractor. In 2004, the practice had 1000 physician-patient encounters. Physicians A, B, and C personally conducted 700 of these encounters, and Physician D conducted 300 of these encounters.

Commentary: Physicians who qualify as "members" conducted only 70% of the practice's physician-patient encounters. As such, the physician practice does not meet the physician-patient encounter requirement and, therefore, cannot qualify as a "group practice" for purposes of the Stark Law.

---

6. Unified business

Next, the Stark Regulations provide that in order for a physician practice to qualify as a "group practice," the practice must be a "unified business."[27] More specifically, the practice must have the following features: (1) centralized decision-making by a body representing the practice that maintains effective control over the practice's assets and liabilities and (2) consolidated billing, accounting, and financial reporting.[28]

In the preamble to the 2004 Stark II, Phase II Regulations, CMS emphasized that this requirement is designed to set "general patterns indicative of integration," but it does not dictate specific practices.[29] CMS also cautioned, however, that the centralized management must exercise "substantial control" over the practice's activities and must not merely "rubber stamp" decisions by various practice cost centers or locations.[30]

7. Group overhead/income

The Stark Law next provides that in order for a physician practice to qualify as a "group practice," the "overhead expenses of and the income from the practice" must be "distributed in accordance with methods previously determined."[31] Recognizing the ambiguity of this requirement, CMS originally proposed modifying it in two ways. First, CMS proposed requiring that the expenses and income of the practice be distributed according to methods that are "determined prior to the time period" during which the practice "earned the income or incurred the costs."[32] Second, CMS proposed requiring that the practice use accounting methods that reflect "a unified business."[33] CMS modified both of these proposed requirements in the 2001 Stark II, Phase I Regulations. The Stark Regulations now permit practices to allocate expenses and income according to methods that are determined prior to *receipt* of payment for the services giving rise to the expenses or producing the revenue,[34] thereby allowing groups to adjust their compensation methodologies prospectively.[35]

8. Compensation

Finally, the Stark Law provides that, with two exceptions, in order for a physician practice to qualify as a "group practice," no "member" may "directly or indirectly" receive "compensation based on the volume or value of [his or her] referrals."[36] (We will refer to this as the "compensation" requirement.) The Stark Regulations mirror this requirement.[37]

In the preamble to the 2001 Stark II, Phase I Regulations, CMS clarified that the compensation requirement applies only to revenues generated by DHS referrals. Thus, a group may allocate overall profits or
award productivity bonuses on the basis of the volume or value of a physician's non-DHS referrals.[38]
Groups that decide to account separately for DHS and non-DHS business, however, must do so carefully to ensure that the group does not distribute revenues based on the volume or value of a physician's DHS referrals.

As noted above, there are two exceptions to this rule: A group may pay its members (1) a "share of
overall profits" of the practice or (2) a "productivity bonus based on services personally performed or
services incident to such personally performed services, so long as the share or bonus is not determined in a manner [that] is *directly* related to the volume or value" of the physician's DHS referrals.[39]

More specifically, with respect to *profit-sharing*, a physician may receive a portion of the practice's
"overall profits" (i.e., the profits earned by the group as a whole or by a component of the practice
that consists of at least five physicians[40]) based on distribution factors that are volume or value neu-
tral, such as (1) an even split (i.e., per capita), (2) a physician's financial investment in the practice, (3) a
physician's seniority, or (4) a distribution methodology used with respect to non-DHS revenues or
profits.[41] The practice may not, however, divide its overall profits in a manner that is "directly related"
to a physician's referrals of DHS that are furnished by others.[42]

Example 6.10

Two physicians (Physician A and Physician B) each own half of a physician practice. The
practice has employed both physicians for five years. The practice's overall profits in
2004 were $100,000. Physician A's *DHS* referrals generated $50,000 of this profit.
Physician A's *non*-DHS referrals generated $25,000 of this profit. Physician B's
non-DHS referrals generated $25,000 of this profit. The practice decides to give both
Physician A and Physician B a 50% share (or $50,000) of the practice's overall profits.

Commentary: The practice's profit-sharing formula meets the "group practice"
definition's compensation requirement (even though the shared profits clearly were
derived indirectly, and in part, from the physicians' DHS referrals).

Example 6.11

This includes the same facts as Example 6.10, except that instead of an even distribution of overall profits, the practice decides to give Physician A (the higher ordering physician) a 75% share (or $75,000) of the practice's overall profits and to give Physician B a 25% share (or $25,000).

Commentary: The practice's profit-sharing formula may not meet the "group practice" definition's compensation requirement because the formula appears to be directly related the physicians' referrals of DHS.

With respect to productivity bonuses, the Stark Law and Regulations provide that a physician may receive such a bonus to the extent it reflects (1) non-DHS referrals, (2) DHS that are personally furnished by the physician (or incident to such personally furnished services), or (3) both.[43] Practices may not determine productivity bonuses in a manner that directly relates to DHS referrals by one physician that are furnished or supervised by another physician.[44] By contrast, bonuses that are determined on the basis of DHS referred by one physician and personally furnished by him or her, or by a nurse or other practitioner under Medicare's "incident to" rules, are permissible. Moreover, basing productivity bonuses on total patient encounters and relative value units generated by the physicians would not, according to CMS, directly relate to the volume or value of their DHS referrals.[45]

Example 6.12

A physician practice has three physicians, Physician A, Physician B, and Physician C. In 2004, Physician A generated $25,000 in revenue for the practice from DHS referrals. These DHS were neither personally furnished by Physician A nor incident to such services. Physician A also generated $25,000 in revenue for the practice from non-DHS referrals. Physician B and Physician C each generated $25,000 in revenue for the practice from non-DHS referrals. Each physician had 1,500 patient encounters during the year. The practice decides to give each physician a $10,000 year-end productivity bonus.

Commentary: The practice's productivity bonuses meet the compensation requirement of the "group practice" definition.

Example 6.13

This includes the same facts as Example 6.12, except (1) Physician A had 2,000 patient encounters and Physicians B and C each had 1,000 patient encounters and (2) the practice decides to give Physician A a $15,000 productivity bonus and Physicians B and C each a $7,500 productivity bonus.

Commentary: The practice's productivity bonuses meet the compensation requirement of the "group practice" definition, insofar as they relate to patient encounters and not to DHS referrals.

Example 6.14

This includes the same facts as Example 6.12 (in which each Physician had 1,500 patient encounters), except the practice decides to give Physician A a $15,000 productivity bonus and Physicians B and C each a $7,500 productivity bonus.

Commentary: The practice's productivity bonuses may not meet the compensation requirement of the "group practice" definition because the bonuses appear to be directly related to the physicians' referrals of DHS that were not personally furnished by the physicians (or incident to such personally furnished services).

CMS has created a *de minimis* exception in the Stark Regulations for the distribution of physician practice profits and productivity bonuses. Pursuant to this exception, the distribution of profits or productivity bonuses will not be related directly to the volume or value of DHS referrals if (1) the total revenues derived by the practice from DHS constitute less than 5% of the practice's total revenues and (2) the allocated portion of those revenues to each physician in the practice constitutes 5% or less of his or her total compensation from the practice.[46]

Example 6.15

A physician practice has four physicians, Physician A, Physician B, Physician C, and Physician D. In 2004, the practice's total revenues were $4 million, $100,000 of which the practice generated from DHS referrals. Physician A made all of these DHS referrals. Each physician received $300,000 in base compensation from the practice, and each physician had 1,500 patient encounters. The practice decides to give Physician A (but none of the other physicians) a $10,000 productivity bonus.

Commentary: This bonus meets the compensation requirement of the "group practice" definition because (1) the total revenues derived by the practice in 2004 from DHS ($100,000) were less than 5% of the group's total revenues ($4 million) and (2) the allocated portion of those revenues ($10,000) to Physician A constitutes less than 5% of his total compensation from the practice ($310,000).

Note: Upon request from CMS, physician practices must produce documentation supporting the calculation and actual payment of profit shares and bonus amounts.[47]

B. In-office ancillary services exception

One of the most important (and complicated) all-purpose exceptions is the "in-office ancillary services" exception. This exception is designed "to allow physicians to furnish DHS that are ancillary to the physician's core medical practice in the location where the core medical services are routinely delivered."[48] The in-office ancillary services exception has four basic requirements, covering *what* types of DHS qualify for protection, *who* may furnish or supervise this DHS, *where* the DHS may be furnished, and *how* the DHS must be billed.

1. DHS requirement

The Stark Law provides that the in-office ancillary services exception covers all DHS except (1) durable medical equipment (DME) (with the exception of infusion pumps) and (2) parenteral and enteral nutrients, equipment, and supplies.[49] Although the Stark Regulations generally follow the Stark Law, the regulations expand the category of DME that may be protected under the in-office ancillary services exception. Under the Stark Regulations, "canes, crutches, walkers and folding manual wheelchairs, and blood glucose monitors" also may be protected under the exception, provided that several conditions are met[50]:

1. The item at issue must be one that the patient "requires for the purposes of ambulating, uses in order to depart from the physician's office, or is a blood glucose monitor (including one starter set of test strips and lancets, consisting of no more than 100 of each)."[51] In addition, if the item is a blood glucose monitor, it must be furnished by a physician, an employee of a physician, or a group practice that also furnishes "outpatient diabetes self-management training to the patient."[52]

2. The item must be furnished (1) in a building that meets the in-office ancillary services exception's "location" requirement (discussed in this chapter) and (2) "as part of the treatment for the specific condition for which the patient-physician encounter occurred."[53] CMS has clarified that it considers DHS "furnished" for purposes of the in-office ancillary services exception when (1) it is provided to the patient in the location where the underlying service is performed or (2) it is dispensed to a patient in a manner sufficient to satisfy Medicare's billing and coverage rules.[54]

3. The item must be furnished personally by the physician who ordered the DME, another physician in his or her group practice, or an employee of the physician or group practice.[55] Also, the physician or group practice that furnishes the DME must meet (1) the Medicare DME supplier standards,[56] (2) the arrangement at issue must not violate the anti-kickback statute or any federal or state law or regulation governing billing or claims submission,[57] and (3) all other requirements of the in-office ancillary services exception must be met.[58]

2. Furnishing/supervision requirement

Assuming the DHS at issue qualifies for protection under the in-office ancillary services exception, the exception next requires that the DHS be furnished (1) "personally by the referring physician," (2) "personally by a physician who is a member of the same group practice as the referring physician," or (3) "personally by individuals who are directly supervised by the physician or by another physician in the group practice."[59] (We will refer to this as the "furnishing/supervision requirement.")

The Stark Regulations largely follow this statutory requirement, with some expansions and clarifications. Specifically, the Stark Regulations provide that the DHS at issue must be "furnished personally" by one of the following individuals: (1) the "referring physician," (2) a "physician who is a member of the same group practice as the referring physician," or (3) an "individual who is supervised by the referring physician or, if the referring physician is in a group practice, by another physician in the group practice," provided that the supervision complies with all applicable Medicare billing and coverage rules.[60] Although the Stark Law uses the term "directly supervised," CMS has relaxed this requirement to allow the level of supervision required by the applicable Medicare billing and coverage rules.

Except where the DHS at issue are personally furnished by the referring physician (or by an individual who is supervised by the referring physician), applying the second and third components of the furnishing/supervision requirement necessitates revisiting what it means to be a "member of" a group practice, as opposed to a physician who merely is "in" a group practice.

As discussed above, the Stark Regulations provide that a "member" of a group practice includes a physician with a direct or indirect ownership interest in the practice, a full or part-time physician-employee of the practice, a *locum tenens* physician, or a physician who provides on-call services for other members of the group practice.[61] Independent contractors and leased physicians (unless the leased physicians meet the definition of "employees" under IRS rules) are not "members" of a group practice.[62] The Stark Regulations define a "physician in the group practice" to mean either a "member" of the group practice or "an independent contractor physician" during the time he or she furnishes patient care services for the group practice "under a contractual arrangement with the group practice to provide services to the group practice's patients in the group practice's facilities."[63] The Stark Regulations further provide that the contract between the group practice and the independent contractor must either contain the same restrictions on compensation that apply to "members" of the group practice or meet the requirements of the personal services exception. Finally, the Regulations provide that the independent contractor's arrangement with the group practice must comply with Medicare's reassignment rules.

Example 6.16

Two physicians (Physician A and Physician B) are employed by (and, therefore, are "members of") a physician practice that (1) is organized as a professional corporation (Group Practice, PC), (2) specializes in furnishing physical therapy (PT) services, and (3) qualifies as a "group practice." A third physician (Physician C) has a contract with Group Practice, PC, and otherwise meets the definition of a "physician in a group practice." Group Practice, PC, also employs nonphysician personnel who furnish PT services, including a therapist. Physician A sees a Medicare patient, determines that he or she needs PT services, orders such services from Group Practice, PC, and personally furnishes the services.

Commentary: The DHS at issue (i.e., the PT services) meet the furnishing/supervision requirement because the "referring physician" (i.e., Physician A) personally furnished them. *Note:* As discussed in Chapter 4 (Referrals), Physician A's "order" probably does not constitute a "referral" in the first instance.

Example 6.17

This includes the same facts as Example 6.16, except Physician B personally furnishes the PT services.

Commentary: The DHS at issue meet the furnishing/supervision requirement because Physician B, who is a member of the same group practice (Group Practice, PC) as the referring physician (Physician A), furnished the DHS.

Example 6.18

This includes the same facts as Example 6.16, except the therapist personally furnishes the PT services under the direct supervision of Physician A.

Commentary: The DHS at issue meet the furnishing/supervision requirement because an individual (the therapist), who the referring physician (Physician A) supervised, personally furnished the services.

Example 6.19

This includes the same facts as Example 6.16, except the therapist personally furnishes the PT services under the direct supervision of Physician B.

Commentary: The DHS at issue meet the furnishing/supervision requirement because an individual (the therapist) who was supervised by another physician (Physician B) in the referring physician's (Physician A) group practice personally furnished the services.

Example 6.20

This includes the same facts as Example 6.16, except the therapist personally furnishes the PT services under the supervision of Physician C.

Commentary: The DHS at issue meet the furnishing/supervision requirement because they were personally furnished by an individual (the therapist) who was supervised by a physician (Physician C) who, although not a "member" of the group practice, is "in" the same group practice as the referring physician (Physician A).

Example 6.21

Three physicians (Physician A, Physician B, and Physician C) are shareholders and employees of a group practice that specializes in orthopedic care. The practice purchases a magnetic resonance imaging (MRI) machine and places it in its office. The physicians order MRI scans for some of their patients, including Medicare beneficiaries, and provide the appropriate level of supervision during the furnishing of the scans. The practice transmits the resulting images to a fourth physician (Physician D), who is a radiologist and, acting as an independent contractor of the practice, interprets the images for Physicians A, B, and C.

Commentary: Physician D's professional services are DHS, but they may not qualify for protection under the in-office ancillary services exception. Physician D, as an independent contractor, is not a "member" of the group practice. Because Physician D, at least arguably, is not providing services to the group practice's patients "in the group practice's facilities," he also may not qualify as a physician who is "in" the group practice.

3. Location requirement

Assuming that the DHS at issue qualify for protection under the in-office ancillary services exception and were provided in accordance with the exception's furnishing/supervision requirement, the next issue relates to *where* practices can furnish DHS. The Stark Law and Stark Regulations require that, in order to be protected by the in-office ancillary services exception, the DHS must be furnished in one of two locations.

a. 'Same building' test

First, the Stark Law provides that the DHS at issue may be furnished "in a building in which the referring physician (or another physician who is a member of the same group practice) furnishes physicians' services unrelated to the furnishing of designated health services."[64] As with many Stark Law provisions, CMS has interpreted—and expanded upon—the "same building" test in the Stark Regulations. As the name of the test implies, there are two basic issues: (1) what is a "building" for purposes of the in-office ancillary services exception and (2) under what circumstances will DHS be deemed to be furnished in the "same" building as services unrelated to the furnishing of DHS?

CMS defines the term "same building" as

> a structure with, or a combination of structures that share, a single street address as assigned by the U.S. Postal Service excluding all exterior spaces (for example, lawns, courtyards, driveways, parking lots) and interior loading docks or parking garages. For purposes of this [rule], the 'same building' does not include a mobile vehicle, van, or trailer.[65]

Although CMS recognizes that the postal address test is imperfect, it views this requirement as a "clear, fair, [and] easily applied standard."[66] Although the Stark Regulations exclude mobile vehicles, vans, and trailers from the definition of "same building," CMS has clarified that the same building test does not preclude physicians and group practices from purchasing the "*technical* components of [such] mobile services" and billing for them in accordance with the purchased diagnostic testing rules.[67] (As discussed in Chapter 4, to effectuate this, CMS has excluded from the definition of "entity" a physician practice that bills for purchased diagnostic tests.)[68] Moreover, if the mobile equipment is placed inside the building at issue (and not in the garage or an internal loading dock), then—assuming the other requirements of the "same building" test are met—use of the equipment may qualify for protection under the in-office ancillary services exception.[69]

Assuming the existence of a CMS-defined "building," the next question is what level of physician services unrelated to DHS must be furnished at that location in order to meet the "same building" test. In the 1998 Stark II Proposed Regulations, CMS stated that the test would be satisfied as long as "any amount" of physician services were furnished in the same building as the DHS in question. In the 2001 Stark II, Phase I Regulations, CMS established a more restrictive rule, requiring (1) that the referring physician or group member furnish "substantial" physician services unrelated to the furnishing of DHS in the same building as the DHS at issue and (2) that these unrelated services represent "substantially the full range" of physician services that the referring physician or group member routinely provides.[70]

In the 2004 Stark II, Phase II Regulations, CMS relaxed its 2001 same building test by eliminating the "substantial physician services" component and adopting three alternate standards, only *one* of which must be satisfied in order to meet the same building test. Specifically, in order to meet the same building test, the DHS at issue must be furnished in a building in which the referring physician or his or her group practice (whichever is applicable) has an office that falls into at least one of the following three categories:

Category one: The office is "normally" open to patients at least 35 hours per week, and the referring physician or one or more "members" of his or her group regularly practices medicine and furnishes physician services to patients in that office at least 30 hours per week. Only "some" of the services furnished in the office must be "unrelated" to the provision of DHS.

CMS explained in the Stark II, Phase II Regulations that "we are not requiring any particular threshold amount of physician services unrelated to DHS—'some' should be interpreted in its common sense meaning."[71] CMS also clarified that the "unrelated" physician services at issue may lead to the ordering of DHS services. According to CMS, "conceptually, this test generally describes buildings that are the principal place of practice for physicians or their groups."[72]

Example 6.22

A group practice has three members (Physician A, Physician B, and Physician C), each of whom is a primary care physician. The group practice has one office (Office No. 1), which is open to patients 40 hours per week. Physician A (who works part-time) furnishes services to patients in Office No. 1 eight hours per week. Physicians B and C furnish physician services to patients in Office No. 1 40 hours per week. Although most of the services that the members furnish to patients in Office No. 1 are not DHS, the office does have an x-ray machine. Physician A orders an x-ray on behalf of a Medicare patient, which the patient receives in Office No. 1.

Commentary: The Category one location requirement is met, because the x-ray was furnished in the same building where the group practice (1) has an office (Office No. 1) that is normally open to patients at least 35 hours per week, (2) two members of the referring physician's (Physician A's) group practice (Physicians B and C) furnish physician services to patients in that office at least 30 hours per week, and (3) some of those services are unrelated to DHS.

Example 6.23

This includes the same facts as Example 6.22, except (1) the group practice has a second office (Office No. 2), which is located in the same building as Office No. 1, and (2) the x-ray machine is located in Office No. 2.

Commentary: The Category one location requirement is met because the x-ray was furnished in the same building where the group practice (1) has an office (Office No. 1) that is normally open to patients at least 35 hours per week, (2) two members of the referring physician's (Physician A's) group practice (Physicians B and C) furnish physician services to patients in that office at least 30 hours per week, and (3) some of those services are unrelated to DHS.

Example 6.24

This includes the same facts as Example 6.23, except Office No. 2 is located in a building that is across the street from Office No. 1.

Commentary: The Category one location requirement is not met, because the x-ray was not furnished in the same building where the group practice has an office that is normally open to patients at least 35 hours per week.

Category two: The office is "normally" open to patients at least eight hours per week, and the referring physician regularly practices medicine and furnishes physician services to patients in that office at least six hours per week. Again, only "some" of the services furnished must be unrelated to the provision of DHS. Note that, unlike the first standard, under this standard the referring physician must furnish physician services at the location at least six hours per week, some of which must be unrelated to the provision of DHS. Services furnished by members of the referring physician's group practice do not count toward the six-hour requirement. Moreover, the building must be the one in which the patient receiving the DHS usually sees the referring physician or a member of his or her group practice for physician services. "Conceptually this test generally describes a building where a referring physician practices medicine at least [one] day per week and that is the principal place in which the physician's patients receive physician services."[73]

Example 6.25

A group practice has three members (Physician A, Physician B, and Physician C), each of whom is a primary care physician. The group practice has two offices (Office No. 1 and Office No. 2), which are in separate buildings. The practice furnishes some non-DHS in each office. Office No. 1 is open to patients on Mondays, Tuesdays, and Wednesdays for eight hours each day. Physicians A, B, and C furnish services to patients 24 hours per week (none of which are DHS) in Office No. 1. Office No. 2 has an x-ray machine and is open on Thursdays and Fridays for eight hours each day. Physicians B and C (but not Physician A) furnish services to patients 16 hours per week in Office No. 2. Physician A orders an x-ray on behalf of a Medicare patient, which the practice furnishes in Office No. 2.

Commentary: The Category two location requirement is not met because the practice did not furnish the x-ray in a building where the group practice has an office where the referring physician (Physician A) regularly practices medicine and furnishes physician services to patients at least six hours per week.

Category three: The office is "normally" open to patients at least eight hours per week; the referring physician or a member of his or her group practice (if any) regularly practices medicine and furnishes physician services to patients in that office at least six hours per week, some of which are unrelated to the provision of DHS; and the referring physician (or a member of the group practice) is present while the DHS is furnished during the time that the office is open. Thus, to meet this third standard, either the referring physician or a member of the referring physician's group practice must be physically present in the building (although not necessarily in the same space or part of the building) during the furnishing of DHS.[74] CMS has stated that "this test generally describes buildings in which the referring physicians (or group practice members, if any) provide physician services to patients at least one day per week and the DHS are ordered during a patient visit or the physicians are present during the furnishing of the designated health service."[75]

Example 6.26

This includes the same facts as Example 6.25. In addition, Physician B is present in Office No. 2 (during its regular hours) when the Medicare patient receives the x-ray.

Commentary: The Category three location requirement is met because (1) the x-ray was furnished in a building where the group practice has an office (Office No. 2) that is open to patients at least eight hours per week, (2) two members (Physicians B and C) of the referring physician's (Physician A's) group practice regularly furnish physician services to patients in Office No. 2 (some of which are unrelated to DHS), and (3) a member of the referring physician's group practice (Physician B) was present in Office No. 2 while the DHS was furnished during normal hours of operation.

In determining "normal" hours of operation, CMS stated that the same building test is "not intended to preclude occasional weeks in which the office is open fewer hours (for example, during vacation periods)."[76] Similarly, in interpreting the requirement that either the referring physician or a member of his or her group practice furnish physician services in the office for a minimum number of hours per week, CMS stated that the requirement

> is not intended to preclude use of the in-office ancillary services exception by physicians or group practices that have unfilled appointment slots, cancellations, or other

occasional gaps in the furnishing of services such that they do not actually provide the requisite number ofhours of physician services in particular weeks. Rather, they must generally (that is, in the customary, usual, and normal course) practice medicine and furnish physician services in the building for the minimum number of hours.[77]

Finally, CMS created a special rule for services provided by physicians whose principal medical practice involves treating patients in their private residences.[78] Pursuant to this special rule, the "same building" requirement is met by a physician furnishing DHS in a patient's private residence, as long as the DHS is furnished contemporaneously with a physician service that is not DHS. CMS stated in the preamble to the 2004 Stark II, Phase II Regulations that the physician does not need to be present throughout the furnishing of the DHS but must be present in the patient's private residence at the inception of the DHS. Note also that a private residence includes an assisted or independent living facility, but does not include a nursing home or long-term care facility.[79]

b. Centralized building test

The Stark Law's location requirement provides group practices (but not solo practitioners) with an alternative to the "same building" test. Pursuant to this alternative, "in the case of a referring physician who is a member of a group practice," the DHS at issue may be furnished "in another building" that is used by the group practice (1) for the provision of some or all of the group's clinical laboratory services" or (2) for the centralized provision of the group's DHS (other than clinical laboratory services).[80] The Stark Regulations define a "centralized building" as

> all or part of a building, including, for purposes of this subpart only, a mobile vehicle, van, or trailer that is owned or leased on a full-time basis (that is, 24 hours per day, seven days per week, for a term of not less than six months) by a group practice and that is used exclusively by the group practice. Space in a building or a mobile vehicle, van, or trailer that is shared by more than one group practice, by a group practice and one or more solo practitioners, or by a group practice and another provider or supplier (for example, a diagnostic imaging facility) is not a centralized building for purposes of this subpart.[81]

Note that, unlike the "same building," a "centralized building" may include a mobile vehicle, van, or trailer, as long as it meets the (24 hour/seven day/six month) exclusivity requirements noted above. In addition, a group practice may have more than one centralized building for the provision of DHS, but each centralized building must meet the exclusive use requirement. Thus, the group may not lease its centralized building to another group for the provision of DHS. However, a group may furnish DHS in its centralized building to other providers or suppliers if furnished as purchased diagnostic tests.

4. Billing requirement

Finally, assuming that the DHS at issue (1) qualify for protection under the in-office ancillary services exception, (2) have been provided in accordance with the exception's furnishing/supervision requirement, and (3) have been furnished in a location that meets either the "same" or "centralized" building test, the final issue relates to *who* may bill for the DHS.

The Stark Law provides that the DHS may be billed by (1) "the physician performing or supervising the services," (2) "a group practice of which such physician is a member under a billing number assigned to the group practice," or (3) "an entity that is wholly owned" by such physician or group practice.[82] The Stark Regulations clarify and expand upon this requirement, providing that the following may bill for DHS:

- the physician furnishing or supervising the services,

- the group practice of which the furnishing or supervising physician is a member, using the group practice's billing number,

- the group practice, if the supervising physician is a "physician in the group practice,"

- an entity that is wholly owned by the furnishing or supervising physician or by that physician's group practice, or

- an independent third party acting as a billing agent.[83]

C. Physicians' services

The second "all-purpose" exception created by Congress is the "physicians' services" exception. This exception is intended to enable a physician within a group practice to make referrals to *other* physicians in the group practice for *physician services* that constitute DHS. More specifically, the Stark Law provides an exception for "physicians' services . . . provided personally by (or under the personal supervision of) another physician in the same group practice . . . as the referring physician."[84] Once again, the Stark Regulations clarify this exception, providing that

- the physician to whom the referral is made must be either (1) a "member" of the referring physician's group practice or (2) a "physician in the same group practice" as the referring physician, and

- the physician services must be furnished either (1) personally by the physician to whom the referral was made or (2) by an individual under the supervision of a physician who is either a member of the referring physician's group practice or a physician in the same group as the referring physician.[85]

"Physician services" for purposes of this exception are defined as "professional services performed by physicians, including surgery; consultation; and home, office, and institutional calls."[86] Importantly, this exception only covers "incident to" services that are themselves "physician services" and specifically excludes all other "incident to" services, such as diagnostic tests or physical therapy. As is the case with the in-office ancillary services exception, the "supervision" required under this exception is the level of supervision required for the particular physician service at issue under Medicare's billing and coverage rules.

II. Academic medical centers

In 2001, CMS created a new exception to protect DHS furnished in an academic medical center (AMC) setting.[87] CMS created the exception in recognition of the unique status of AMCs, which typically are composed of multiple affiliated organizations that jointly deliver healthcare services to patients pursuant to a common mission. Frequently money and other types of remuneration are transferred between the various components of the AMC, and physician members of an AMC's faculty refer patients to the AMC's teaching hospital. According to CMS, such a relationship "raises the possibility of indirect remuneration for referrals."[88]

The Stark Regulations define the term "AMC" as a group of entities consisting of (1) an accredited medical school or an accredited academic hospital;[89] (2) one or more faculty practice plans (irrespective of how they are organized), which are affiliated with the medical school or academic hospital; and (3) one or more affiliated hospitals "in which a majority of the physicians on the medical staff consist of physicians who are faculty practice plan members and a majority of all hospital admissions are made by physicians who are faculty members."

For purposes of the third component of the definition, a "faculty member" is a "physician who is either on the faculty of the affiliated medical school or on the faculty of one or more of the educational programs at the accredited academic hospital." In addition, (1) "faculty from any affiliated medical school or accredited academic hospital education program may be aggregated," (2) "residents and nonphysician professionals need not be counted," and (3) "any faculty member may be counted, including courtesy and volunteer faculty."[90]

Assuming the existence of an AMC as defined in the Stark Regulations, the exception imposes additional requirements that focus primarily on the status of referring physicians, the compensation paid by the AMC to the referring physicians, and the relationship between and among the components of the AMC.

A. Referring physicians

Each referring physician must (1) be a full- or part-time *bona fide* employee of a component of the AMC (e.g., medical school, faculty practice plan, or hospital); (2) be licensed to practice medicine in the state(s) in which he or she practices; (3) have a *bona fide* faculty appointment at the affiliated medical school or one or more of the educational programs at the accredited hospital; and (4) furnish (and receive compensation for) substantial academic or clinical teaching services as part of his or her employment with the AMC.

CMS has created a "safe harbor" for determining whether a physician meets the "substantial services" requirement. Pursuant to this safe harbor, if the physician spends at least 20% of his or her professional time (i.e., eight hours per week) providing academic or clinical teaching services (or a combination thereof) to the AMC, then the "substantial services" requirement will be met. CMS emphasizes, however, that physicians who do not fit into this safe harbor may nonetheless meet this requirement, as long as the AMC uses a "reasonable and consistent" method for calculating a physician's academic or clinical teaching services.[91]

In the preamble to the 2004 Stark II, Phase II Regulations, CMS rejected the suggestion that it eliminate the requirement that the referring physician be an employee of a component of the AMC. According to CMS, if the referring physician is not an employee, "the relationship between the physician and the party paying the remuneration should not be sufficiently different from the usual arrangements of entities or organizations that are not AMCs, and one of the other exceptions" (e.g., the personal services, employment, or fair market value (FMV) exception) "should apply."[92]

B. Referring physician compensation

The next set of requirements of the AMC exception focuses on the compensation paid to the referring physician. Specifically, the referring physician's total compensation from all components of the AMC must (1) be set in advance, (2) be FMV for the services provided by the referring physician, and (3) not be determined in a manner that takes into account the volume or value of any referrals or other business generated by the referring physician within the AMC.[93] In addition, the referring physician's compensation must not violate the anti-kickback statute.[94] CMS has clarified that the FMV of a referring physician's compensation may be measured based on the compensation received by physicians at other AMCs or by comparable private practice physicians in the area, even if the latter figure is higher.[95]

Many commenters objected to the requirement that the physician's total compensation be "set in advance." In response, CMS noted that the changes made to the "set in advance" definition in the Stark II, Phase II Regulations (see Chapter 2) should address the commenters' concerns.[96] As discussed below, however, the inclusion of the "set in advance" requirement may be relevant for parties deciding whether to rely on the AMC exception or the indirect compensation arrangements exception (see Chapter 9) when analyzing referrals made by referring physicians in the context of an AMC.

C. AMC components

The AMC exception includes three specific requirements that the AMC components collectively must meet:

1. All money transferred between and among the components of the AMC must support (directly or indirectly) the missions of teaching, indigent care, research, or community service.

2. The relationship between and among the components of the AMC must be set forth in a written agreement or other documents that have been adopted by the governing body of each component of the AMC.[97]

3. Any money paid to a referring physician for research must support *bona fide* research or teaching and must be consistent with the terms of the research grant.[98]

CMS rejected the request to expand the third requirement to protect grants to referring physicians for other purposes, such as the provision of indigent care and community service, suggesting that AMCs should structure these types of payments to fit into other, existing Stark Law exceptions.[99]

D. AMC exception v. indirect compensation arrangements exception

It is interesting to compare the requirements and benefits of the AMC exception to those of the indirect compensation arrangements exception. The AMC exception does not protect financial relationships between a teaching hospital and physicians who are not faculty practice plan members, and the indirect compensation arrangements exception, in turn, does not protect direct compensation arrangements between faculty practice plan members and a teaching hospital.

With respect to indirect compensation arrangements between individual faculty practice plan physicians and a teaching hospital, however, both the AMC exception and the indirect compensation arrangements exception may be viable options, and in many cases, the latter exception may be preferred. As with the AMC exception, the indirect compensation arrangements exception will protect DHS referrals by faculty practice plan physicians to a teaching hospital, even though the faculty practice plan receives financial support payments from the teaching hospital.

In general, the indirect compensation arrangements exception will apply if the physician's compensation is consistent with FMV and is not determined in a manner the takes into account the value or volume of referrals or other business generated by the referring physician for the AMC. The benefit of relying on this exception, rather than on the AMC exception, is that it does not require an assessment of the relationship between the referring physician and the affiliated medical school or hospital (e.g., there is no need to consider whether the referring physician furnishes substantial academic or clinical teaching services as part of the physician's employment relationship with the AMC), and there is no need to consider the relationship among the various components of the AMC. In addition, unlike the AMC exception, the indirect compensation arrangements exception does not include a "set in advance" requirement, which may offer AMCs greater flexibility (and protections) when structuring their compensation arrangements with faculty physicians.

III. Services furnished to enrollees of prepaid plans

Both the Stark Law and Stark Regulations include a "prepaid plans exception."[100] This exception generally protects DHS that are furnished by a managed care organization (MCO), or by one of its contractors or subcontractors, to enrollees of certain types of prepaid health plans, provided that the DHS are covered by the plan at issue (and not by another "plan or line of business offered or administered by the same organization").[101] Examples of covered prepaid health plans include certain Medicare+Choice and healthcare prepayment plans, as well as plans offered by demonstration project MCOs, Public Health Service Act qualifying health maintenance organizations, and certain Medicaid MCOs.[102]

IV. Implants furnished in ASCs

CMS created an exception for prosthetic devices that the referring physician or a member of the referring physician's group practice implants in a Medicare-certified ambulatory surgery center (ASC).[103] As discussed in Chapter 3, CMS revised its definition of DHS in the 2001 Stark II, Phase I Regulations to exclude items and services billed as a part of a composite rate payment. At the same time, however, CMS recognized that the bundled ASC payment does not include many prosthetic devices and DME that physicians implant in an ASC; therefore, they continue to retain their character as DHS. Thus, without this exception, surgeons with ownership interests in ASCs (e.g., ophthalmologists) could not refer their patients to these ASCs if the procedures included the implantation of certain prosthetic devices (e.g., cataract surgery and the implantation of an intraocular lens) or DME.[104]

This exception applies to implants, including cochlear implants; intraocular lenses; and other implanted prosthetics, prosthetic devices, and DME.[105] To qualify for the exception, the following conditions must be met:

- the referring physician or a member of the referring physician's group practice must implant the item in a Medicare-certified ASC,

- the item must be implanted in the patient during a surgical procedure paid for by the Medicare program,

- the arrangement for furnishing the implant must not violate the anti-kickback statute, and

- the implant must be billed in a manner that complies with all federal and state billing laws and regulations.[106]

Finally, the exception applies only when the ASC bills for the implants; if the physician bills for the implants, CMS has suggested that a different exception, such as the in-office ancillary services exception, must be satisfied.[107] (CMS's suggestion notwithstanding, it is not clear whether the in-office ancillary services exception could, in fact, apply when the physician bills the implants at issue.) Furthermore, the exception does not apply to any financial relationships between a referring physician and any entity other than the ASC in which the physician implants the item at issue.[108]

V. Dialysis-related outpatient prescription drugs

This exception, initially created in the 2001 Stark II, Phase I Regulations, applies to the furnishing of dialysis-related outpatient drugs (collectively, "dialysis drugs") in or by an end-stage renal disease (ESRD) facility.[109] As used in this exception, the term "furnished" means that the dialysis drugs are administered to the patient in the ESRD facility or, for certain drugs, are dispensed by the ESRD facility for the patient's use at home.

This exception requires that (1) the arrangement for furnishing dialysis drugs not violate the anti-kickback statute, (2) the dialysis drugs be billed in a manner that complies with all federal and state laws and regulations, and (3) the dialysis drugs be listed on CMS's Web site (as well as in any annual updates published in the *Federal Register*).[110] Note that the scope of this exception specifically excludes any financial relationships between the referring physician and any entity other than the ESRD facility that furnishes the dialysis drugs to the patient.

VI. Preventative screening, immunizations, and vaccines

This exception applies to legislatively mandated preventative screening tests, immunizations, and vaccines (collectively, "preventative services") that are (1) subject to CMS-imposed frequency limits, (2) billed in a manner that complies with all federal and state billing laws and regulations, (3) covered by Medicare, and (4) listed as eligible on CMS's list of current procedural terminology/healthcare common procedure coding system codes.[111]

CMS removed a proposed requirement that the preventative services be paid based on a fee schedule in order to accommodate vaccines and other preventative services that may be paid by Medicare using different reimbursement methodologies.[112] However, CMS refused to expand the definition of preventative services in the 2004 Stark II, Phase II Regulations to include diagnostic Pap tests or diagnostic radiology services. According to CMS, there is no distinction between these diagnostic tests and any other diagnostic laboratory tests to which the Stark Law's referral prohibition applies.[113]

VII. Eyeglasses and contact lenses

The Medicare program covers the provision of one pair of either eyeglasses or contact lenses when furnished to patients following cataract surgery during which an intraocular lens is inserted.[114]

Consistent with this coverage policy, CMS created a regulatory exception that applies to the provision of eyeglasses and contact lenses furnished under such circumstances, as long as facilities billing for these items comply with all federal and state billing laws and regulations and offer the contacts/glasses in a manner that does not violate the anti-kickback statute.[115]

As with the preventative services discussed above, Medicare's coverage of eyeglasses or contact lenses following cataract surgery is subject to a frequency limitation (i.e., the beneficiary is limited to one pair of either item after each cataract surgery).[116]

VIII. Rural intra-family referrals

The 2004 Stark II, Phase II Regulations include what CMS refers to as a "narrow" exception for intra-family referrals in rural areas,[117] which is designed to "ensure access for patients in remote or sparsely served areas."[118] This exception permits a physician to refer patients for DHS to an IFM, or to an entity with which the IFM has a financial relationship, if the following conditions are met: (1) The patient resides in a rural area; (2) except for services furnished to patients where they reside (e.g., in their home), no other person or entity is available within 25 miles of the patient's residence to furnish the services in a timely manner (in light of the patient's condition); (3) for services furnished to patients where they reside (such as home health services), no other person or entity is available to furnish the services in a timely manner (in light of the patient's condition); and (4) the financial relationship does not violate the anti-kickback statute or any federal or state laws or regulations governing billing and claims submission.[119]

CMS stated in the preamble to the Stark II, Phase II Regulations that the 25-mile radius of care provision will satisfy its need to ensure access, preclude the risk of program abuse, and minimize the potential for any unfair competition for nonphysician-owned entities in rural areas.[120] CMS also noted that the exception focuses on where the services are furnished, not where the DHS entity is located, and gives the example of a physician who knows that a home health agency located 50 miles away from the patient's residence is willing to provide home health services to the patient. In such a case, the physician may not refer the patient to a family-owned home health agency under this exception.[121] Indeed, the exception provides that the referring physician or the IFM must make "reasonable inquiries" as to the availability of other persons or entities to furnish the DHS (e.g., consulting telephone directories, professional associations, other providers, or Internet resources), but neither the referring physician nor the IFM has an affirmative obligation to inquire as to the availability of persons or entities located farther than 25 miles from the patient's residence.[122]

Finally, noting the difficulty of crafting objective, qualitative measures in this exception, CMS indicated that although the exception takes into account "timely availability of DHS, it does not take into account the quality of other available DHS entities."[123] Thus, a physician may not refer a patient to her spouse's home health agency, for example, simply because she is dissatisfied with the quality of care provided by an otherwise available DHS provider.

Notes

1. 42 United States Code (USC) §1395nn(h)(4)(A).
2. 42 Code of Federal Regulations (CFR) §411.352(a). A hospital that employs physicians is not a "group practice," although a hospital could form and own a group practice as a separate legal entity, provided that doing so is permitted under applicable state law.
3. 42 CFR §411.352(a).
4. 42 CFR §411.352(a).
5. 42 CFR §411.352(a)(1)-(3).
6. 42 CFR §411.352(b).
7. 42 CFR §411.351.
8. 42 CFR §411.351.
9. 42 USC §1395nn(h)(4)(A)(i).
10. 42 CFR §411.352(c).
11. 42 CFR §411.351.
12. 42 CFR §411.351.
13. Stark II Proposed Regulations (Preamble), 63 *Federal Register* (*FR*) 1659, 1708 (1998).
14. Stark II, Phase I Regulations (Preamble), 66 *FR* 856, 904 (2001).
15. 42 USC §1395nn(h)(4)(A)(ii).
16. 42 CFR §411.352(d)(1). With respect to the billing and receipt components of this require-

ment, CMS takes the position that these will be satisfied by any physician services that are billed by the group under any group number, regardless of the payer. Stark II, Phase I Regulations (Preamble), 66 *FR* 856, 905 (2001). In other words, physician services furnished to another entity in return for a contractual fee will satisfy this requirement, provided that the fees are treated as receipts of the group.

17. Stark I Regulations (Preamble), 60 *FR* 41914, 41934 (1995).

18. Stark I Regulations (Preamble), 60 *FR* 41914, 41934 (1995).

19. 42 CFR §411.352(d)(1). The data used to calculate compliance with this requirement must be made available to CMS upon request. 42 CFR §411.352(d)(2).

20. Stark II Proposed Regulations (Preamble), 63 *FR* 1659, 1688 (1998)

21. 42 CFR §411.352(d)(5). This provision "does not apply when an existing group practice admits a new member or reorganizes." 42 CFR §411.352(d)(5).

22. 42 CFR §411.352(d)(6). This provision "does not apply when an existing group practice reorganizes or admits a new member who is not relocating his or her practice." 42 CFR §411.352(d)(6). It also should be noted that the substantially all services requirement does not apply to physician practices that are located in a healthcare professional shortage area (HPSA). 42 CFR §411.352(d)(3). Moreover, where a physician practice is located outside of a HPSA, "any time spent by a . . . member providing services in an HPSA should not be used to calculate whether the . . . practice has met" the substantially all services requirement, "regardless of whether the member's time in the HPSA is spent in a . . . practice, clinic, or office setting." 42 CFR §411.352(d)(4).

23. 42 USC §1395nn(h)(4)(A)(v).

24. "Members of the group must personally conduct no less than 75% of the physician-patient encounters of the group practice." 42 CFR §411.352(h).

25. Stark II Proposed Regulations (Preamble), 63 *FR* 1659, 1689 (1998).

26. Stark II, Phase I Regulations (Preamble), 66 *FR* 856, 905 (2001).

27. 42 CFR §411.352(f). The Stark Law definition of "group practice" contains no similar provision.

28. 42 CFR §411.352(f)(1).

29. Stark II, Phase II Regulations (Preamble), 69 *FR* 16054, 16080 (2004).

30. Stark II, Phase II Regulations (Preamble), 69 *FR* 16054, 16080 (2004). Also note that the unified business requirement specifically permits location and specialty-based compensation practices that relate to (1) revenues not derived from DHS or (2) revenues derived from DHS when the com-

pensation is distributed in a manner consistent with the special rules for productivity bonuses and profit shares discussed below. 42 CFR §411.352(f)(2).

31. 42 USC §1395nn(h)(4)(A)(iii).

32. Stark II Proposed Regulations (Preamble), 63 *FR* 1659, 1690 (2001).

33. Stark II Proposed Regulations (Preamble), 63 *FR* 1659, 1690 (2001).

34. 42 CFR §411.352(e).

35. 42 CFR §411.352(e).

36. 42 USC §1395nn(h)(4)(A)(iv).

37. 42 CFR §411.352(g).

38. Stark II, Phase I Regulations (Preamble), 66 *FR* 856, 908 (2001).

39. 42 USC §1395nn(h)(4)(B)(i); 42 CFR §411.352(i).

40. 42 CFR §411.352(i)(2). It is through the concept of the "five-physician component," introduced in the 2001 Stark II, Phase I Regulations, that CMS permits groups to compensate their physicians in a manner that reflects locality/specialty factors.

41. 42 CFR §411.352(i)(2).

42. 42 CFR §411.352(i)(2).

43. 42 USC §1395nn(h)(4)(B)(i); 42 CFR §411.352(i) .

44. Stark II, Phase I Regulations (Preamble), 66 *FR* 856, 908 (2001).

45. 42 CFR §411.352(i)(3).

46. 42 CFR §411.352(i)(2)(iii).

47. 42 CFR §411.352(i)(4).

48. Stark II, Phase I Regulations (Preamble), 66 *FR* 856, 888 (2001).

49. 42 USC §1395nn(b)(2).

50. 42 CFR §411.355(b)(4).

51. 42 CFR §411.355(b)(4)(i).

52. 42 CFR §411.355(b)(4)(i).

53. 42 CFR §411.355(b)(4)(ii).

54. Stark II, Phase I Regulations (Preamble), 66 *FR* 856, 882-83 (2001).

55. 42 CFR §411.355(b)(4)(iii).

56. 42 CFR §411.355(b)(4)(iv).

57. 42 CFR §411.355(b)(4)(v).

58. 42 CFR §411.355(b)(4)(vi).

59. 42 USC §1395nn(b)(2)(A)(i).

60. 42 CFR §411.355(b)(1)(iii). Thus, in the case of general supervision, the referring physician or another physician in the group does not necessarily have to be physically present in the office suite where the DHS is being provided in order to satisfy the supervision requirements of the in-office ancillary services exception. 42 CFR §410.32(b)(3)(i).

61. 42 CFR §411.351.

62. 42 CFR §411.351.

63. 42 CFR §411.351.

64. 42 USC §1395nn(b)(2)(A)(ii)(I).

65. 42 CFR §411.351.

66. Stark II, Phase II Regulations (Preamble), 69 *FR* 16054, 16073 (2004).

67. Stark II, Phase II Regulations (Preamble), 69 *FR* 16054, 16073 (2004).

68. 42 CFR §411.351.

69. Stark II, Phase II Regulations (Preamble), 69 *FR* 16053, 16074 (2004). See also Stark II, Phase I Regulations (Preamble), 66 *FR* 856, 891 (2001) ("[A] group practice can move any piece of equipment from office to office and use that 'in-office' piece of equipment for the provision of DHS . . .").

70. Stark II, Phase I Regulations (Preamble), 66 *FR* 856, 890 (2001).

71. Stark II, Phase II Regulations (Preamble), 69 *FR* 16054, 16073 (2004).

72. Stark II, Phase II Regulations (Preamble), 69 *FR* 16054, 16073 (2004).

73. Stark II, Phase II Regulations (Preamble), 69 *FR* 16054, 16073 (2004).

74. 42 CFR §411.355(b)(2)(i)(C).

75. Stark II, Phase II Regulations (Preamble), 69 *FR* 16054, 16073 (2004).

76. Stark II, Phase II Regulations (Preamble), 69 *FR* 16054, 16073 (2004).

77. Stark II, Phase II Regulations (Preamble), 69 *FR* 16054, 16073 (2004).

78. 42 CFR §411.355(b)(6).

79. Stark II, Phase II Regulations (Preamble), 69 *FR* 16054, 16074 (2004).

80. 42 USC §1395nn(b)(2)(A)(ii)(II).

81. 42 CFR §411.351.

82. 42 USC §1395nn(b)(2)(B).

83. 42 CFR §411.355(b)(3). Note that in the 2001 Stark II, Phase I Regulations, CMS resolved a

potential ambiguity in the billing requirement in connection with independent contractors supervising the provision of DHS by clarifying that independent contractors qualify as "physicians in the group" for both supervision and billing purposes under the in-office ancillary services exception. Stark II, Phase I Regulations (Preamble), 66 *FR* 856, 893-94 (2001). Note also that in the 2004 Stark II, Phase II Regulations, CMS made it clear that it was not permissible for a shared DHS facility in the "same building" to bill under the shared facility's own billing number. Stark II, Phase II Regulations (Preamble), 69 *FR* 16054, 16076 (2004).

84. 42 USC §1395nn(b)(1).

85. 42 CFR §411.355(a).

86. 42 CFR §410.20(a).

87. 42 CFR §411.355(e).

88. Stark II, Phase I Regulations (Preamble), 66 *FR* 856, 916 (2001).

89. The Stark II, Phase II Regulations provide that a hospital or healthcare system with four or more approved medical education programs will be viewed as an "accredited academic hospital." 42 CFR §411.355(e)(3).

90. 42 CFR §411.355(e)(2)(iii).

91. Stark II, Phase II Regulations (Preamble), 69 *FR* 16054, 16110 (2004).

92. Stark II, Phase II Regulations (Preamble), 69 *FR* 16054, 16109 (2004).

93. 42 CFR §411.355(e)(1)(ii).

94. 42 CFR §411.355(e)(1)(iv).

95. Stark II, Phase II Regulations (Preamble), 69 *FR* 16054, 16110 (2004).

96. Stark II, Phase II Regulations (Preamble), 69 *FR* 16054, 16110 (2004).

97. The Regulations also provide that if the AMC is a single legal entity, this requirement will be met if transfers of funds between components of the AMC are reflected in the routine financial reports of the AMC. 42 CFR §411.355(e)(1)(iii)(B).

98. 42 CFR §411.355(e)(1)(iii).

99. Stark II, Phase II Regulations (Preamble), 69 *FR* 16054, 16110–111 (2001).

100. 42 USC §1395nn(b)(3); 42 CFR §411.355(c).

101. 42 CFR §411.355(c).

102. The prepaid health plans that are covered by this exception are enumerated in the Stark Regulations at 42 CFR §411.355(c)(1)-(9). CMS also has created an exception for risk sharing

compensation arrangements that involve MCOs not covered by the prepaid plans exception.

103. 42 CFR §411.355(f).

104. Stark II, Phase I Regulations (Preamble), 66 *FR* 856, 934 (2001).

105. Note that CMS declined to expand the exception to apply to the implantation of radioactive brachytherapy seeds.

106. 42 CFR §411.355(f).

107. Stark II, Phase II Regulations (Preamble), 69 *FR* 16054, 16111 (2004).

108. 42 CFR §411.355(f)(5).

109. 42 CFR §411.355(g).

110. The following list of covered dialysis drugs was published by CMS in the November 15, 2004 *Federal Register* as part of CMS's Final Physician Fee Schedule rule for calendar year 2005: J0630 (Calcitonin salmon injection); J0636 (Inj calcitriol per 0.1 mcg); J0895 (Deferoxamine mesylate inj); J1270 (Injection, doxercalciferol); J1750 (Iron dextran); J1756 (Iron sucrose injection); J1955 (Inj levo-carnitine per 1 gm); J2501 (Paricalcitol); J2916 (Na ferric gluconate complex); J2993 (Reteplase injection); J2995 (Inj streptokinase/250000 IU); J2997 (Alteplase recombinant); J3364 (Urokinase 5000 IU injection); P9041 (Albumin (human), 5%, 50 ml); P9045 (Albumin (human), 5%, 250ml); P9046 (Albumin (human), 25%, 20ml); P9047 (Albumin (human), 25%, 50ml); Q4054 (Darbepoetin alfa, ESRD use); and Q4055 (Epoetin alfa, ESRD use). CMS also expanded the definition of EPO to include new drugs that are therapeutically equivalent, as long as the drug is included on the CMS List of covered dialysis drugs. Note that the industry has expressed concerns about the ability or willingness of CMS to keep its list of approved dialysis drugs current and to include new covered dialysis drugs as they become available.

111. 42 CFR §411.355(h).

112. Stark II, Phase II Regulations (Preamble), 69 *FR* 16054, 16116 (2004).

113. Stark II, Phase II Regulations (Preamble), 69 *FR* 16054, 16116 (2004).

114. 42 CFR §§410.36(a)(2)(ii) and 414.228.

115. 42 CFR §411.355(i).

116. Stark II, Phase I Regulations (Preamble), 66 *FR* 856, 936 (2001).

117. 42 CFR §411.355(j).

118. Stark II, Phase II Regulations (Preamble), 69 *FR* 16054, 16083 (2004).

119. 42 CFR §411.355(j).

120. Stark II, Phase II Regulations (Preamble), 69 *FR* 16054, 16083-84 (2004).

121. Stark II, Phase II Regulations (Preamble), 69 *FR* 16054, 16084 (2004).

122. 42 CFR §411.355(j)(2).

123. Stark II, Phase II Regulations (Preamble), 69 *FR* 16054, 16084 (2004).

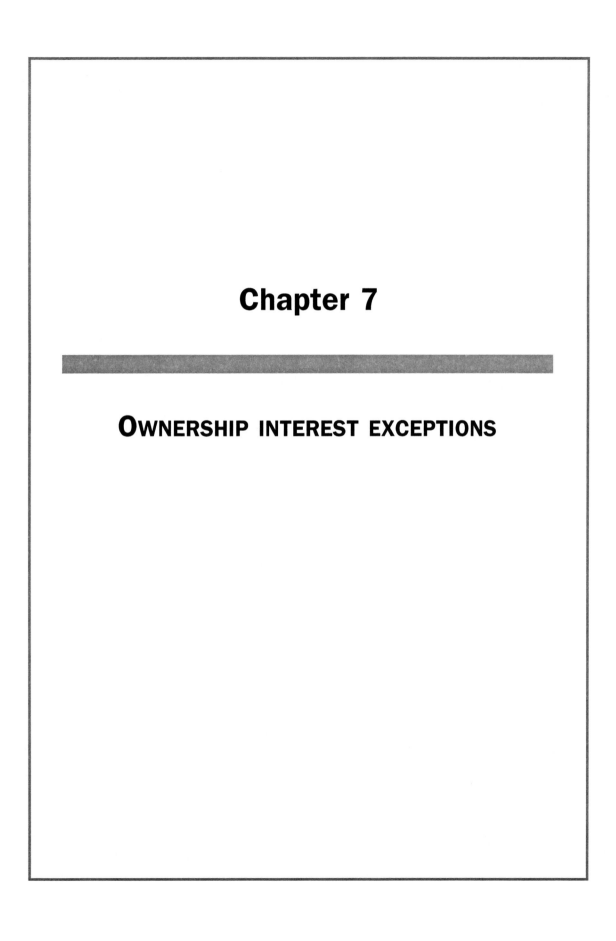

Chapter 7

OWNERSHIP INTEREST EXCEPTIONS

Chapter 7

Ownership interest exceptions

Where the financial relationship at issue takes the form of an ownership or investment interest—which we will refer to as an "ownership interest"—exceptions falling into either the "all purpose" category or the "ownership interest" category may protect referrals by the physician-owner to the entity. This chapter discusses the five ownership interest exceptions—the publicly traded securities exception, the mutual funds exception, the Puerto Rican hospital exception, the rural provider exception, and the whole hospital exception.

I. Publicly traded securities exception

The Stark Law provides an exception for ownership of "investment securities (including shares or bonds, debentures, notes, or other debt instruments)" that "may be purchased on terms generally available to the public" and meet two conditions.[1] First, they must be (1) "securities listed on the New York Stock Exchange, the American Stock Exchange, or any regional exchange in which quotations are published on a daily basis, or foreign securities listed on a recognized foreign, national, or regional exchange in which quotations are published on a daily basis," or (2) "traded under an automated interdealer quotation system operated by the National Association of Securities Dealers."[2] Second, the securities must be "in a corporation that had, at the end of the corporation's most recent fiscal year, or on average during the previous [three] fiscal years, stockholder equity exceeding $75,000,000."[3]

The Stark Regulations largely track the Stark Law with respect to the publicly traded securities exception.[4] Over the years, however, the Centers for Medicare & Medicaid Services (CMS) has clarified the publicly traded securities exception. In the preamble to the 1998 Proposed Stark II Regulations, CMS explained that the purpose of this exception "is to allow physicians or family members to acquire stock in large companies," provided that the acquisition "does not particularly favor the physicians over other purchasers."[5]

Consistent with this purpose, CMS has interpreted the requirement that the investment securities be "purchased on terms generally available to the public" to mean that the securities could have been bought on the open market at the time they were acquired by the physician or immediately family member (IFM), even if the physician/IFM, in fact, acquired them through other means (e.g., an inheritance).[6]

CMS further clarified this requirement in the 2004 Stark II, Phase II Regulations, indicating that it is sufficient for the ownership interest to be in securities that are generally available to the public when the physician makes the diagnosed health service (DHS) referral at issue, rather than when the physician (or IFM) acquires the securities.[7] Thus, securities acquired by a physician before a public offering will be protected, as long as they are available to the public at the time of any DHS referrals by the physician.[8]

Example 7.1

In 1997, a physician's friend purchased 1000 shares in a privately held hospital holding company with shareholder equity of $150 million. In 2000, the holding company went public. In January 2003, the physician's friend died, leaving him all of her 1000 shares. The physician has medical staff privileges at one of the hospitals owned by the holding company.

Commentary: The physician may make referrals to the hospital for the furnishing of DHS covered by Medicare without violating the Stark Law's referral prohibition because shares of the holding company are readily available on the open market. The fact that the holding company was not publicly traded when the physician's friend acquired her ownership interest (in 1997) does not alter the analysis.

Example 7.2

This includes the same facts as Example 7.1, except that in 2004, one year after the physician received the 1000 shares, the holding company engaged in a leveraged buy-out and took the company private. The physician remains one of the company's private owners.

Commentary: The physician cannot rely on the publicly traded securities exception and, in the absence of another exception, could not make referrals to the hospital for the furnishing of DHS covered by Medicare.

Providers have urged CMS to expand the publicly traded securities exception to cover investments in smaller companies. To date, however, CMS has declined this invitation, contending that the $75 million threshold is important "because it effectively severs any tie between referrals and returns on investment" and, as such, "strikes an appropriate balance between excepting legitimate investments and precluding abusive 'sweetheart' deals predicated on referrals."[9]

II. Mutual funds exception

The Stark Law also provides an exception for ownership of "shares in a regulated investment company"—also known as a mutual fund—"as defined in section 851(a) of the Internal Revenue Code of 1986, if such company had, at the end of the company's most recent fiscal year, or on average during the previous [three] fiscal years, total assets exceeding $75,000,000."[10] The Stark Regulations mirror this exception.[11]

III. Puerto Rican hospital exception

Under both the Stark Law and Stark Regulations, an ownership interest in a hospital located in Puerto Rico does not give rise to a financial relationship for purposes of the Stark Law.[12] Thus, where a physician/IFM has an ownership interest in a hospital located in Puerto Rico, the physician may make referrals to the hospital for the furnishing of DHS covered by Medicare without triggering the Stark Law's referral prohibition.

IV. Rural provider exception

The Stark Law provides that an ownership interest in an entity that furnishes DHS in a "rural area" does not give rise to a financial relationship within the meaning of the Stark Law, provided that "substantially all of the [DHS] furnished by the entity are furnished to individuals residing in" the rural area at issue.[13]

Although the Stark Law itself does not define the terms "substantially all" or "rural area," the terms have been defined by CMS. In the 1998 Proposed Stark II Regulations, CMS defined "substantially all" to mean not less than 75% of the relevant entity's total DHS.[14] CMS adopted this definition in its 2004 Stark II, Phase II Regulations.[15] The 2004 regulations also adopted the agency's earlier proposals (1) to eliminate the requirement that the provider at issue be based in the rural area at issue, as long as the DHS at issue are furnished in that rural area, and (2) to define "rural area" as any area that is not designated as an urban area (i.e., a "metropolitan statistical area") by the Office of Management and Budget.[16]

Example 7.3

A physician owns a physical therapy company headquartered in County A, which the government designates an urban area. Although located in County A, the company furnishes 80% of its services in County B to patients residing in County B, which is a rural area. A Medicare beneficiary resides in County B. The physician refers this beneficiary to the company for the furnishing of DHS covered by Medicare.

Commentary: The referral will not violate the Stark Law, provided the patient receives the services in County B.

CMS has declined requests to "grandfather" investments for providers located in an area originally treated as rural but subsequently reclassified as urban.[17] CMS has indicated, however, that the new "grace period" exception created by CMS in the Stark II, Phase II Regulations may be available to the owners of such entities.[18] Finally, in 2004, CMS clarified that the rural provider exception will not protect ownership interests in a "specialty hospital" during the moratorium imposed by Section 507 of the Medicare Prescription Drug, Improvement and Modernization Act of 2003 (MMA), discussed below.[19]

V. Whole hospital exception

The Stark Law provides that an ownership interest in a hospital located outside of Puerto Rico will not give rise to a financial relationship if (1) the ownership interest is in the entire hospital (as opposed to a subdivision of the hospital) and (2) the referring physician is authorized to perform services at the hospital.[20]

In 1998, CMS proposed that this exception would cover (1) both direct and indirect ownership interests;[21] (2) DHS furnished by a hospital only, and not by non-hospital entities owned by a hospital (e.g., a hospital-owned home health agency or skilled nursing facility);[22] and (3) all services furnished by a hospital, even if such services are not inpatient or outpatient hospital services.[23] CMS adopted these proposals in the 2004 Stark II, Phase II Regulations.[24]

Example 7.4

A physician is a member of a limited liability company that owns and operates three hospitals (Hospital A, Hospital B, and Hospital C). The physician has medical staff privileges at Hospitals A and B, but not C. Hospitals A and C operate diagnostic clinical laboratories that serve both hospital and non-hospital patients. Hospital B services non-hospital patients through a wholly owned, but separately organized, diagnostic clinical laboratory.

Commentary: (1) The physician may refer Medicare patients to Hospital A's lab, because Hospital A and the lab are part of the same corporate entity; (2) the physician may not refer Medicare patients to Hospital C's lab because he is not authorized to perform services at Hospital C; and (3) the physician may not refer Medicare patients to the lab owned by Hospital B, because Hospital B and the lab are separate corporate entities.

In addition to incorporating the 1998 proposed rule, the 2004 Stark II, Phase II Regulations modified the whole hospital exception to reflect the provisions of Section 507 of the MMA. Section 507 implemented an 18-month moratorium—running from December 8, 2003, to June 8, 2005—on the application of the whole hospital exception to certain "specialty hospitals."[25]

More specifically, during the 18-month moratorium, a physician's ownership in a specialty hospital did not qualify for the whole hospital exception, and a physician with an ownership interest in a specialty hospital could not refer a Medicare patient to that hospital for the furnishing of DHS (even if the specialty hospital was located in a rural area), unless the specialty hospital was "in operation or under development prior to November 18, 2003," and several other conditions were satisfied.[26]

CMS defined a "specialty hospital" to include a hospital reimbursed under Medicare's inpatient prospective payment system that was primarily or exclusively engaged in the care and treatment of (1) patients with a cardiac condition, (2) patients with an orthopedic condition, (3) patients receiving a surgical procedure, or (4) any other special category that the Secretary of the Department of Health and Human Services designated as inconsistent with the purpose of permitting physician ownership of a hospital.[27]

Although the Medicare Payment Advisory Commission (MedPAC) recommended that the moratorium be extended for up to two additional years,[28] Congress had not extended the moratorium as of June 8, 2005. On the next day, however, CMS announced that it was undertaking a six-month review of specialty hospitals, which—by virtue of freezing certifications of new specialty hospitals—had the practical effect of extending the moratorium until January 2006.[29]

Notes

1. 42 United States Code (USC) §§1395nn(c)(1).
2. 42 USC §1395nn(c)(1)(A).
3. 42 USC §1395nn(c)(1)(B).
4. 42 USC §4.11356(a).
5. Proposed Stark II Regulations (Preamble), 63 *Federal Register (FR)* 1659, 1698 (1998).

6. Proposed Stark II Regulations (Preamble), 63 *FR* 1659, 1698 (1998).

7. Stark II, Phase II Regulations (Preamble), 69 *FR* 16054, 16081 (2004).

8. Stark II, Phase II Regulations (Preamble), 69 *FR* 16054, 16081 (2004).

9. Stark II, Phase II Regulations (Preamble), 69 *FR* 16054, 16082 (2004). As we will discuss in Chapter 11, in 2004, CMS eliminated the reporting requirement for shareholder information regarding financial relationships that satisfy the publicly traded company exception.

10. 42 USC §1395nn(c)(2).

11. 42 CFR §411.356(b).

12. 42 USC §1395nn(d)(1); 42 CFR §411.356(c)(2).

13. 42 USC §1395nn(d)(2).

14. Proposed Stark II Regulations (Preamble), 63 *FR* 1659, 1724 (1998).

15. 42 CFR §411.356(c)(1). See also Stark II, Phase II Regulations (Preamble), 69 *FR* 6054, 16082 (2004).

16. Stark II, Phase II Regulations (Preamble), 69 *FR* 16054, 16082-16083 (2004); 42 CFR §411.356(c)(1), citing 42 CFR §412.62(f)(1)(ii).

17. Stark II, Phase II Regulations (Preamble), 69 *FR* 16054, 16083 (2004).

18. Stark II, Phase II Regulations (Preamble), 69 *FR* 16054, 16083 (2004).

19. Stark II, Phase II Regulations (Preamble), 69 *FR* 16054, 16083 (2004).

20. 42 USC §1395nn(d)(3).

21. Proposed Stark II Regulations (Preamble), 63 *FR* 1659, 1713 (1998).

22. Proposed Stark II Regulations (Preamble), 63 *FR* 1659, 1698 (1998).

23. Proposed Stark II Regulations (Preamble), 63 *FR* 1659, 1699 (1998).

24. Stark II, Phase II Regulations (Preamble), 69 *FR* 16054, 16084 (2004); 42 CFR §411.356(c)(3).

25. Stark II, Phase II Regulations (Preamble), 69 *FR* 16054, 16084 (2004);42CFR §411.356(c)(3)(iii). See also "Physician Self-Referral Prohibition; 18-Month Moratorium on Physician Investment in Specialty Hospitals," CMS Pub. No. 100-20, Transmittal No. 62 (March 19, 2004).

26. 42 CFR §411.351.

27. 42 CFR §411.351.

28. MedPAC Report to the Congress: Physician-Owned Specialty Hospitals (March 2005).

29. CMS Fact Sheet, "CMS Outlines Next steps as Moratorium on New Speciality Hospitals Expires" (June 9, 2005), available online at *www.cms.hhs.gov/media/pressrelease.asp?counter=1478*.

Chapter 8

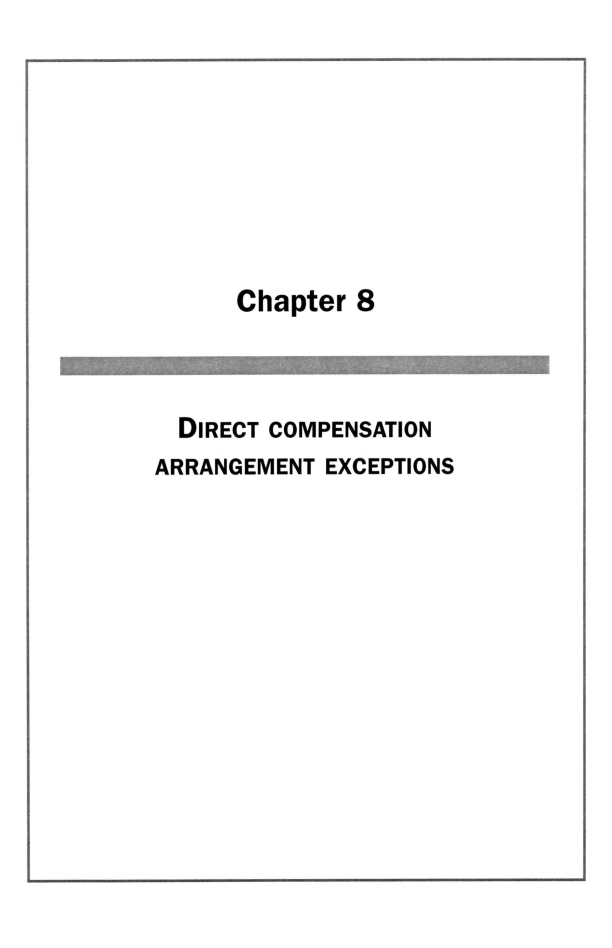

DIRECT COMPENSATION ARRANGEMENT EXCEPTIONS

Chapter 8

DIRECT COMPENSATION ARRANGEMENT EXCEPTIONS

As discussed in Chapter 1, there are four types of financial relationships and four general categories of Stark Law exceptions. When the financial relationship at issue takes the form of a direct compensation arrangement, two of the four exception categories may apply: the "all-purpose" exceptions and the "direct compensation arrangement" exceptions. Chapter 6 discusses the all-purpose exceptions. The following exceptions are available for direct compensation arrangements:

- Space rental

- Equipment rental

- Employment

- Personal services arrangements

- Physician recruitment

- Isolated transactions

- Remuneration unrelated to designated health services (DHS)

- Group practice arrangements with hospitals

- Payments by a physician

- Charitable donations

- Compensation under $300

- Fair market value (FMV) compensation

- Medical staff incidental benefits

- Risk-sharing arrangements

- Compliance training

- Referral services

- Obstetrical malpractice insurance
- Professional courtesy
- Physician retention
- Community-wide health information systems

Chapter 10 discusses the physician recruitment and physician retention exceptions. This chapter will discuss the remaining 18 exceptions.

Before summarizing each direct compensation arrangement exception, note that the application of these exceptions is not uniform. For example:

- **Unilateral vs. bilateral.** Some exceptions, by their terms, only protect compensation flowing in one direction, whereas others are not limited in this way. For example, the exception for charitable donations only protects charitable gifts given by a physician or his or her immediate family member (IFM) to a DHS entity—not the other way around. Other exceptions are structured to cover compensation that flows both ways. For example, the exceptions for space and equipment rentals cover payments made by the lessee to the lessor, as well as the provision of space or equipment by the lessor to the lessee.

- **Direct vs. hybrid.** Although all of the exceptions discussed in this chapter cover direct compensation arrangements, a few of the exceptions, as drafted, appear to be applicable to a broader array of arrangements. For example, the exception for FMV compensation protects compensation between an entity and a physician or a group of physicians. Given the evolution of the exception for indirect compensation arrangements, it is unclear whether CMS intended the FMV compensation arrangements exception to protect certain indirect compensation arrangements or whether it simply has not made technical corrections to the exception.

- **Hospital vs. all DHS entities.** Certain exceptions only cover direct compensation arrangements with a hospital, while others relate to compensation arrangements with any type of DHS entity. For example, the exception for remuneration unrelated to DHS only protects remuneration provided by a hospital to a physician. Most other exceptions (e.g., employment, personal services, charitable donations, and compensation under $300) protect compensation provided by all types of DHS entities.

- **Physician vs. IFM.** Certain exceptions protect compensation received or provided by a physician only, whereas others include the physician's IFM. For example, the exceptions for compliance training and professional courtesy protect compensation provided by an entity to a physician and his or her IFM. In contrast, the exception for community-wide health information systems only protects compensation provided by an entity to a physician.

- **Anti-kickback statute adoption.** Several exceptions, namely the exceptions for referral services and obstetrical malpractice insurance, simply incorporate parallel safe harbors from the anti-kickback statute. CMS has provided little guidance about how such safe harbors will apply under the Stark Law.

I. Space rental exception

Recognizing that hospitals and physicians often lease space from each other and that such arrangements, although beneficial for the efficient delivery of healthcare services, create a financial relationship between the parties, Congress established an exception to the Stark Law for space rental arrangements.[1] CMS, in turn, has created an exception for space rental arrangements in the Stark Regulations.[2]

A. Law and regulations

The Stark Law provides that "payments made by a lessee to a lessor for the use of premises" do not give rise to a financial relationship, provided that seven conditions are met:

1. The lease is set out in writing, is signed by the parties to the lease, and "specifies the premises covered by the lease."

2. The term of the lease is for at least one year.

3. The space leased "does not exceed that which is reasonable and necessary for the legitimate business purposes of the lease."

4. The space leased is used exclusively by the lessee, unless the lease is for use of space consisting of common areas, in which case lease payments may be based on the lessee's pro rata share of expenses for the common space.

5. The lease charges are "set in advance, are consistent with FMV, and are not determined in a manner that takes into account the volume or value of any referrals or other business generated between the parties."

6. The terms of the lease would be "commercially reasonable even if no referrals were made between the parties."

7. The lease meets such other requirements as "CMS may impose by regulation as needed to protect against program or patient abuse."[3]

With limited exceptions (related to the "one-year term" requirement and holdover lessees), the Stark Regulations track these statutory provisions.[4] Specifically, the Regulations provide that "payments for the use of office space made by a lessee to a lessor" do not give rise to a financial relationship under the Stark Law, provided that there is a rental or lease agreement that meets the following seven conditions:

1. The agreement is set out in writing, is signed by the parties, and specifies the premises it covers.

2. The term of the agreement is at least one year. To meet this requirement, if the agreement is terminated during the term (with or without cause), the parties may not enter into a new agreement during the first year of the original term of the agreement.

3. The space rented or leased does not exceed that which is reasonable and necessary for the legitimate business purposes of the lease or rental and is used exclusively by the lessee when being used by the lessee (and is not shared with or used by the lessor or any person or entity related to the lessor), except that the lessee may make payments for the use of space consisting of common areas if the payments do not exceed the lessee's pro rata share of expenses for the space based on the ratio of the space used exclusively by the lessee to the total amount of space (other than common areas) occupied by all persons using the common areas.

4. The rental charges over the term of the agreement are set in advance and are consistent with FMV.

5. The rental charges over the term of the agreement are not determined in a manner that takes into account the volume or value of any referrals or other business generated between the parties.

6. The agreement would be commercially reasonable even if no referrals were made between the lessee and the lessor.

7. A holdover month-to-month rental for up to six months immediately following an agreement of at least one year that met the conditions of this exception will satisfy this exception, provided that the holdover rental is on the same terms and conditions as the immediately preceding agreement.[5]

B. *Discussion*

1. One-year term requirement

Both the Stark Law and Regulations require that a space lease agreement have a term of at least one year. The Regulations clarify that a lease agreement that permits termination (with or without cause) during the first year satisfies the one-year term requirement. Thus, lease agreements that are actually terminated before the expiration of the first year of the original term (and, as such, do not run for a term of one year) still may satisfy the exception, provided that its other requirements are met. On the other hand, a space lease agreement that, by its terms, is for a period of less than one year (e.g., five months), will not meet the one-year term requirement. [6]

What remains unclear, however, is whether parties may terminate a lease arrangement for one location and enter into a subsequent lease arrangement for a second, separate location during the first year of the original lease term.[7] A comment that first appeared in the preamble to the 1998 Stark II Proposed Regulations, and is repeated in the preamble to the 2004 Stark II, Phase II Regulations, provides some insight into CMS's likely approach to this issue. CMS stated in both rulemakings that a lease arrangement may be terminated during the first year, provided that (1) no further agreement is entered into during the first year of the original term (which is consistent with the current provision in the Stark Regulations) and (2) "any new lease fits on its own terms in an exception."[8] The reference to a "new lease" suggests that a "new lease" arrangement was contemplated. Moreover, a subsequent lease arrangement that meets the requirements for the space lease exception poses no additional risk of program fraud and abuse. For these reasons, it appears that parties to a lease that is terminated during the first year may enter into another lease within the same one-year period, provided that the second lease relates to different space and otherwise meets the terms of the space rental exception.

2. Exclusive use requirement

To fit within the space rental exception, the leased space must be "used exclusively by the lessee when being used by the lessee."[9] Although this requirement was originally interpreted to prohibit lessees from subletting leased space, CMS clarified in the 2004 Stark II, Phase II Regulations that the exclusive use requirement does not preclude a lessee from subleasing space, provided that, as with the original lease, the sublessee does not share the space with the lessor.[10] CMS cautioned, however, that a sublease arrangement may result in an indirect compensation arrangement between the sublessee and the original lessor through a "chain of leases."[11]

Note: Chapter 5 discusses the definition of an indirect compensation arrangement and Chapter 9 discusses the indirect compensation arrangements exception.

Notwithstanding the exclusive use requirement's prohibition against sharing space with the lessor or a related entity, the Stark Regulations do provide that lease payments may include compensation for the use of common areas if the payments do not exceed the lessee's pro rata share of the expenses for such space. The calculation of the pro rata share of expenses underlying the lease payment must be based on the ratio of space used exclusively by the lessee to the total amount of space leased (other than the common areas) to all persons using the common areas.[12]

Example 8.1

Four independent, unaffiliated physicians each lease an office and an examination room in a four-office suite in a hospital's medical office building. Each physician also is entitled to use the suite's common waiting room and reception area. Each office and examination room is exactly the same size.

Commentary: Each of the four physicians may pay one-quarter of the rental amount for the common waiting room and reception area.

Finally, although neither the Stark Law nor Regulations expressly address timeshare arrangements, many such arrangements could likely be structured to fit within the exception. With respect to such arrangements, the precise intervals (e.g., day, time) during which the lessees would have "exclusive use" of the space would need to be specified in the relevant agreements.

Example 8.2

Three independent, unaffiliated physicians (Physicians A, B, and C) lease the same medical office and examination room on a timeshare basis. Physician A's lease agreement permits her to use the space on Mondays, Wednesdays, and Fridays, from 8:00 a.m. to 12:00 p.m. Physician B's lease agreement permits her to use the space on Mondays, Wednesdays, and Fridays, from 1:00 p.m. to 5:00 p.m. Physician C's lease agreement permits her to use the space all day on Tuesdays and Thursdays.

Commentary: Each space lease arrangement would appear to satisfy the requirement of the space lease exception that the physician have exclusive use of the space during the designated days and times to which the lease applies.

---

3. Set in advance and FMV requirement

CMS has provided some guidance regarding the meaning of FMV in connection with leases. Specifically, the definition of FMV provides that "[w]ith respect to rentals and leases ... FMV means the value of rental property for general commercial purposes (not taking into account its intended use). In the case of a lease of space, this value may not be adjusted to reflect the additional value the prospective lessee or lessor would attribute to the proximity or convenience to the lessor when the lessor is a potential source of patient referrals to the lessee."[13] The definition of FMV provides that a rental payment will not be deemed to take into account intended use if it "takes into account costs incurred by the lessor in developing or upgrading the property or maintaining the property," including office build-outs and other tenant improvements.[14]

Finally, CMS has made it clear that the lease amount may not reflect any past or future referrals of DHS payable by Medicare. The "other business generated" language also precludes the parties from structuring the lease amount to reflect referrals of non-Medicare business.[15]

Example 8.3

A physician specializing in orthopedic medicine leases space to a physical therapy (PT) company in a medical office building that she owns. The lease agreement provides for a fixed monthly lease amount that does not vary with the value or volume of referrals of Medicare patients. The lease agreement provides, however, that the PT company will pay an additional lease amount of $100 per month for every 25 non-Medicare patients that the physician refers to the PT company. This additional payment is to cover additional costs that the physician landlord may incur as the result of "increased wear and tear" from additional patient flow through the space.

Commentary: The lease arrangement does not satisfy the space rental exception because the additional payment for non-Medicare referrals does not meet the requirement that the lease amount not reflect "other business" generated between the parties.

Note: The "FMV" and "other business generated" standards are discussed in further detail in Chapter 2.

4. Holdover lessees

The Stark Regulations expand on the statutory space rental exception by providing special require-ments for holdover tenancies (i.e., when the lessee continues to occupy the leased space beyond the last day of the lease term).[16] A lease arrangement with a month-to-month holdover lessee will satisfy the space lease exception for a period of up to six months, provided that the holdover period imme-diately follows the expiration of a lease agreement that met the requirements of the space rental exception in the first instance and provided that the lessee continues to occupy the premises on the same terms and conditions set forth in the original lease.[17] Before the end of the six months, the par-ties must enter into a new, signed rental agreement or renew the original lease. This new clarification in the Stark Regulations is particularly helpful in situations where a lease agreement's original term has expired before the parties are able to conclude successfully negotiations for a new or renewed lease arrangement.

Example 8.4

A physician leases office space in a hospital's medical office building. The lease agree-ment has a term of two years. At the end of two years, the parties begin to renegotiate the lease, but they cannot agree on a new rental amount. After seven months, the par-ties reach an agreement and sign a new lease.

Commentary: At a minimum, the seventh month of the holdover period would not satis-fy the space rental exception, as its provisions permitting holdover tenants only apply for six months after the expiration of the lease.

II. Equipment rental exception

Similar to the treatment of space rentals, the Stark Law and Regulations provide an exception for equipment rental arrangements. This exception recognizes that it is common for physicians to lease equipment from, and to, entities to which they may make DHS referrals.

A. Law and regulations

Like its space rental counterpart, the exception for equipment leases is fairly straightforward, providing that a "compensation arrangement" does not include "[p]ayments made by a lessee of equipment to the lessor of the equipment for the use of the equipment," as long as seven requirements are met:

1. The lease is set out in writing, signed by the parties to the lease, and "specifies the equipment covered by the lease."

2. The term of the lease is for at least one year.

3. The equipment leased "does not exceed that which is reasonable and necessary for the legitimate business purposes of the lease."

4. The equipment leased is used exclusively by the lessee.

5. The lease charges are "set in advance, are consistent with FMV, and are not determined in a manner that takes into account the volume or value of any referrals or other business generated between the parties."

6. The terms of the lease would be "commercially reasonable even if no referrals were made between the parties."

7. The lease meets such other requirements as CMS "may impose by regulation as needed to protect against program or patient abuse."[18]

The provisions in the Stark Regulations that address the equipment rental exception are nearly identical to the statutory provisions, with the exception of language that (1) sets forth what CMS will accept as meeting the "one-year term requirement" and (2) addresses holdover situations.[19] Specifically, the Stark Regulations provide that payments "made by a lessee to a lessor for use of equipment" will not give rise to a financial relationship under the Stark Law if:

1. The rental or lease agreement is set out in writing, signed by the parties, and specifies the equipment it covers.

2. The equipment rented or leased does not exceed that which is reasonable and necessary for the legitimate business purposes of the lease or rental, is used exclusively by the lessee when being used by the lessee, and is not shared with or used by the lessor or any person or entity related to the lessor.

3. The agreement provides for a term of rental or lease of at least one year. To meet this requirement, if the agreement is terminated during the term with or without cause, the parties may not enter into a new agreement during the first year of the original term of the agreement.

4. The rental charges over the term of the agreement are set in advance, are consistent with FMV, and are not determined in a manner that takes into account the volume or value of any referrals or other business generated between the parties.

5. The agreement would be commercially reasonable even if no referrals were made between the parties.

6. A holdover month-to-month rental for up to six months immediately following an agreement of at least one year that met the conditions of this exception, provided that the holdover rental is on the same terms and conditions as the immediately preceding agreement. [20]

B. Discussion

1. One-year term requirement

As with space rental arrangements, equipment lease arrangements must be for a term at least one year (the "one-year term requirement").[21] Also like the space rental exception, however, the parties to an equipment lease may terminate the arrangement during the first year of the lease (with or without cause), provided that they do not enter into a new agreement during the first year of the original term of the lease. Once again, it is unclear whether the parties can enter into a subsequent arrangement for the lease of different equipment during the first year of the original lease. The language in the

Stark Regulations suggests that this is permissible, provided that the new lease itself meets an exception to the Stark Law.[22]

2. Exclusive use requirement

The equipment lease exception also requires that the equipment be used exclusively by the lessee during the lease period (i.e., like the space lease exception, the lessee must not share the leased equipment with any other person or entity during those times that the lessee is entitled to use the equipment).[23] As discussed below, however, the Stark Regulations do permit lessees to lease equipment on a "per-click" or "per-use" basis. As such, the equipment lease exception does not appear to require exclusive use or full-time possession of the equipment covered by the lease.

In addition, as with space leases, subleases of equipment meet the exclusive use requirement as long as the sublessee does not share the leased equipment with the original lessor during the time of the lease.[24] As noted above, however, a sublease may, through a chain of leases, create an indirect compensation arrangement between the sublessee and the original lessor.[25] In that event, the sublease arrangement would need to be evaluated under the indirect compensation arrangement definition and exception (see Chapters 5 and 9, respectively).

3. Set in advance and FMV requirement

CMS has explained that per-use or per-click equipment lease arrangements satisfy the set in advance and FMV requirements as long as the per-use/click lease amount is itself set in advance, is FMV, and does not vary with the volume or value of referrals between the parties.[26] The Stark Regulations do not require that the lease arrangement specify a minimum or maximum number of uses per month (or any other time period) or a schedule of use.

Example 8.5

A physician leases office space in a hospital's medical office building. Separate and apart from the office space lease arrangement, the hospital offers the physician tenant the option of entering into an equipment lease arrangement for certain equipment that the hospital has located in the medical office building, including a computed tomography (CT) scanning machine. The physician would like to lease the CT scanning machine from the hospital but does not have enough volume to warrant leasing the machine for a full day each week. The physician also is concerned about the logistics of trying to schedule all CT scans on a single day of the week. Accordingly, the physician negotiates a first-come, first-served equipment lease arrangement with the hospital, whereby the physician rents the CT machine on a "per-use" basis and, assuming that the machine is not being used by other physicians, schedules his patients at times that are convenient for them.

Commentary: The lease arrangement is consistent with the equipment lease exception, provided that the lease amount does not vary with the volume or value of the physician's DHS referrals to the hospital.

CMS has also clarified that an equipment lease can be combined with another compensation arrangement, such as a personal services arrangement, as long as the agreement assigns a separate FMV to each component of compensation.[27] Thus, a physician can enter into an arrangement to lease a diagnostic machine from a hospital and purchase the services of the technician who operates the equipment, provided that (1) the agreement separately enumerates the payment amounts for the equipment lease and the technical personal services and (2) the parties undertake a separate FMV evaluation of each.

Finally, CMS has explained that, under the appropriate circumstances, equipment leases (but not office space leases) may be eligible for protection under the exception for FMV compensation.[28]

4. Holdover lessees

As with space leases, the Stark Regulations expand on the statutory provisions governing the equipment lease exception by providing special requirements for holdover month-to-month equipment rentals.[29] A lease arrangement with a month-to-month holdover lessee will satisfy the equipment lease exception for a period of up to six months, provided the holdover period immediately follows the expiration of a lease agreement that met the requirements of the equipment lease exception in the first instance, and provided that the lessee continues to lease the equipment on the same terms and conditions as contained in the original lease.[30] Before the end of the six months, the parties must enter into a new, signed lease agreement or renew the original lease. Once again, this aspect of the Stark Regulations is particularly helpful in situations where a lease agreement's original term has expired before the parties are able to conclude successfully negotiations for a new or renewed lease arrangement.

III. Employment exception

Although many physicians have historically resisted employment arrangements outside of their own group practice (often preferring to remain independent contractors), the employment of physicians by DHS entities has become more common. Consequently, Congress and CMS created an exception to protect certain bona fide employment arrangements.

A. Law and regulations

The Stark Law provides that any amount paid by an employer to a physician (or an IFM) "who has a bona fide employment relationship with the employer for the provision of services" will not constitute remuneration—and, as such, will not give rise to a financial relationship—if four conditions are met:

1. The employment is for identifiable services.

2. The amount of remuneration under the employment arrangement is consistent with the FMV of the services and is not determined in a manner that takes into account (directly or indirectly) the volume or value of any referrals by the referring physician.

3. The remuneration is provided pursuant to an agreement that would be commercially reasonable even if no referrals were made to the employer.

4. The employment meets such other requirements as CMS may impose by regulation to protect against program or patient abuse. [31]

The Law further provides that the exception does "not prohibit the payment of remuneration in the form of a productivity bonus based on services performed personally" by the physician (or an IFM).[32] Finally, the law defines an "employee" as an individual who would be considered an employee under the usual common law rules relied on by the Internal Revenue Service.[33]

The Stark Regulations generally parallel the Stark Law, providing that "[a]ny amount paid by an employer "to a physician (or IFM)" who has a bona fide employment relationship with the employer for the provision of services" will not give rise to a financial relationship under the Stark Law if three conditions are met:

1. The employment is for identifiable services.

2. The amount of the remuneration under the employment is consistent with the FMV of the services, and is not determined in a manner that takes into account (directly or indirectly) the volume or value of any referrals by the referring physician. Note, however, that the exception does not prohibit payment of remuneration in the form of a productivity bonus based on services performed personally by the physician (or IFM).

3. The remuneration is provided under an agreement that would be commercially reasonable even if no referrals were made to the employer.[34]

B. Discussion

This exception is premised upon the existence of a bona fide employer-employee relationship. CMS has explained that there "is no presumption of employment," meaning that the DHS entity seeking protection under this exception has the burden of establishing the "necessary indicia of employment."[35] As such, it is incumbent upon DHS entities to ensure that their employment arrangements with physicians (and IFMs) are indeed *bona fide*. For example, paying a physician on a W-2 basis, and withholding taxes appropriately, are indicia of a *bona fide* employer-employee relationship, although this may be insufficient in and of itself.[36]

Second, unlike many of the other compensation arrangement exceptions, the employment exception does not require that the agreement be in writing and signed by both parties. Thus, many employment arrangements that do not involve a written employment agreement may still be protected by this exception.

Third, although not favored by CMS, arrangements that require employed physicians to refer patients to specific DHS entities may nevertheless fit within this exception, provided that certain conditions are satisfied. [37] In particular, and as discussed further in Chapter 2, both patient and insurer choice must be preserved and respected, the physician's independent medical judgment must be protected, the required referrals must relate solely to the physician's services covered under the employment arrangement, and the referral requirement must be reasonably necessary to effectuate the legitimate purposes of the employment relationship. [38]

Fourth, non-compete provisions generally are acceptable under the employment exception, as long as any compensation paid for the non-compete does not take into account referrals and is commercially reasonable even if the physician makes no referrals to the DHS entity. [39]

Fifth, by its terms, the employment exception permits a DHS entity to pay an employed physician a productivity bonus based on services "personally performed" by the physician. [40] CMS has explained that this aspect of the employment exception was designed to ensure that physicians could be compensated "in a manner that directly correlates to their own personal labor, including labor in the provision of DHS," but not for generating referrals of DHS performed by others. [41]

Example 8.6

A hospital employs a physician to provide physician services in its emergency department. The physician is paid $160,000 annually, plus a productivity bonus based on the value of the services that the physician personally furnishes.

Commentary: Because the bonus payment is based on the physician's personally furnished services, the arrangement will satisfy the employment exception, provided its other requirements are met.

Note, however, that the technical component or facility fees associated with a professional service may not be considered when calculating a physician's productivity bonus, as those fees do not reflect personally furnished services.

Example 8.7

A physician enters into an employment agreement to oversee the vascular ultrasound lab at an independent diagnostic testing facility. Under the agreement, the physician will interpret ultrasound tests performed by technicians. The physician will reassign his right to receive payment to the hospital, which will bill and receive payment for both the technical and professional component of the ultrasound exams. The hospital will pay the physician $200 per hour, plus 25% of the net collections attributable to all of the ultrasound tests.

Commentary: The employment exception cannot be satisfied because the 25% of net collections payment provision is calculated not only on professional interpretations personally furnished by the physician, but also on the vascular ultrasound tests performed by the technicians.

Similarly, productivity bonuses may not take into account "incident to" services (i.e., revenue furnished by a physician extender, such as a nurse). However, such "incident to" income may be included in a physician's bonus if the physician is employed by a group practice, the services are furnished pursuant to the "in-office ancillary exception" (see Chapter 6), and the bonus pool is derived from overall practice profits.

Finally, payments to physicians based on reduced use of DHS are not protected by the employment exception.[42] Although CMS was urged to interpret the employment exception to "permit hospitals to pay incentives to employed physicians based on meeting hospital or drug utilization targets," it declined, explaining that it believes "Congress intended to limit these kind of incentives consistent with the civil monetary [penalties law] . . . [which] prohibits a hospital from paying physicians to reduce or limit care to hospital patients." As such, CMS was unwilling to say that payments based on lowering utilization present no risk of fraud or abuse.[43]

IV. Personal services arrangements exception

Arrangements between hospitals (and other DHS entities) and physicians (or their IFMs) for the provision of personal services are commonplace in the healthcare industry. Because such arrangements are often critical to the delivery of healthcare items and services and are not necessarily abusive, both the Stark Law and Regulations include an exception for personal services arrangements.

A. Law and regulations

The Stark Law provides that remuneration "from an entity" will not give rise to a financial relationship under the Stark Law if seven conditions are met:

1. The arrangement is set out in writing, signed by the parties, and specifies the services covered by the arrangement.

2. The arrangement covers all of the services to be provided by the physician (or IFM) to the entity.

3. The aggregate services contracted for do not exceed those that are reasonable and necessary for the legitimate business purposes of the arrangement.

4. The term of the arrangement is for at least one year.

5. The compensation to be paid over the term of the arrangement is set in advance, does not exceed FMV, and, except in the case of a physician incentive plan, is not determined in a manner that takes into account the volume or value of any referrals or other business generated between the parties.

6. The services to be furnished under the arrangement do not involve the counseling or promotion of a business arrangement or other activity that violates any state or federal law.

7. The arrangement meets such other requirements as CMS may impose by regulation to protect against program or patient abuse.[44]

The Stark Regulations generally track the Stark Law, providing that remuneration from a DHS entity to a physician or IFM, or to a "single physician-owned professional corporation" will not give rise to a financial relationship under the Law as long as six requirements are met:

1. The arrangement is set out in writing, is signed by the parties, and specifies the services covered by the arrangement.

2. The arrangement covers all of the services to be furnished by the physician (or IFM) to the entity. Note that this requirement will be met if any separate arrangements between the entity and the physician (or IFM) incorporate the others by reference or cross-reference a master list of contracts that is maintained and updated centrally, is available for review by CMS upon request, and preserves the historical record of contracts. Note further that a physician or IFM can "furnish" services through employees hired for the purpose of performing the services, through a wholly owned entity, or through *locum tenens*[45] physicians.

3. The aggregate services contracted for do not exceed those that are reasonable and necessary for the legitimate business purposes of the arrangement.

4. The term of the arrangement is for at least one year. To meet this requirement, if the arrangement is terminated during the term (with or without cause), the parties may not enter into the same or substantially the same arrangement during the first year of the original term of the arrangement.

5. The compensation to be paid over the term of the arrangement is set in advance, does not exceed FMV and, except in the case of a physician incentive plan, is not determined in a manner that takes into account the volume or value of any referrals or other business generated between the parties.

6. The services to be furnished under the arrangement do not involve the counseling or promotion of a business arrangement or other activity that violates any state or federal law.[46]

B. Discussion

1. Services "furnished" by the physician

Under this exception, a physician (or IFM) may "furnish" services personally, or through an employee, wholly owned company, or a *locum tenens* physician. However, the exception does not permit a physician to use an independent contractor to furnish services that the physician has covenanted to provide personally under a personal services agreement.

2. All services are "covered" by the arrangement

The personal services arrangements exception requires that the arrangement cover all services furnished by the physician or IFM. Issues relating to this requirement generally arise where the parties at issue contract for more than one service, or are contemplating doing so. Under these circumstances, this prong of the exception may be satisfied in several ways. First, the DHS entity and the physician/IFM may enter into a single agreement that contemplates all services to be provided by the physician/IFM to the entity. Second, the entity and physician/IFM may enter into several separate agreements, each of which incorporate the others by reference. Third, the parties may enter into separate agreements that each reference a master list of contracts. If the latter approach is selected, more than one master list may be maintained and cross-referenced, provided that all of the master lists, taken together, cover all of the contracts at issue. In addition, if an entity chooses to cross-reference one or more master lists, the list(s) must be maintained in a manner that preserves the historical record of the contracts, and must be updated centrally and available for review by CMS upon request.

3. Termination of personal services agreements

The fourth requirement of the exception provides that agreements for personal services must be for at least one year. The agreement, however, may include provisions for termination of the agreement during the first year of the term, and such provisions may permit termination with or without cause. However, if the agreement is terminated before the end of the first year, the parties cannot enter into an agreement for the "same" or "substantially the same" services until one year has passed from the commencement date of the agreement.

Example 8.8

A hospital enters into a two-year contract with a surgeon to provide medical director services to the hospital's surgery department. The contract permits either party to terminate the arrangement without cause upon 30 days notice. The physician terminates the contract after three months.

Commentary: The arrangement would meet the personal services exception (provided all of the other requirements of the exception were met), as long as the parties did not enter into another contract for medical director services for at least nine months.

---

4. Equipment combined with personal services agreements

Contrary to its earlier interpretation of this exception, CMS now permits equipment to be included as part of a personal services agreement, for the purposes of the personal services arrangements exception. CMS has explained that "[i]t is common practice for many independent contractors to provide the tools of their trade in connection with service contracts."[47] As such, and in recognition of the fact that the equipment rental and personal services exceptions are similar (e.g., both require FMV compensation), CMS concluded that excluding items and equipment from the personal services exception would be "unnecessarily formalistic."[48] For example, where a hospital contracts with a nephrologist to provide dialysis services to its patients, as well as certain dialysis equipment, the arrangement may fall within the personal services exception.[49] However, in determining the FMV of an arrangement that includes both services and equipment, an entity must be able to demonstrate that the services and equipment separately satisfy the FMV requirement.[50]

5. Establishing compensation

The fifth requirement of the personal services arrangements exception provides that the compensation under the arrangement must be set in advance, not exceed FMV and, except in the case of a physician incentive plan, not be determined in a manner that takes into account the volume or value of referrals or other business generated between the parties. As discussed further in Chapter 2, with respect to the FMV requirement, the Stark II, Phase II Regulations create a "safe harbor" of sorts by providing that an hourly payment for a physician's personal services will be considered FMV if (1) the hourly rate is determined by averaging the 50th percentile national compensation level for physicians in the same specialty (or general practice if the specialty is not identified in the survey) in at least four national surveys (e.g., Medical Group Management Association, Mercer, etc.) and dividing by 2000 hours or (2) the hourly rate is less than or equal to the average hourly rate for emergency room services in the relevant physician market, provided that there are at least three hospitals providing emergency room services in the market.

Note that hourly compensation not determined using this methodology is not presumptively outside the range of FMV. That said, it is likely that CMS will look to these provisions if FMV for particular personal services is ever called into question. Thus, if parties to an arrangement use an alternative methodology that yields a result that is significantly lower or higher than the "safe harbor" provisions, CMS may question—and, in some cases reject—the methodology.

6. FMV exception

Certain arrangements that qualify for protection under the personal services arrangements exception also may qualify for protection under the FMV exception (discussed below). The FMV exception, however, differs in two significant respects from the personal services arrangements exception. First, unlike the personal services arrangement exception, the FMV exception protects arrangements that have a term of less than one year. Second, the FMV exception does not require that separate agreements incorporate each other by reference or cross-reference a master list of contracts.

V. Isolated transactions exception

In recognition of the fact that certain one-time financial transactions between a DHS entity and a physician or IFM (e.g., the sale of a medical office building) would create a financial relationship between the parties under the Stark Law—but would not necessarily pose a significant risk of program abuse—Congress and CMS created an exception for so-called "isolated transactions."[51] In a nutshell, this exception protects certain one-time transactions between a physician/IFM and DHS entities, provided that the terms are commercially reasonable and consistent with FMV.

A. Law and regulations

The Stark Law provides that "an isolated financial transaction, such as a one time sale of property or practice," shall not give rise to a financial relationship, if the amount of the remuneration is consistent with FMV and is not determined in a manner that takes into account (directly or indirectly) the volume or value of any referrals by the referring physician.[52] In addition, the remuneration must be provided pursuant to an agreement that would be commercially reasonable even if no referrals were made to the entity.[53] Finally, the transaction must meet such other requirements as CMS may impose by regulation to protect against program or patient abuse.[54]

The Stark Regulations provide that an "isolated financial transaction, such as a one time sale of property or a practice" does not give rise to a financial relationship under the Stark Law if three conditions are met:

1. The amount of remuneration under the isolated transaction is consistent with the FMV of the transaction, and is not determined in a manner that takes into account (directly or indirectly) the volume or value of any referrals by the referring physician or other business generated between the parties.

2. The remuneration is provided under an agreement that would be commercially reasonable even if the physician made no referrals.

3. There are no additional transactions between the parties for six months after the isolated transaction, except for transactions that are specifically excepted under another exception and commercially reasonable post-closing adjustments that do not take into account (directly or indirectly) the volume or value of referrals or other business generated by the referring physician.[55]

The term "isolated transaction" is defined in the Stark Regulations as part of the definition of "transaction":

> Transaction means an instance or process of two or more persons or entities doing business. An isolated transaction means one involving a single payment between two or more persons or entities or a transaction that involves integrally related installment payments provided that— (1) [t]he total aggregate payment is fixed before the first payment is made and does not take

into account, directly or indirectly, the volume or value of referrals or other business generated by the referring physician; and (2) [t]he payments are immediately negotiable or are guaranteed by a third party, secured by a negotiable promissory note, or subject to a similar mechanism to ensure payment even in the event of default by the purchaser or obligated party.[56]

B. Discussion

A few aspects of this exception are worthy of note. First, although the exception is designed to protect one-time transactions, all payments related to the transaction need not be exchanged at the time of the transaction. The exception permits the parties to make installment payments well after the relevant "isolated" transaction has occurred. In fact, provided that the terms of the installment payments are fixed before the transaction occurs (and the payments are negotiable, guaranteed, or otherwise secured), there is no time limit by which all such payments must be made.

Example 8.9

A hospital sells a medical office building to a physician for $100,000 on May 1, 2005. The physician pays the hospital $50,000 on May 1, 2005, and executes a promissory note to pay the remaining $50,000, in equal monthly installments, over the ensuing 12 months.

Commentary: Although the parties will exchange remuneration after the sale of the medical office building, this arrangement could meet the isolated transactions exception, provided all of its other requirements are met.

In contrast, however, the parties to an isolated transaction must make all post-closing adjustments—such as collections on accounts receivable, escrow agreements, and "other adjustments that are made shortly after the initial closing and are designed to remedy unknown conditions, shortfalls in accounts receivable, or similar contingencies"[57]—within six months of the transaction.

VI. Remuneration unrelated to DHS exception

Both the Stark Law and Stark Regulations have an exception for certain remuneration furnished by a hospital that is unrelated to the provision of DHS. Although this exception appears broad, CMS has interpreted it to be "very narrow" and available only if the remuneration at issue is "wholly unrelated" to the provision of DHS.[58]

A. Law and regulations

The Stark Law provides that remuneration that is "provided by a hospital to a physician" that "does not relate to the provision of DHS" will not give rise to a financial relationship.[59] The Stark Regulations build on this general rule, providing that remuneration given by a hospital to a physician that "does not relate, directly or indirectly, to the furnishing of DHS" does not create a financial relationship.[60] To qualify as "unrelated," however, the remuneration must be wholly unrelated to the furnishing of DHS and must not take into account the volume or value of a physician's referrals.

Remuneration relates to the furnishing of DHS if it (1) is an item, service, or cost that could be allocated in whole or in part to Medicare or Medicaid under cost reporting principles; (2) is furnished, directly or indirectly, explicitly or implicitly, in a selective, targeted, preferential, or conditioned manner to medical staff or other persons in a position to make or influence referrals; or (3) otherwise takes into account the volume or value of referrals or other business generated by the referring physician.[61]

B. Discussion

Plainly, the most challenging aspect of applying this exception to an arrangement is determining whether the remuneration at issue is "wholly unrelated" to the provision of DHS. CMS has set forth several guideposts and provided several examples that are instructive in this regard.

- First, CMS considers costs that could be included under Medicare cost-reporting principles as allowable costs to be related to the provision of DHS. This is true regardless of whether a particular hospital actually includes the costs on its cost report.[62]

- Second, the exception does not provide leeway regarding the type of entities and individuals providing or receiving the remuneration at issue. The entity providing the remuneration must be a hospital (as opposed to some other type of DHS entity, such as a clinical laboratory or home health agency),[63] and the person receiving the remuneration must be a physician (as opposed to an IFM).[64]

- Third, although a payment that is wholly unrelated to the provision of DHS does not have to be FMV for the exception to apply, CMS has noted that it will scrutinize carefully any payments that are above FMV to ensure that they are not, in fact, "disguised payments related to DHS."[65]

- Finally, CMS has provided a series of examples illustrating what it considers to be related to the provision of DHS.

Example 8.10

A hospital makes a loan to a physician to finance the physician's purchase of an interest in a limited partnership that owns the hospital.

Commentary: The loan is related to the provision of DHS.[66]

Example 8.11

A hospital leases office space in a nearby medical building to physicians in a position to refer to the hospital.

Commentary: The lease is related to the provision of DHS.[67]

Example 8.12

A hospital provides malpractice insurance to physicians who would otherwise have to pay for such insurance.

Commentary: The subsidy is related to the provision of DHS.[68]

> ### Example 8.13
>
> A hospital makes payments to a physician for a covenant not to compete.
>
> **Commentary:** The payments are related to the provision of DHS. (Although CMS acknowledges that a covenant not to compete is not necessarily equivalent to an obligation to make referrals, it still views such payments as "plainly related to the provision of DHS.")[69]

In contrast, CMS has provided only one example of payments made for items and services that are unrelated to DHS.

> ### Example 8.14
>
> A teaching hospital makes FMV payments to rent a house owned by a physician for use by visiting fellows.
>
> **Commentary:** The rental payments would not be considered related to the provision of DHS.[70]

VII. Group practice arrangements with hospitals exception

The Stark Law and Regulations include a narrow exception that protects certain arrangements—established prior to December 19, 1989—between a hospital and a group practice, "under which DHS are provided by the group but are billed by the hospital."

A. Law and regulations

The Stark Law provides that in order to qualify for this exception seven conditions must be met:

1. With respect to services furnished to an inpatient of the hospital, the arrangement must be pursuant to the provision of inpatient hospital services under section 1861(b)(3) of the Social Security Act (defining "inpatient hospital services" to include diagnostic and therapeutic items or services furnished by a hospital or by others under arrangement with the hospital).

2. The arrangement must have begun before December 19, 1989, and must have continued in effect without interruption since that date.

3. With respect to the DHS covered under the arrangement, substantially all of the services furnished to patients of the hospital must be furnished by the group under the arrangement at issue.

4. The arrangement must be pursuant to an agreement that is set out in writing and specifies the services to be provided by the parties and the compensation for these services.

5. The compensation paid over the term of the agreement must be consistent with FMV, and the compensation per unit of services must be fixed in advance and not determined in a manner that takes into account the volume or value of any referrals or other business generated between the parties.

6. The compensation must be provided pursuant to an agreement that would be commercially reasonable even if no referrals were made to the entity.

7. The arrangement between the parties must meet such other requirements as CMS may impose by regulation to protect against program or patient abuse.[71]

The Stark Regulations generally parallel the Law, providing that an "arrangement between a hospital and a group practice under which DHS are furnished by the group but are billed by the hospital" does not give rise to a financial relationship if six conditions are met:

1. With respect to services furnished to an inpatient of the hospital, the arrangement must be pursuant to the provision of inpatient hospital services under section 1861(b)(3) of the Social Security Act.

2. The arrangement must have begun before, and continued in effect without interruption since, December 19, 1989.

3. With respect to the DHS covered under the arrangement, at least 75% of the services furnished to patients of the hospital must be furnished by the group under the arrangement.

4. The arrangement must be in accordance with a written agreement that specifies the services to be furnished by the parties and the compensation for services furnished under the agreement.

5. The compensation paid over the term of the agreement must be consistent with FMV, and the compensation per unit of service must be fixed in advance and not determined in a manner that takes into account the volume or value of any referrals or other business generated between the parties.

6. The compensation must be provided in accordance with an agreement that would be commercially reasonable, even if no referrals were made to the hospital.[72]

B. Discussion

Although this exception covers a narrow category of arrangements and inevitably will become less and less relevant over time, it is flexible in one important respect: Arrangements that have changed or otherwise varied over time (i.e., since 1989) are not necessarily disqualified. That is, even if the services covered by the arrangement at issue, or the physicians providing those services, have changed over the years (e.g., services have been provided by different individuals within the same practice), the arrangement can still meet the exception, provided that it otherwise has continued in effect without interruption since December 19, 1989.[73]

Example 8.15

A physician group has been furnishing services at a hospital since 1987. In 1990, the group hired two new physicians.

Commentary: The parties could meet the group practice arrangements with hospitals exception, provided that the other requirements of the exception are met.

VIII. Payments by a physician exception

Recognizing that a financial relationship is created between a physician and a DHS entity where the physician (or an IFM) purchases items or services from the entity—but also recognizing that certain transactions of this type pose little risk of fraud and abuse—the Stark Law and Regulations include an exception for payments by a physician to an entity as compensation for items or services.

A. Law and regulations

The Stark Law provides that payments by a physician do not constitute compensation if the payments are made (1) to a laboratory for the provision of clinical laboratory services, or to any other entity for other items or services and (2) the items or services are furnished at a price that is consistent with FMV.[74]

Similarly, the Stark Regulations provide that a financial relationship is not created if (1) a physician (or IFM) pays a laboratory for clinical laboratory services, or any other entity for other items or services, (2) the items or services are furnished at a price consistent with FMV, and (3) the items or services are not specifically covered by another exception.[75]

B. Discussion

There are several noteworthy aspects of this exception. First, in addition to covering payments by a physician, this exception covers payments by a referring physician's IFM.[76] This is important because, as a practical matter, family members frequently have occasion to purchase items or services from DHS entities (e.g., a hospital) and, in the absence of this exception, a financial relationship would be created with any physician related to such family members.

Second, the exception covers items or services of any kind, not just those covered by Medicare. For example, if a physician purchases flower arrangements from a hospital gift shop, this purchase may be protected by this exception, provided that the price is set at FMV. CMS also has made clear that the exception protects purchases made at a "legitimate discount."[77]

Example 8.16

A physician regularly buys books, candy, and flowers from a hospital's gift shop. Every Monday, the gift shop sells all candy at 25% off.

Commentary: Because the discount is offered to all buyers and otherwise appears legitimate, the physician's purchase of discounted candy would not preclude the applicability of this exception.

Finally, this exception is not available for items or services that are specifically covered by any other exception, such as the exceptions for leases or personal services. [78]

Example 8.17

A hospital enters into a lease for office space with a staff physician.

Commentary: The hospital and physician cannot rely on this exception for payments by a physician, but must comply with the space lease exception.

IX. Charitable donations exception

Recognizing that charitable donations from a physician to a DHS entity would create a financial relationship—but rarely pose a risk of program abuse—CMS has created an exception for bona fide charitable donations made by a physician (or IFM) to a DHS entity.

A. Law and regulations

The Stark Regulations provide that "[b]ona fide charitable donations" made by a physician (or IFM) to an entity do not give rise to a financial relationship under the Stark Law if three conditions are satisfied:

1. The charitable donation is made to an organization exempt from taxation under the Internal Revenue Code (or a supporting organization).

2. The donation is neither solicited nor made in a manner that takes into account the volume or value of referrals or other business generated between the physician and the entity.

3. The arrangement does not violate the federal healthcare program anti-kickback statute or any federal or state law or regulation governing billing or claims submission.[79]

B. Discussion

Provided that the donation at issue is made to a tax-exempt organization and meets the other requirements outlined above, there is no restriction on the type of donation that may qualify for protection under this exception.

Example 8.18

Physician A donates $1,000 in cash to a tax-exempt hospital where she has medical staff privileges. Physician B donates office equipment to the hospital. Physician C buys a ticket to a charity dinner sponsored by the hospital.

Commentary: The donation made by each physician is eligible for protection under the charitable donations exception.

CMS has clarified that "[b]road-based solicitations not targeted specifically at physicians, such as sales of charity ball tickets or general fundraising campaigns," do not constitute "solicitation" and will qualify for protection under this exception.[80] More selective or targeted fundraising also may qualify, provided that such activity is performed in a manner that does not reflect or take into account referrals or other business generated between the parties.[81]

Example 8.19

A tax-exempt community hospital sponsors a charity golf tournament each year to support its charitable mission. The hospital's chief executive officer invites area businesses and the hospital's entire medical staff. Tickets are sold on a first-come, first-served basis.

Commentary: The invitations would not be viewed as a "solicitation" under the charitable donations exception, as they were not specifically targeted to a particular group of physicians nor tied in any way to physician referrals.

X. Compensation under $300 per year exception

Physicians (and IFMs) often receive meals, gift baskets, theater or sporting event tickets, and other free items from entities with which they do business. CMS has created a regulatory exception for such non-monetary compensation, provided that certain conditions are satisfied.

A. Law and regulations

The Stark Regulations provide that "[c]ompensation from an entity in the form of items or services (not including cash or cash equivalents) that does not exceed an aggregate of $300 per year," does not give rise to a financial relationship under the Stark Law if three conditions are satisfied:

1. The compensation must not be determined in any manner that takes into account the volume or value of referrals or other business generated by the referring physician.

2. The compensation must not be solicited by the physician or the physician's practice (including employees and staff members).

3. The compensation arrangement must not violate the anti-kickback statute or any federal or state law or regulation governing billing or claims submission.[82]

The Stark Regulations further provide that the $300 limit "will be adjusted each calendar year to the nearest whole dollar by the increase in the Consumer Price Index-Urban All Items (CPI-U) for the 12-month period ending the preceding September 30." CMS "intends to display as soon as possible after September 30 each year, both the increase in the CPI-U for the 12-month period and the new non-monetary compensation limit on the physician self-referral Web site *(http://cms.hhs.gov/medlearn/ref-phys.asp)*." [83]

B. Discussion

Note that, in CMS's view, the Stark Law "clearly intended to make DHS entities responsible for monitoring their compensation arrangements with physicians."[84] As such, compliance with this exception requires DHS entities to track the value of any gifts (e.g., meals, gift baskets) provided to referring physicians (or their IFMs). Although CMS believes that such a tracking system should not be "unduly burdensome,"[85] as a practical matter, it will require hospitals to develop and implement a system for tracking all gifts provided to physicians (or IFMs). In the absence of a tracking system, it may be difficult for hospitals to ensure compliance with the exception.

Example 8.20

A hospital routinely gives all physicians joining its staff a welcome gift basket (valued at $200). The hospital does not have a system for tracking gifts given to its staff physicians. Physician A joins the hospital staff and receives a basket. Two months later, but in the same calendar year, the hospital offers all of its staff physicians tickets for a local sporting event. Each ticket is valued at $30. Physician A receives five tickets (valued at $150).

Commentary: The compensation provided to Physician A (totaling $350), would not meet the exception.

The tracking system must be designed to account for several specific aspects of the exception. First, to the extent that an entity wants to take advantage of the increases to the $300 limit set by CMS, the tracking system will need to be designed to accommodate such adjustments. CMS will update the annual cap each October, based upon the CPI-U index for the preceding 12-month period ending on September 30. Therefore, DHS entities will either have to track gifts from October to September (instead of on a calendar-year basis) against the current limit or make separate calculations for the first 10 months of the year (January–September) and for the remaining three months (October–December), for which the higher, adjusted cap will apply.

Second, a hospital may not multiply the $300 limit by the number of physicians in a group practice for purposes of providing the practice with a more expensive gift. This exception only permits gifts to individual physicians, not to group practices, although individual gifts of up to $300 annually may be given to each physician in a group.[86]

Third, note that if a physician or member of his or her practice requests or solicits an item (e.g., free office supplies or a free meal), the exception will not apply.

Example 8.21

A physician regularly serves on-call duty in the evening at a hospital. The physician asks the hospital whether it will provide him with a free meal when he is called to the hospital during the dinner hour. The hospital agrees.

Commentary: The provision of such meals to the physician cannot meet the exception because the physician solicited the meals. (The arrangement may be protected by the medical staff incidental benefits exception, however.)

One final note: The plain language of the exception only covers compensation "from an entity" to a physician and, as such, does not appear to apply to gifts or other things of value given to physicians by a non-DHS entity, such as a hospital system. Depending on the corporate structure and relationship between the DHS entity (e.g., a hospital) and the non-DHS entity (e.g., a hospital system) at issue, however, CMS may attribute the value of any gifts or other things of value given by the non-DHS entity to certain DHS entities (e.g., each hospital in the system where the physician receiving the gift is on the medical staff).

XI. Fair market value compensation exception

The Stark Regulations protect FMV compensation resulting from an arrangement between a DHS entity and a physician, IFM, or a group of physicians for the provision of items or services furnished by the physician, IFM, or a group of physicians to the DHS entity. The Stark Law does not contain a counterpart to this regulatory exception.

A. Law and regulations

Under the FMV compensation exception, compensation resulting from an arrangement between an entity and a physician (or IFM) or any group of physicians (regardless of whether the group meets the definition of a "group practice") for the provision of items or services by the physician (or IFM) or group of physicians to the entity does not give rise to a financial relationship under the Stark Law, provided that six conditions are met:

1. The arrangement is in writing, signed by the parties, and covers only identifiable items or services, all of which are specified in the agreement.

2. The writing specifies the timeframe for the arrangement, which can be for any period of time and have a termination clause, provided that the parties enter into only one arrangement for the same items or services during the course of a year. An arrangement made for less than one year may be renewed any number of times if the terms of the arrangement and the compensation for the same items or services do not change.

3. The writing specifies the compensation that will be provided under the arrangement. The compensation must be set in advance, must be consistent with FMV, and must not be determined in a manner that takes into account the volume or value of referrals or other business generated by the referring physician.

4. The arrangement is commercially reasonable (i.e., taking into account the nature and scope of the transaction) and furthers the legitimate business purposes of the parties.

5. The arrangement does not violate the anti-kickback statute or any federal or state law or regulation governing billing or claims submission.

6. The services to be furnished under the arrangement do not involve the counseling or promotion of a business arrangement or other activity that violates state or federal law.[87]

B. Discussion

A detailed discussion of the definition of "FMV" is set forth in Chapter 2. Note that the FMV compensation exception only applies to arrangements that involve "items" or "services." Thus, for example, the FMV exception does not apply to the transfer, lease, or license of real or intangible property, property rights, or covenants not to compete.[88] CMS has refused to expand the scope of the exception in this regard, despite repeated requests.[89]

Similarly, this exception does not apply to arrangements in which a DHS entity provides items or services to a physician, IFM, or group. CMS has refused to broaden the exception to accommodate such arrangements, citing concerns regarding possible fraud and abuse.[90]

Example 8.22

A hospital provides medical record transcription services to a community-based physician on its medical staff. The physician pays the hospital FMV for such services.

Commentary: The arrangement is not eligible for protection under the FMV compensation exception, as the exception does not apply where an entity is furnishing the item or service at issue to a physician. (The arrangement may be eligible for protection under the payments by a physician exception, however.)

By the same token, and unlike the exception for payments by a physician (discussed earlier in this chapter), the FMV exception may be used even if another exception potentially applies to the arrangement at issue. Thus, for example, it may be used in situations involving personal services where the requirements of the personal services arrangements exception cannot be satisfied.

Example 8.23

A hospital has an existing contract with a physician to provide on-call coverage. The hospital decides to enter into another contract with the same physician to serve as the part-time medical director of the hospital's cardiology department. The new contract does not reference the existing contract for on-call coverage or a master list of contracts (a requirement under the personal services arrangements exception).

Commentary: The arrangement may not meet the exception for personal services arrangements, but it would still be eligible to meet the FMV exception.

XII. Medical staff incidental benefits exception

Recognizing that many benefits given by a hospital to its staff physicians do not pose a material risk of overutilization or other program or patient abuse,[91] CMS has created an exception for certain "incidental benefits," such as free or discounted parking or meals provided by hospitals (and certain other facilities) to members of their medical staff.[92] The purpose of this exception, according to CMS, is to protect medical staff benefits that are "incidental to services being provided by the medical staff at the hospital."[93]

A. Law and regulations

The Stark Regulations provide that "[c]ompensation in the form of items or services (not including cash or cash equivalents)" furnished by "a hospital to a member of its medical staff"—or by any other facility with a bona fide medical staff—will not give rise to a financial relationship under the Stark Law "when the item or service is used on the hospital's campus," and the following seven conditions are met:

1. The compensation is provided to all members of the medical staff practicing in the same specialty (but not necessarily accepted by every member to whom it is offered) without regard to the volume or value of referrals or other business generated between the parties.

2. Except with respect to identification of medical staff on a hospital Web site or in hospital advertising, the compensation is provided only during periods when the medical staff members are making rounds or are engaged in other services or activities that benefit the hospital or its patients.

3. The compensation is provided by the hospital and used by the medical staff members only on the hospital's campus. (Compensation, including, but not limited to, Internet access, pagers, or two-way radios, used away from the campus only to access hospital medical records or information or to access patients or personnel who are on the hospital campus, as well as the identification of the medical staff on a hospital Web site or in hospital advertising, will meet the "on campus" requirement.)

4. The compensation is reasonably related to the provision of, or designed to facilitate directly or indirectly the delivery of, medical services at the hospital.

5. The compensation is of low value (i.e., less than $25) with respect to each occurrence of the benefit (e.g., each meal given to a physician while he or she is serving patients who are hospitalized must be of low value). The $25 limit will be adjusted each calendar year to the nearest whole dollar by the increase in the CPI-U for the 12-month period ending the preceding September 30. CMS intends to display as soon as possible after September 30 each year both

the increase in the CPI-U for the 12-month period and the new limits on the physician self-referral Web site (*http://cms.hhs.gov/medlearn/refphys.asp*).[94]

6. The compensation is not determined in any manner that takes into account the volume or value of referrals or other business generated between the parties.

7. The compensation arrangement does not violate the anti-kickback statute or any federal or state law or regulation governing billing or claims submission.[95]

B. Discussion

Provided that its various requirements are met, this exception permits hospitals to provide their staff with a variety of incidental medical staff benefits, including, but not limited to, reduced or free parking,[96] meals at the hospital,[97] free computer/Internet access,[98] pagers and two-way radios,[99] lab coats[100] and a listing or identification on the hospital's Web site.[101]

As noted above, with respect to the third requirement of the exception (i.e., that the compensation be provided on the hospital's campus), CMS has created an exception for certain off-site technology. This exception is extremely narrow, however, and is limited to specific technology-related benefits. In all other instances, the compensation must be provided to the physician while he or she is physically present on the hospital's campus (e.g., a meal given to a physician during the time period he or she is in the hospital treating patients). Note, however, that CMS has not defined "campus" in connection with this exception (or in any other part of the Stark Regulations).[102]

With respect to the fifth requirement of the exception (i.e., the $25 per occurrence limit), note that, unlike the exception for compensation under $300 per year (discussed in a previous section of this chapter), the hospital is not required to track the aggregate value of benefits furnished to physicians. Accordingly, a hospital may provide as many incidental benefits to physicians as it desires, as long as each individual benefit is under $25 and the benefits meet the other requirements of the exception.

> **Example 8.24**
>
> A hospital provided the following incidental benefits to a staff physician in 2004: 15 free meals in the hospital cafeteria (15 x $20 = $300); free parking ($10/day x 250 days = $2,500); and a free lab coat ($20). Thus, the hospital provided the physician with incidental benefits totaling $2,820.
>
> **Commentary:** Provided that the other requirements of the exception are met, the benefits provided by the hospital are eligible to meet the exception for medical staff incidental benefits because each single benefit was less than $25.

Finally, CMS has made it clear that incidental benefits provided by a hospital to its medical staff that do not fit within this exception may nevertheless be protected by other exceptions, including those for (1) employment, (2) FMV, (3) compensation under $300 per year, and (4) remuneration unrelated to DHS.[103] However, temporary lapses in compliance with this exception are not eligible for protection under the exception for temporary non-compliance. As CMS has stated, "[t]o provide otherwise would effectively negate" the limit set forth in the medical staff incidental benefit exception.[104]

XIII. Risk-sharing arrangements exception

As discussed in Chapter 6, the Stark Law includes an exception for services furnished to enrollees of certain "prepaid" health plans.[105] That exception, however, does not cover services furnished to enrollees of managed care organizations (MCO) operating commercial or employer-sponsored health plans that do not qualify as "prepaid" plans under the Stark Law. The exception for risk-sharing arrangements fills this gap and applies to certain compensation arrangements between an MCO or an independent physicians' association and a physician.[106]

A. Law and regulations

The Stark Regulations provide that "[c]ompensation pursuant to a risk-sharing arrangement (including, but not limited to, withholds, bonuses, and risk pools) between a managed care organization or an independent physicians' association and a physician (either directly or indirectly through a subcontractor) for services provided to enrollees of a health plan," will not give rise to a financial relationship under the Stark Law, provided that the arrangement does not violate the anti-kickback statute or any federal or state law or regulation governing billing or claims submission.[107]

A "health plan" is defined as "an entity that furnishes or arranges under agreement with contract health providers for the furnishing of items or services to enrollees or furnishes insurance coverage for the provision of such items and services, in exchange for a premium or a fee," where the entity does one of the following:

1. operates in accordance with a contract, agreement, or statutory demonstration authority approved by CMS or a state healthcare program,

2. charges a premium and its premium structure is regulated under a state insurance statute or a state enabling statute governing health maintenance organizations or preferred provider organizations,

3. is an employer, if the enrollees of the plan are current or retired employees, or is a union welfare fund, if the enrollees of the plan are union members, or

4. is licensed in the state, is under contract with an employer, union welfare fund, or a company furnishing health insurance coverage as described in requirements (2) and (3) above, and is paid a fee for the administration of the plan that reflects the FMV of those services. [108]

An "enrollee" is defined in the Stark Regulations as "an individual who has entered into a contractual relationship with a health plan (or on whose behalf an employer, or other private or governmental entity has entered into such a relationship) under which the individual is entitled to receive specified healthcare items and services, or insurance coverage for such items and services, in return for payment of a premium or a fee." [109]

B. Discussion

According to CMS, this exception is intended to be very broad. For example, the exception is available for all qualifying risk-sharing arrangements, regardless of whether the physician is a member of a group practice, is employed, is an independent contractor, or is an academic medical center physician. [110] Moreover, CMS has stated that it has "purposefully" refused to define "MCO" so as to create "a broad exception with maximum flexibility." [111]

CMS also has noted that the exception is meant to cover all risk-sharing compensation paid to physicians by an entity that is "downstream" of any type of health plan, insurance company, health maintenance organization, or independent practice association, provided that the other requirements of the exception are met.[112] CMS also has confirmed that "[a]ll downstream entities are included."[113] Finally, CMS has noted that this exception would cover payments to physicians based on their utilization of DHS in contrast to most other exceptions, which would not permit payments of this type.[114]

XIV. Compliance training exception

Recognizing that compliance training programs provided by a DHS entity to physicians are "beneficial and do not pose a risk of fraud or abuse" but that the provision of such programs might create a compensation arrangement between the entity and physicians, CMS has created an exception for compliance training programs.[116]

A. Law and regulations

The Stark Regulations provide that compliance training provided by an entity to a physician (or to the physician's IFM or office staff) who practices in the entity's local community or service area, will not give rise to a financial relationship under the Stark Law, provided the training is held in the "local community or service area."[117] "Compliance training" is defined as any of the following:

1. training regarding the basic elements of a compliance program (e.g., establishing policies and procedures, training of staff, internal monitoring, reporting),

2. specific training regarding the requirements of federal and state healthcare programs (e.g., billing, coding, reasonable and necessary services, documentation, unlawful referral arrangements), or

3. training regarding other federal, state, or local laws, regulations, or rules governing the conduct of the party for whom the training is provided (but not including continuing medical education [CME]).[118]

B. Discussion

Although this exception is generally straightforward, uncertainty exists in certain respects. The first, and perhaps most critical ambiguity, relates to whether bona fide compliance training that also qualifies for CME credit can meet the exception. Because hospitals often use CME credit to secure physician attendance at training courses, resolution of this issue is important to many hospitals (and certain other DHS entities).

According to CMS, CME is not considered "compliance training" for purposes of this exception because CME is not "primarily intended to promote legal compliance."[119] It is unclear, however, whether CMS intended to exclude from the exception compliance training that also qualifies for CME credit. Given the purpose of the exception—to encourage physicians to receive compliance training—CME programs regarding legal compliance logically should be protected under this exception. (Of course, training programs that do not meet this exception are not necessarily prohibited. For example, provision of CME to physicians could be covered under the exception for non-monetary compensation up to $300.)[120] A second issue concerns the exception's scope. For example, would the exception cover a meal served by a hospital to staff physicians during a four-hour compliance training session? Arguably, the meal could be viewed as a separate stream of compensation being provided by the hospital to the physicians, which would need to be protected by another exception (e.g., the exception for medical staff incidental benefits).

XV. Referral services exception

In recognition of the fact that the anti-kickback statute contains a "safe harbor" for certain types of referral services,[121] CMS has created a parallel exception to the Stark Law.[122] In a nutshell, this exception protects remuneration paid by a physician to a referral service.

A. Law and regulations

The Stark Regulations provide that "[r]emuneration that meets all of the conditions set forth in 42 Code of Federal Regulations (CFR) §1001.952(f)"—i.e., the anti-kickback statute safe harbor for referral services—will not give rise to a financial relationship under the Stark Law.[123] The anti-kickback statute's referral services safe harbor, in turn, provides that remuneration does not include "any payment or exchange of anything of value between an individual or entity (participant) and another entity serving as a referral service," as long as four requirements are met:

1. The referral service does not exclude as a participant in the referral service any individual or entity who meets the qualifications for participation.

2. Any payment the participant makes to the referral service is assessed equally against and collected equally from all participants, and is only based on the cost of operating the referral service, and not on the volume or value of any referrals to or business otherwise generated by either party for the referral service for which payment may be made in whole or in part under Medicare, Medicaid, or other federal healthcare programs.

3. The referral service imposes no requirements on the manner in which the participant provides services to a referred person, except that the referral service may require that the participant charge the person referred at the same rate as it charges other persons not referred by the referral service, or that these services be furnished free of charge or at reduced charge.

4. The referral service makes the following five disclosures to each person seeking a referral, with each such disclosure maintained by the referral service in a written record certifying such disclosure and signed by either the person seeking a referral or by the individual making the disclosure on behalf of the referral service:

   - the manner in which the referral source selects the group of participants in the service to which it could make a referral,
   - whether the participant has paid a fee to the referral service,
   - the manner in which it selects a particular participant from this group for that person,
   - the nature of the relationship between the referral service and the group of participants to whom it could make the referral, and
   - the nature of any restrictions that would exclude such an individual or entity from continuing as a participant.[124]

B. Discussion

As noted above, this exception was incorporated by reference to the anti-kickback statute, with little additional guidance from CMS.[125] As such, its provisions do not neatly fit within the analytical framework of the Stark Law, and it is unclear how certain terms should be interpreted under the Stark Law. For example, "participant," a term used in the safe harbor, is not defined under the Stark Law. Assuming, however, that a physician can qualify as a "participant," this exception would appear to protect a physician's payment of a fee to a referral service, such as a hospital, to be included in the hospital's online referral service.

XVI. Obstetrical malpractice insurance exception

In recognition of the fact that the anti-kickback statute includes a "safe harbor" for obstetrical malpractice insurance subsidies, CMS has created a parallel exception to the Stark Law.[126] Under this exception, a hospital (or other entity) may pay a medical malpractice insurer for certain premiums for an obstetrics-gynecology physician who practices in a health professional shortage area (HPSA),[127] provided certain conditions are satisfied.[128]

A. Law and regulations

The Stark Regulations provide that remuneration provided "to the referring physician that meets all of the conditions set forth in [42 CFR] §1001.952(o)"—i.e., the anti-kickback statute safe harbor for obstetrical malpractice insurance subsidies—will not give rise to a financial relationship under the Stark Law.[129]

The anti-kickback statute safe harbor provides that remuneration does not include any payment made by a hospital or other entity to another entity that is providing malpractice insurance (including a self-funded entity), where such payment is used to pay for some or all of the costs of malpractice insurance premiums for a practitioner who engages in obstetrical practice as a routine part of his or her medical practice in a primary care HPSA, provided that eight requirements are met:

1. The payment is made in accordance with a written agreement between the entity paying the premiums and the practitioner, which sets out the payments to be made by the entity, and the terms under which the payments are to be provided.

2. The practitioner must certify that, for the initial coverage period (not to exceed one year), the practitioner has a reasonable basis for believing that at least 75% of the practitioner's obstetrical patients treated under the coverage of the malpractice insurance will either (a) reside in an HPSA[130] or medically underserved area (MUA)[131] or (b) be part of a medically underserved population (MUP).[132]

3. Thereafter, for each additional coverage period (not to exceed one year), at least 75% of the practitioner's obstetrical patients treated under the prior coverage period (not to exceed one year) must have (a) resided in an HPSA or MUA or (b) been part of an MUP.

4. There is no requirement that the practitioner make referrals to, or otherwise generate business for, the entity as a condition of receiving the benefits.

5. The practitioner is not restricted from establishing staff privileges at, referring any service to, or otherwise generating any business for, any other entity of his or her choosing.

6. The amount of payment may not vary based on the volume or value of any previous or expected referrals to or business otherwise generated for the entity by the practitioner for which payment may be made in whole or in part under Medicare, Medicaid, or any other federal healthcare programs.

7. The practitioner must treat obstetrical patients who receive medical benefits or assistance under any federal healthcare program in a nondiscriminatory manner.

8. The insurance is a bona fide malpractice insurance policy or program, and the premium, if any, is calculated based on a bona fide assessment of the liability risk covered under the insurance. [133]

The "costs of malpractice insurance premiums" is defined under the safe harbor as follows: (1) for practitioners who engage in obstetrical practice full-time, any costs attributable to malpractice insurance; and (2) for practitioners who engage in obstetrical practice on a part-time or sporadic basis, the costs, attributable exclusively to the obstetrical portion of the practitioner's malpractice insurance and related exclusively to obstetrical services provided in a primary care HPSA.[134]

B. Discussion

Like the exception for referral services, this exception was incorporated into the Stark Regulations by reference, with little additional discussion.[135] CMS has explained, however, that malpractice insurance subsidies that do not fit within this narrow exception may be protected under the employment exception (provided the physician is an employee of the entity at issue) or the FMV compensation exception.[136] In both instances, however, the total compensation paid to the physician must be FMV.

XVII. Professional courtesy exception

In recognition of the "longstanding tradition" and "widespread practice" among hospitals and group practices of providing free or reduced-cost healthcare items and services to physicians and their family members, CMS has established a fairly broad exception for "professional courtesy."[137] In general, the exception permits the extension of professional courtesies to physicians, members of a physician's office staff, and IFMs.[138]

A. Law and regulations

The Stark Regulations define "professional courtesy" as "the provision of free or discounted healthcare items or services" to a physician or his or her IFMs or office staff.[139] Under the Regulations, "[p]rofessional courtesy" offered by an entity to a physician or a physician's IFM or office staff will not give rise to a financial relationship under the Stark Law if six conditions are met:

1. The professional courtesy is offered to all physicians on the entity's bona fide medical staff or in the entity's local community or service area without regard to the volume or value of referrals or other business generated between the parties.

2. The healthcare items and services provided are of a type routinely provided by the entity.

3. The entity's professional courtesy policy is set out in writing and approved in advance by the entity's governing body.

4. The professional courtesy is not offered to a physician (or IFM) who is a federal healthcare

program beneficiary, unless there has been a good faith showing of financial need.

5. If the professional courtesy involves any whole or partial reduction of a coinsurance obligation, the insurer is informed in writing of the reduction.

6. The arrangement does not violate the anti-kickback statute or any federal or state law or regulation governing billing or claims submission.[140]

B. Discussion

Several aspects of the professional courtesy exception merit discussion. First, there is no restriction on the type of professional courtesy that may be offered to physicians, provided that the items and services are of the type routinely provided by the entity. As such, professional courtesy may include free or discounted flu vaccines, "check ups," or diagnostic tests provided to a physician (or his or her office staff or IFMs).

Second, arrangements that involve professional courtesy but do not meet this exception may fit into other exceptions to the Stark Law. For example, CMS has indicated that professional courtesy extended to employees may fall within the employee exception (and, as such, would not need to meet the requirements outlined above). Similarly, some professional courtesy may meet the exception for incidental medical staff benefits.

Third, the exception requires that an entity must have a written professional courtesy policy in place (which has been approved by the entity's governing body, such as the board of directors) before the provision of professional courtesy will be protected.

Example 8.25

A hospital offers flu vaccines to staff physicians and their families for half price. The hospital has a written policy providing for such professional courtesy, approval of which is pending before the hospital's board.

Commentary: The exception for professional courtesy would not apply to any of the vaccines until the governing body approves the hospital's policy.

Finally, although professional courtesy is common in the hospital context, the exception is not limited to hospital-physician arrangements. Physician practices may take advantage of this exception as well. In other words, professional courtesy offered by a physician practice to other referring physicians could be structured to fit within the exception.

XVIII. Community-wide health information systems exception

In an effort to improve the exchange of health information among healthcare providers, CMS has created an exception for the provision of information technology by a DHS entity to a physician to permit him or her to access and participate in a community-wide health information system.[141] The exception contemplates a system that affords access to electronic healthcare records and related information systems and that facilitates the sharing of medical information and alerts.[142]

A. Law and regulations

The Stark Regulations provide that "[i]tems or services of information technology provided by an entity to a physician that allow access to, and sharing of, electronic healthcare records and any complimentary drug information systems, general health information, medical alerts, and related information for patients served by community providers and practitioners, in order to enhance the community's overall health," will not give rise to a financial relationship under the Stark Law if three conditions are met:

1. The items or services are available as necessary to enable the physician to participate in a community-wide health information system, are principally used by the physician as part of the community-wide health information system, and are not provided to the physician in any manner that takes into account the volume or value of referrals or other business generated by the physician.

2. The community-wide health information systems are available to all providers, practitioners, and residents of the community who desire to participate.

3. The arrangement does not violate the anti-kickback statute, or any federal or state law or regulation governing billing or claims submission. [143]

B. Discussion

CMS has provided guidance on certain aspects of this exception. First, CMS has explained that "information technology" includes both hardware and software. [144] As such, this exception covers computers and hand-held devices, as well as software programs.

Second, CMS has emphasized that the exception only covers the provision of "technology items and services that are necessary to enable the physician to participate in the health information system." [145] In other words, an entity cannot provide a physician with redundant technology (e.g., the same type of technology the physician already owns) or superfluous technology (e.g., items and services that are not integral to the community-wide information system).

Example 8.26

A hospital would like to develop and implement an Internet-based health information system to improve access and quality of care in its community. As part of its plan, the hospital will provide physicians with Internet service to facilitate their access to the system.

Commentary: If any physician already has Internet service, the provision of such service by the hospital will not fit within this exception.

Third, the Stark Regulations do not define "community" for purposes of a "community-wide health information system." Assessing compliance with this exception, therefore, will necessarily involve developing a reasonable definition of community.

Fourth, the exception requires that the community-wide health information system be available to all providers, practitioners, and residents of the community who desire to participate. This requirement may narrow the potential utility of this exception, as it will not protect systems that are not made available to all persons in these categories.

Finally, the provision of information technology to a physician by a DHS entity may implicate the anti-kickback statute. For example, the provision of hardware or software for free or at a reduced charge to a physician who is an actual or potential referral source may be construed as a kickback for the referral of patients. Unlike the Stark Law, the anti-kickback statute does not include a safe harbor for the provision of information technology to a physician in conjunction with a community-wide health system. The OIG is, however, considering developing a safe harbor for certain information technology, which may end up paralleling the Stark Law exception.[146]

Notes

1. 42 United States Code (USC) §1395nn(e)(1).

2. 42 CFR §411.357(a).

3. 42 USC §1395nn(e)(1)(A).

4. 42 CFR §411.357(a).

5. 42 CFR §411.357.

6. The FMV compensation exception is not available under these circumstances either, as CMS has indicated that the space rental exception is "limited to items and services provided by physicians," and, as such "does not apply to space leases." Stark II, Phase II Regulations (Preamble), 69 *Federal Register* (*FR*) 16054, 16086 (2004).

7. Note that, although strongly implied by the text of the exception and the preamble to the 1998 Stark II Proposed Regulations, this requirement of the space rental exception does not expressly state that this prohibition is limited to instances in which the parties enter into a new agreement for the same space during the first year of the original term of the agreement.

8. Stark II, Phase II Proposed Regulations (Preamble), 63 *FR* 1659, 1713 (1998).

9. 42 CFR §411.357(a)(3).

10. Stark II, Phase II Regulations (Preamble), 69 *FR* 16054, 16085 (2004).

11. Stark II, Phase II Regulations (Preamble), 69 *FR* 16054, 16086 (2004). Similarly, an indirect compensation arrangement may exist between an individual physician and a lessor, where the physician's medical practice group leases the office space from the lessor.

12. 42 CFR §411.357(a)(3).

13. 42 CFR §411.351.

14. 42 CFR §411.351. For a more complete discussion of this issue, see *United States ex rel. Goodstein v. McLaren Regional/FDA*, 202 F. Supp. 2d 671 (E.D. Mich. 2002).

15. Stark II, Phase II Regulations (Preamble), 69 *FR* 16054, 16086 (2004).

16. 42 CFR §411.357(a)(7).

17. 42 CFR §411.357(a)(7). See also Stark II, Phase II Regulations (Preamble), 69 *FR* 16054, 16085 (2004).

18. 42 USC §1395nn(e)(1)(B).

19. 42 CFR §411.357(b).

20. 42 CFR §411.357.

21. 42 CFR §411.357(b)(3).

22. Stark II, Phase II Regulations (Preamble), 69 *FR* 16054, 16085-86 (2004).

23. 42 CFR §411.357(b)(2).

24. Stark II, Phase II Regulations (Preamble), 69 *FR* 16054, 16085-86 (2004).

25. Stark II, Phase II Regulations (Preamble), 69 *FR* 16054, 16086 (2004).

26. Stark II, Phase II Regulations (Preamble), 69 *FR* 16054, 16085 (2004). Note that in its preamble discussion concerning the "volume or value" standards, CMS addressed the situation where a per-use based methodology of determining an equipment lease amount incorporates decreasing payments as volume increases. CMS reserved judgment on this type of lease payment, stating that such arrangements would have to be reviewed on a case-by-case basis. CMS did indicate, however, that if the basis for the decreasing payments was a distribution of fixed costs over the term of the lease (as is customary with leased equipment), the payments remained FMV, and the decline in amount was not based on volume, such payments would be permitted. Id. at 16069.

27. Stark II, Phase II Regulations (Preamble), 69 *FR* 16054, 16091 (2004).

28. Stark II, Phase II Regulations (Preamble), 69 *FR* 16054, 16086 (2004).

29. 42 CFR §411.357(a)(7).

30. 42 CFR §411.357(a)(7). See also Stark II, Phase II Regulations (Preamble), 69 *FR* 16054, 16085 (2004).

31. 42 USC §1320a-7b(b)(3)(B).

32. 42 USC §1320a-7b(b)(3)(B).

33. Common law rules for employees are set forth in 20 CFR §404.1007 and 26 CFR §31.3121(d)-1(c).

34. 42 CFR §411.357(c).

35. 69 *FR* 16054, 16087 (2004).

36. 69 *FR* 16054, 16087 (2004).

37. 69 *FR* at 16089.

38. See 42 CFR §411.354(d)(4), 69 *FR* 16068, 16069, and 16087.

39. 69 *FR* 16088. As discussed in Chapter 10, covenants not to compete between an employer and its physician employee are prohibited in the context of certain physician recruitment arrangements.

40. 69 *FR* 16087.

41. 69 *FR* 16087.

42. 69 *FR* 16089.

43. 69 *FR* 16088.

44. 42 USC §1395nn(e)(3).

45. Under the Phase II Regulations, a *locum tenens* physician is defined as a physician who substitutes (i.e., "stands in the shoes") in exigent circumstances for a physician, in accordance with applicable reassignment rules and regulations, including §3060.7 of the Medicare Carriers Manual (CMS Pub. 14-3), Part 3—Claims Process, as amended or replaced from time to time.

46. 42 CFR §411.357(d).

47. 69 *FR* 16091.

48. 69 *FR* 16091.

49. 63 *FR* 1701; 69 *FR* 16091.

50. 69 *FR* 16091.

51. 42 USC §1395nn(3)(6); 42 CFR §411.357(f).

52. 42 USC §1395nn(e)(2)(B) (incorporated by reference at 42 USC §1395nn(e)(6)(A)).

53. 42 USC §1395nn(e)(2)(C) (incorporated by reference at 42 USC §1395nn(e)(6)(A)).

54. 42 USC §1395nn(e)(6)(B).

55. 42 CFR §411.357(f).

56. 42 CFR §411.351.

57. 69 *FR* 16098.

58. 69 *FR* 16093.

59. 42 USC §1395nn(e)(4).

60. 42 CFR §411.357(g).

61. 42 CFR §411.357(g).

62. 69 *FR* 16094.

63. This exclusion applies even if such entity is related to a hospital, such as a hospital-owned home health agency. 69 *FR* 16094. As such, "[d]epending on the circumstances, payments from a legal entity related to the hospital would be analyzed as a direct compensation arrangement subject to the direct compensation exceptions or an indirect compensation arrangement to which the indirect compensation exception may apply." Id.

64. 69 *FR* 16094.

65. 69 *FR* 16094.

66. 69 *FR* 16094.

67. 69 *FR* 16094.

68. 69 *FR* 16094.

69. 69 *FR* 16094.

70. 69 *FR* 16093.

71. 42 USC §1395nn(e)(7)(A).

72. 42 CFR §411.357(h).

73. 69 *FR* 16099.

74. 42 USC §1395nn(e)(8).

75. In this context, "services" means any kind of services, and not just those defined as "services" for purposes of the Medicare program in §400.202. 42 CFR §411.375(i).

76. 69 *FR* 16099.

77. 69 *FR* 16099. This obviates the need for a separate exception for discounts.

78. 69 *FR* 16099. This obviates the need for a separate exception for discounts.

79. 42 CFR §411.357(j).

80. 69 *FR* 16116.

81. 69 *FR* 15116.

82. 42 CFR §411.357(k).

83. 42 CFR §411.357(k).

84. 69 *FR* 16112.

85. 69 *FR* 16112.

86. 69 *FR* 16112.

87. 42 CFR §411.357(l).

88. *69 FR* 16111.

89. *69 FR* 16111.

90. *69 FR* 16111.

91. *66 FR* 921.

92. 42 CFR §411.357(m).

93. *69 FR* 16112.

94. *69 FR* 16112.

95. 42 CFR §411.357(m).

96. *66 FR* 921.

97. *63 FR* 1713.

98. *63 FR* 921.

99. *69 FR* 16112.

100. *69 FR* 16113.

101. *69 FR* 16113.

102. CMS has, however, defined "campus" in other regulations. For example, in the regulations governing provider-based entities, CMS defines "campus" as "the physical area immediately adjacent to the provider's main buildings, other areas and structures that are not strictly contiguous to the main buildings but are located within 250 yards of the main buildings, and any other areas determined on an individual case basis, by the CMS regional office, to be part of the provider's campus." 42 CFR §413.65(a)(2).

103. *66 FR* 920-921.

104. *69 FR* 16057.

105. 42 USC §1395nn(b)(3).

106. *66 FR* 913.

107. 42 CFR §411.357(n).

108. 42 CFR §1001.952(l)(2).

109. 42 CFR §1001.952(l)(2).

110. *69 FR* 16067.

111. *69 FR* 16114.

112. *69 FR* 16114.

113. *69 FR* 16114.

114. 69 *FR* 16088.

115. 66 *FR* 921.

116. 42 CFR §411.357(o).

117. 42 CFR §411.357(o).

118. 42 CFR §411.357(o).

119. 69 *FR* 16115.

120. 69 *FR* 16115.

121. 42 CFR §1001.952(f).

122. 69 *FR* 16115; 42 CFR §411.357(q).

123. 69 *FR* 16115; 42 CFR §411.357(q).

124. 42 CFR §1001.952(f).

125. 69 *FR* 16115.

126. 42 CFR §411.357 (r).

127. HPSA is defined as an area designated under section 332(a)(1)(A) of the Public Health Service Act for primary medical care professionals. See 42 CFR §411.351.

128. 69 *FR* 16115.

129. 42 CFR §411.357(r).

130. Supra note 2.

131. 42 CFR §1001.952 (a)(4); see also 42 CFR §51c.102(e); *http://bhpr.hrsa.gov/shortage/muaguide.htm* (as of July 07, 2005)

132. 42 CFR §1001.952 (a)(4).

133. 42 CFR §1001.952(o).

134. 42 CFR §1001.952(o).

135. In contrast, the OIG has addressed the anti-kickback statute safe harbor in both a letter and two advisory opinions. See OIG Letter re: Malpractice Insurance Assistance, January 15, 2003, posted on the OIG web site at *http://oig.hhs.gov/fraud/docs/alertsandbulletins/MalpracticeProgram.pdf*; OIG Advisory Opinion No. 04-11 (September 2, 2004) (obstetrical malpractice support) and Advisory Opinion No. 04-19 (Dec. 30, 2004) (neurosurgeon malpractice support).

136. 63 *FR* 1713-1714; 66 *FR* 920-21.

137. 59 *FR* 16141, 16115-116.

138. 59 *FR* 16116.

139. 42 CFR §411.351.

140. 42 CFR §411.357 (s).

141. *69 FR* 16053, 16113.

142. *69 FR* 16053, 16113.

143. 42 CFR §411.357(u); *69 FR* at 16142.

144. *69 FR* 16113.

145. *69 FR* 16113.

146. See e.g., S.B. 1262, "The Health Technology to Enhance Quality Act of 2005" (109th Congress, June 2005); U.S. Department of Health and Human Services, "Decade of Health Information Technology" available at *www.hhs.gov/news/press/2004pres/20040721a.html;* GAO Report "HHS's Efforts to Promote Health Information Technology and Legal Barriers to Its Adoption," GAO-04-991R (August 13, 2004).

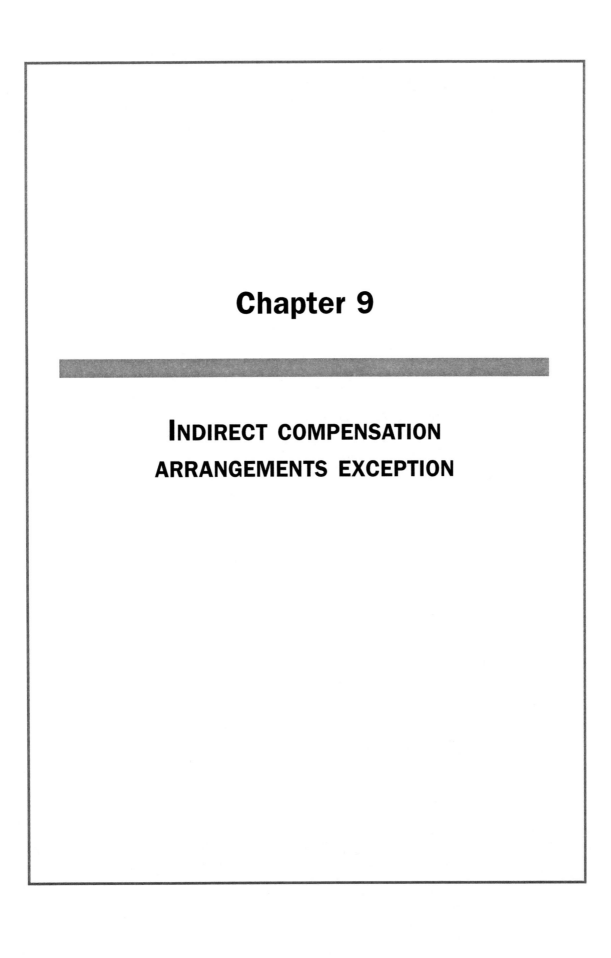

Chapter 9

INDIRECT COMPENSATION ARRANGEMENTS EXCEPTION

Chapter 9

INDIRECT COMPENSATION ARRANGEMENTS EXCEPTION

As noted in Chapter 1, there are four types of financial relationships and four general categories of Stark Law exceptions. When a physician or his or her immediate family member (IFM) has a financial relationship with an entity in the form of an indirect compensation arrangement (ICA)(see Chapter 5), the arrangement may be protected by an all-purpose exception (see Chapter 6) or the ICA exception.

The Stark Law does not include an exception for ICAs. The Centers for Medicare & Medicaid Services (CMS) proposed the ICA exception in 1998 as part of the Stark II Proposed Regulations. CMS modified the exception in 2001 as part of the Stark II, Phase I Regulations, and in 2004, as part of the Stark II, Phase II Regulations. Currently, the ICA exception has three requirements:

- The compensation received by the referring physician or IFM must be fair market value (FMV) for services and items actually provided and must not be determined in any manner that takes into account the value or volume of referrals or other business generated by the referring physician for the entity furnishing designated health services (DHS).

- The compensation arrangement must be set out in writing and signed by the parties, and must specify the services covered by the arrangement, except in the case of a bona fide employment relationship between an employer and an employee, in which case the arrangement need not be set out in a written contract but must be for identifiable services and be commercially reasonable even if no referrals are made to the employer.

• The compensation arrangement must not violate the anti-kickback statute or any federal or state law or regulation governing billing or claims submission.[1]

I. Fair market value and volume or value requirement

As discussed in Chapter 5, in order for a physician/IFM to have an indirect compensation arrangement with an entity, there must be an unbroken chain of financial relationships between the physician/IFM and entity. Assuming that there is such an unbroken chain, one must determine whether the physician/IFM has a compensation arrangement or an ownership interest in the chain of financial relationships at issue. If the physician/IFM has a compensation arrangement, the ICA definition focuses on that arrangement. If the physician/IFM has an ownership interest, the ICA definition focuses on the compensation arrangement that is closest to the physician/IFM.

As with the ICA definition, the first requirement of the ICA exception focuses on the compensation arrangement that is closest to the physician/IFM at issue.

Example 9.1

A physician is employed by a nursing home that has a services contract with a physical therapy company.

Commentary: The physician has a direct compensation arrangement with the nursing home in the chain of financial relationships at issue. Thus, the ICA exception focuses on the compensation arrangement between the physician and the nursing home.

Example 9.2

A physician has an ownership interest in a nursing home that has a services contract with a physical therapy company.

Commentary: The physician has a direct ownership interest in the chain of financial relationships at issue. Thus, the ICA exception focuses on the compensation arrangement between the nursing home and the physical therapy company.

> **Example 9.3**
>
> A physician owns a company that leases imaging equipment to a hospital on a fixed, per-procedure basis.
>
> **Commentary:** The ICA exception focuses on the compensation arrangement between the company and the hospital because this is the closest compensation arrangement to the physician.

We will refer to the compensation arrangement that is the focus of the ICA exception as the "relevant compensation arrangement." Having identified the relevant compensation arrangement, the first requirement of the ICA exception necessitates determining (1) whether the compensation under that arrangement is "FMV for services and items actually provided" and (2) whether the compensation under the arrangement is "determined in any manner that takes into account the value or volume of referrals or other business generated by the referring physician for the entity furnishing DHS."[2] To meet the first requirement of the ICA exception, the answer to the first question must be "yes," and the answer to the second question must be "no."

A. Fair market value

The term FMV, "volume or value," and "other business generated" standards, as well as the special compensation rules that supplement these standards, appear throughout the Stark Regulations and are discussed in detail in Chapter 2. In this chapter, we will discuss some of the issues that may arise when applying these standards in the context of the ICA exception. To begin the discussion, we will return to an example from Chapter 5 which is based on a 2004 Office of Inspector General advisory opinion.

Example 9.4

Two neurosurgeons who are shareholders of a practice group have privileges at a local hospital. The group informs the hospital that (1) its insurance carrier will no longer provide malpractice coverage to the two neurosurgeons; (2) another carrier has agreed to pick up the coverage, but at a much steeper premium; and (3) the two neurosurgeons intend to retire unless the hospital will compensate the group for the difference between the old and new premiums. The hospital agrees.

If we assume that both neurosurgeons have an ICA with the hospital (and that no all-purpose exception is available), then the neurosurgeons will not be able to refer Medicare patients to the hospital for DHS unless the ICA exception applies. Because the physicians have an ownership interest in the chain of financial relationships at issue (i.e., their ownership interests in the practice group), the relevant compensation arrangement for the ICA exception is the compensation arrangement between the practice group and the hospital.[3]

For the first requirement of the ICA exception to apply, the compensation provided by the hospital to the practice group must be "fair market value for services and items actually provided" by the group to the hospital. The compensation from the hospital to the group takes the form of "support payments" equal to the difference between the physicians' old and new malpractice insurance premiums. Under our example, however, it is unclear whether the hospital is receiving "services or items" from the group.

It is true that, in exchange for the support payments, the neurosurgeons will remain in the community and be able to refer Medicare and other patients to the hospital, which will benefit the hospital financially. (Indeed, this benefit may greatly exceed the value of the support payments.) The problem, however, is that the Stark Law is intended to prevent hospitals from paying physicians for referrals, not to encourage such arrangements.[4]

B. *Volume or value and other business generated*

Assuming that the relevant compensation arrangement constitutes a FMV exchange, then the next question is whether the compensation at issue is "determined in a manner that takes into account the value or volume of patient referrals or other business generated by the referring physician for the entity furnishing DHS."

1. ICA definition v. ICA exception

Unlike the similar condition that is part of the ICA definition, the first requirement of the ICA exception permits the parties to rely on the Stark Regulations' special compensation rules (and relatedly, uses the term "compensation" as opposed to "aggregate compensation").[5] In general, the special compensation rules provide that certain per-procedure or per-click payments will not trigger the Stark Law's "volume or value" or "other business generated" standards, provided the per unit measure at issue (1) is consistent with FMV and (2) will not vary during the compensation arrangement in any manner that takes into account DHS referrals or other business generated by the referring physician for the DHS entity.[6]

Example 9.5

This example includes the same facts as Example 9.3 (i.e., a physician owns a company that leases imaging equipment to a hospital on a fixed, per-procedure basis).

Commentary: CMS might conclude that the hospital's per-procedure payments to the equipment company trigger the volume or value standard when considered in the "aggregate," and without regard to the special compensation rules—thereby satisfying the second condition of the ICA definition. However, provided that each fixed, per-procedure fee is FMV and the amount of the fee does not vary during the arrangement, the compensation could meet the first requirement of the ICA exception (which permits application of the special compensation rules).

---

2. 'Set in advance' standard not applicable

The 2001 Stark II, Phase I Regulations caused confusion about whether the "volume or value" or "other business generated" standards require that the compensation at issue also be "set in advance." In the preamble to those regulations, CMS stated that a "compensation arrangement does not take into account the volume or value of referrals or other business generated between the parties if the compensation is fixed in advance . . ."[7] This statement caused some commenters to assume that the "set in advance" standard was indirectly incorporated into the "volume or value" and "other business generated" standards and, therefore, into the ICA exception. In the preamble to the 2004 Stark II, Phase II Regulations, CMS clarified this, confirming that—consistent with the regulatory text of the ICA exception—the exception "does not include a 'set in advance' requirement."[8]

II. Written agreement requirement

The second requirement of the ICA exception is that the relevant compensation arrangement (i.e., the one closest to the physician/IFM) must be "set out in writing, signed by the parties, and specify the services covered by the arrangement."[9]

Example 9.6

This includes the same facts as Example 9.3 (i.e., a physician owns a company that leases imaging equipment to a hospital on a fixed, per-procedure basis).

Commentary: The lease between the company and the hospital is the relevant compensation arrangement. Assuming that the lease arrangement (1) is in writing, (2) specifies the equipment being leased, (3) specifies the rental rate, and (4) is signed by both parties, the arrangement should meet the second requirement of the ICA exception. However, if the lease agreement expired on June 30, 2005 (and the parties didn't renew it), but the parties continued the equipment rental arrangement without interruption, then the arrangement arguably would not meet the second requirement of the ICA exception.

The second requirement provides one exception to its "written agreement" rule. Where the relevant compensation arrangement is an employment arrangement, the arrangement need not be in writing, but it must be for identifiable services and commercially reasonable even in the absence of referrals to the employer.[10]

Finally, although the first requirement of the ICA exception refers to compensation for "services and items," the second requirement simply refers to "services." Presumably, the omission of "items" from the second requirement is inadvertent and, as such, arrangements that provide for the payment of compensation in exchange for services or items may satisfy the second requirement of the ICA exception.

III. Violation of law requirement

The third requirement of the ICA exception provides that the compensation arrangement does "not violate the anti-kickback statute ... or any Federal or State law or regulation governing billing or claims submission."[11] This requirement is discussed in detail in Chapter 2. Note, however, that unlike the first and second requirements of the ICA exception—which focus exclusively on the compensation arrangement closest to the physician/IFM at issue—the third requirement focuses on the "entire arrangement ... include[ing] each link in the chain as well as the overall arrangement viewed as a whole."

Example 9.7

This example includes the same facts as Example 9.3. (i.e., a physician owns a company that leases imaging equipment to a hospital on a fixed, per-procedure basis).

Commentary: It is not enough that the relevant compensation arrangement (i.e., the lease arrangement between the company and hospital) does not violate the anti-kickback statute. To meet the third requirement of the ICA exception, the entire financial relationship—which includes each link in the chain of financial relationships, as well as the chain as a whole—must not violate the anti-kickback statute.

Notes

1. 42 Code of Federal Regulations (CFR) §411.357(p).

2. More specifically, the first requirement of the ICA exception provides that the compensation "received by the referring physician (or immediate family member)" must be fair market value and not determined in a manner that takes into account the value or volume of referrals or other business generated by the referring physician for the DHS entity. Although the first requirement of the ICA exception (as written) can be applied where the physician/IFM has a compensation arrangement, it cannot be applied (as written) where the physician/IFM has an ownership interest. The reason is simple: In the latter case, the focus is on a compensation arrangement that *does not* involve the physician/IFM, but the first requirement of the ICA exception focuses on the compensation received by the physician/IFM. Presumably, this is a drafting error and the provision actually should read to the following effect: "The compensation received by the referring physician (or immediate family member), *or other relevant individual or entity*, is fair market value for services and items actually provided and not determined in any manner that takes into account the value or volume of referrals or other business generated by the referring physician for the entity furnishing DHS."

3. To the extent that the physicians also are employed by the practice group or have another compensation arrangement with the practice group, there would be a second potential indirect compensation arrangement between each physician and the hospital, which would need to be analyzed separately. In such a case, however, the relevant compensation arrangement would be the arrangement between each physician and the group—not the group and the hospital.

4. CMS addressed a similar issue relating to the Stark Law's recruitment exception (see Chapter 10). Where there is a shortage of physicians in a particular specialty in a hospital's community, the hospital may try to recruit a physician in that specialty to relocate to the hospital's geographic service area. Upon relocation, the physician will not become an employee or independent contractor of the hospital or furnish any items or services to the hospital. Once relocated, however, the physician may refer patients to the hospital for inpatient and outpatient hospital services. As part of a recruitment effort, hospitals will often offer the physician a variety of benefits, such as an income guarantee and reimbursement of moving expenses.

In the 2001 Stark II, Phase I Regulations, CMS suggested that, when a hospital provided remuneration to a physician as part of a recruitment arrangement, the Stark Law's FMV exception may protect the resulting compensation arrangement. In the 2004 Stark II, Phase II Regulations, however, CMS reconsidered its position:

> In the preamble to the [Stark II, Phase I Regulations], we stated that physician recruitment arrangements might fit in the new fair market value exception, depending on the specific facts . . . We concluded that we would consider the issue further in Phase II of the rulemaking. Upon further consideration, we do not believe that recruitment incentives can fit in the fair market value exception…We agree that the physician's relocation is not properly viewed as a benefit to the hospital, except as a potential source of DHS referrals—a consideration that is antithetical to the premise of the statute.

Presumably, CMS would take a similar position for the malpractice premium support arrangement discussed in Example 9.4, which effectively amounts to a physician "retention" (as opposed to a physician "relocation") arrangement. In other words, CMS might conclude that the decision by the neurosurgeons to remain in the hospital's community (provided the hospital makes the insurance support payments at issue) "is not properly viewed as a benefit to the hospital, except as a potential source of DHS referrals—a consideration that is antithetical to the premise of the statute."

Were CMS to take this position, any indirect compensation arrangement between each neurosurgeon and the hospital could not meet the FMV component of the first requirement of the ICA exception. This would preclude the neurosurgeons from making referrals to the hospital for DHS covered by Medicare.

5. Stark II, Phase II Regulations (Preamble), 69 *FR* 16056, 16069 (2004).

6. 42 CFR §411.354(d)(2)-(3).

7. Stark II, Phase I Regulations (Preamble), 66 *FR* 856, 877 (2001).

8. Stark II, Phase II Regulations (Preamble), 69 *FR* 16056, 16061 (2004).

9. 42 CFR §411.357(p)(2).

10. Stark II, Phase I Regulations (Preamble), 66 *FR* 856, 878 (2001).

11. Stark II, Phase II Regulations (Preamble), 69 *FR* 16056, 16066 (2004).

12. 42 CFR §§411.354(d)(2), (3).

13. Stark II, Phase II Regulations (Preamble), 69 *FR* 16056, 16069 (2004).

14. Stark II, Phase II Regulations (Preamble), 69 *FR* 16056, 16069 (2004).

15. Stark II, Phase II Regulations (Preamble), 69 *FR* 16056, 16069 (2004).

16. 42 CFR §411.357(p)(2).

17. 42 CFR §411.357(p)(2).

18. 42 CFR §411.357(p)(3).

19. Stark II, Phase II Regulations (Preamble), 69 *FR* 16056, 16061 (2004).

Chapter 10

PHYSICIAN RECRUITMENT
AND RETENTION EXCEPTIONS

Chapter 10

PHYSICIAN RECRUITMENT AND RETENTION EXCEPTIONS

Chapter 8 addresses all but two of the direct compensation arrangement exceptions. This chapter covers the two direct compensation arrangement exceptions not addressed in Chapter 8—the "physician recruitment" exception and the "physician retention" exception. We discuss these two exceptions separately for the following reasons:

- The physician recruitment exception is particularly complex and, as such, warrants a more extensive discussion and treatment than many of the other, more straightforward, direct compensation arrangement exceptions.

- The physician retention exception relates closely to the physician recruitment exception. For example, both involve payments to physicians to relocate to or—in the case of a retention payment, to remain in—a particular service area.

- Although these two exceptions may be characterized as direct compensation arrangement exceptions, the recruitment exception in particular arguably qualifies as a "hybrid" exception, protecting both direct (i.e., physician-hospital) recruitment arrangements and indirect (i.e., physician-group-hospital) recruitment arrangements.

- Perhaps more than any other type of physician-hospital arrangement, hospital-physician recruitment and retention arrangements—which, virtually by definition, involve a hospital providing something of value to a physician or physician group and receiving nothing (in the way of money, services, or items) in return—are viewed by federal healthcare law enforcement agencies as potentially abusive. Because of this, hospitals and physicians must ensure that their recruitment and retention arrangements, which often involve the exchange of significant amounts of money, comply with the Stark Law.

I. Physician recruitment exception

Not unlike other industries (where a company may be forced to provide financial incentives to attract talented personnel), a hospital interested in recruiting a new physician to its community (i.e., a "sponsoring hospital") may need to pay for certain recruitment-related expenses, such as headhunter fees and moving expenses, to attract a talented physician. In addition, the sponsoring hospital may need to offer the physician an income or collections guarantee. (*Note:* The need to offer such benefits is particularly evident in regions where certain factors, such as escalating malpractice premiums, make physician recruitment and retention difficult.) This remuneration, in turn, may create a direct or indirect compensation arrangement (1) between the recruited physician and the sponsoring hospital and (2) if the physician is joining an existing (i.e., "host") practice, between the sponsoring hospital and any physician-owner, physician-employee, or physician-contractor of the host practice.

Recognizing that physician recruitment is a common and beneficial practice in the healthcare industry, Congress created an exception for physician recruitment arrangements in the Stark Law.[1] The Centers for Medicare & Medicaid Services (CMS), in turn, has created an exception for physician recruitment arrangements in the Stark Regulations.[2] CMS overhauled its regulatory exception in the 2004 Stark II, Phase II Regulations to establish, among other things, "bright-line" rules for applying the exception. Although CMS met this objective, the Stark II, Phase II Regulations also created additional ambiguities and left numerous unanswered questions, many of which this chapter will address.

The Stark Law's recruitment exception provides that a "compensation arrangement" does not include "remuneration" furnished by a "hospital to a physician to induce the physician to relocate to the geographic area served by the hospital in order to be a member of the medical staff of the hospital," if the arrangement meets the following conditions:

• The physician is not required to refer patients to the hospital.

• The amount of the remuneration under the arrangement is not determined in a manner that takes into account (directly or indirectly) the volume or value of any referrals by the referring physician.

• The arrangement meets such other requirements as CMS may impose by regulation as needed to protect against program or patient abuse.[3]

The Stark Regulations modify and expand upon these statutory provisions in several ways. Most significantly, perhaps, the regulations clearly distinguish between (1) "solo relocations" (i.e., arrangements where the recruited physician will establish his or her own medical practice upon relocation) and (2) "host practice relocations" (i.e., arrangements where the recruited physician will join an existing medical practice upon relocation).

A. Solo relocations

The Stark Regulations provide that "[r]emuneration provided by a hospital to recruit a physician that is paid directly to the physician and is intended to induce the physician to relocate his or her medical practice to the geographic area served by the hospital in order to become a member of the hospital's medical staff" will not create a compensation arrangement if several conditions are met.[4] Before turning to these conditions, however, four threshold issues warrant discussion.

First, with the exception of federally qualified health centers (FQHC)[5], the recruitment exception only applies to recruitment arrangements that involve "hospitals." Similar arrangements involving other types of designated health services (DHS) entities do not qualify for protection under the physician recruitment exception.

Second, the physician recruitment exception applies only to remuneration intended to "induce the physician to relocate his or her medical practice . . ."[6] In most cases, the application of this requirement is straightforward (and the requirement is easily met). In a few cases, however, this "inducement to relocate" requirement can pose an obstacle to meeting the recruitment exception.

Example 10.1

A neurosurgeon from Boise, ID, practiced medicine in New York City between 1994 and 2004. In November 2004, the physician decided to move back to Boise, sold his condominium in New York, purchased a house in Boise, and entered into a medical office space lease in Boise with a January 1, 2005, start date. For several years, a hospital in Boise had been attempting to recruit a neurosurgeon. In December 2004, the hospital contacted the physician in New York and offered him a recruitment package that included reimbursement of his moving expenses and a two-year income guarantee.

Commentary: The proposed recruitment arrangement arguably would not fit into the physician recruitment exception because the "remuneration" at issue (i.e., the moving expenses and income guarantee) could not serve as an "inducement" to the physician to relocate his medical practice to Boise because—before the offer of remuneration—the physician had already decided to relocate his medical practice to Boise.

Third, the recruitment exception applies only to remuneration intended to induce the physician to relocate his or her medical practice "in order to become a member of the hospital's medical staff . . ."[7] Again, in most cases, physician recruitment arrangements easily meet this requirement, but in a few cases it can pose an obstacle to meeting the recruitment exception.

Example 10.2

A primary care physician had a medical practice in Arlington, VA, between August 1, 2000, and July 31, 2004. During that time, the physician was a member of a hospital's medical staff. In July 2004, the physician decided to take two years off and obtain a masters degree at the University of West Virginia. In December 2004, however, the physician changed his mind and contacted the hospital, indicating that he might be interested in returning to Arlington, and to private practice. The hospital, in turn, offered the physician a recruitment package that included a one-year income guarantee, effective January 1, 2005. As of January 1, 2005, however, the physician was still a member of the hospital's medical staff.

Commentary: The proposed recruitment arrangement arguably would not fit into the recruitment exception because the "remuneration" at issue (i.e., the income guarantee) could not serve as an "inducement" to the physician to join the hospital's medical staff because—at the time of the offer of the remuneration—the physician already was a member of the hospital's medical staff.

Fourth, the recruitment exception applies only to remuneration intended to induce the physician to "relocate" his or her "medical practice" "to" the "geographic area served by the hospital."[8] The Stark Regulations provide that a physician will be considered to have "relocated his or her medical practice" if (1) the "physician moves his or her medical practice at least 25 miles" (i.e., the "25 mile test") or (2) the "physician's new medical practice derives at least 75% of its revenues from professional services furnished to patients (including hospital inpatients) not seen or treated by the physician at his or her prior medical practice site during the preceding [three] years, measured on an annual basis (fiscal or calendar year)" (i.e., the "75% test").[9] *Note:* CMS has made it clear that the focus is on the relocation of the physician's "medical practice," not his or her residence.

The Stark Regulations define the term "geographic area served by the hospital" as "the area composed of the lowest number of contiguous ZIP codes from which the hospital draws at least 75% of its inpatients."[10] Although seemingly straightforward, this test raises a variety of interesting issues. For example, if a hospital draws 10% of its inpatients from each of 10 contiguous ZIP codes (imagine a pizza having 10 slices with the hospital in the center), could the hospital pick any eight ZIP codes as its geographic service area (GSA)? Similarly, what if a hospital does not draw 75% of its inpatients from contiguous ZIP codes (i.e., there are certain ZIP codes not served by the hospital that form "gaps" among the contiguous ZIP codes surrounding the hospital)? Does that mean that the hospital does not (and cannot) have a GSA for Stark Law purposes and, therefore, cannot rely on the recruitment exception?

Set forth below are a few examples demonstrating the application of the requirement that the remuneration provided by the sponsoring hospital must be intended to induce the recruited physician to "relocate" his or her "medical practice" "to" the "geographic area served by the hospital."

Example 10.3

A hospital's GSA consists of five ZIP codes: 99991, 99992, 99993, 99994, and 99995. The recruited physician will be moving 3,000 miles; his medical practice will derive 100% of its revenues from professional services furnished to patients the physician has never seen or treated; and he will reside in ZIP code 99995. The physician's medical office, however, will be in ZIP code 99996.

Commentary: The arrangement will not qualify for protection under the physician recruitment exception. Although the physician is relocating his residence to the hospital's GSA, he is not relocating his medical practice to the hospital's GSA.

> ### Example 10.4
>
> A hospital's GSA consists of five ZIP codes: 99991, 99992, 99993, 99994, and 99995. The recruited physician will be moving his medical practice 30 miles from ZIP code 99991 to ZIP code 99995. After relocating, the physician's new medical practice will derive 80% of its revenues from professional services furnished to patients the physician has never seen or treated.
>
> **Commentary:** The arrangement will not qualify for protection under the physician recruitment exception. Although the physician will meet both the 25 mile and 75% tests, the physician is not relocating his medical practice "to" the hospital's GSA; rather, he is relocating his medical practice "within" the hospital's GSA.

> ### Example 10.5
>
> This includes the same facts as Example 10.4, except the recruited physician will be moving his medical practice one mile (not 30 miles) and from ZIP code 99996 to ZIP code 99995.
>
> **Commentary:** The arrangement will qualify for protection under the recruitment exception because the physician is "relocating" his medical practice to the hospital's GSA (i.e., from ZIP code 99996 to ZIP code 99995) and will meet the 75% test.

The Stark Regulations provide that residents and physicians who have been in practice for one year or less (i.e., new physicians) do not have to meet the 25 mile or 75% tests. However, in addition to meeting the other requirements of the physician recruitment exception, the "recruited resident or physician must establish his or her medical practice in the geographic area served by the hospital."[11]

Assuming that the recruitment arrangement involves a "hospital" paying remuneration to a physician that is intended to "induce" the physician to "relocate" his or her "medical practice" "to" the "geographic area served by the hospital" in order to become a "member of the hospital's medical staff," then the arrangement will qualify for protection under the physician recruitment exception, provided that it meets four additional requirements:

1. The arrangement must be in writing and signed by both the hospital and the recruited physician.[12]

2. The hospital may "not determine (directly or indirectly) the amount of the remuneration to the physician based on the volume or value of any actual or anticipated referrals by the physician or other business generated between the parties."[13]

3. The arrangement cannot be "conditioned on the physician's referral of patients to the hospital."[14]

4. The physician must be "allowed to establish staff privileges at any other hospital(s) and to refer business to any other entities."[15] (CMS has indicated that "reasonable credentialing restrictions" on the ability of physicians to compete with the sponsoring hospital are acceptable.[16])

B. Host practice relocations

When a physician decides that, upon relocation, he or she will join an existing practice, the sponsoring hospital, recruited physician, and host practice must meet the requirements discussed above and several additional requirements.[17] (*Note:* We will refer to these additional requirements as the "host practice relocation requirements.") In general, the host practice relocation requirements are designed to ensure that hospitals do not use physician recruitment arrangements to induce physician practices to make referrals to the hospital or to reward physician practices for past referrals.

The host-practice relocation requirements apply to any arrangement where the "remuneration provided by a hospital" flows either (1) "indirectly" to a recruited physician "through payments made to another physician or physician practice" or (2) "directly" to a recruited physician "who joins a physician practice."[18]

Assuming that there is an arrangement pursuant to which the "remuneration provided by a hospital" flows either (1) "indirectly" to a recruited physician "through payments made to another physician or physician practice" or (2) "directly" to a recruited physician "who joins a physician practice," then the sponsoring hospital, recruited physician, and host practice must meet seven requirements, each of which is discussed below.

Example 10.6

A Los Angeles hospital recruits a New York physician who will join an existing physician practice upon relocation as an employee at a salary of $120,000 (or $10,000 per month). As part of the recruitment package, the hospital agrees to provide the physician with a one-year income guarantee of $120,000 (i.e., the hospital agrees that if the collections attributable to the physician minus the non-salary related costs [e.g., overhead] attributable to the physician are less than $120,000, then the hospital will make up the difference). For example, if the collections attributable to the physician are $360,000 and the non-salary related costs attributable to the physician are $240,000, then the hospital will pay nothing (because the collections minus the non-salary related costs leave exactly enough to cover the "income" to the recruited physician [i.e., the $120,000] that was "guaranteed"). If the collections attributable to the physician are $240,000 and the non-salary related costs attributable to the physician are $240,000, then the hospital will pay $120,000. If the collections attributable to the physician are $0 and the non-salary-related costs attributable to the physician are $240,000, then the hospital will pay $360,000.

The recruitment agreement provides that the hospital will pay monies pursuant to the income guarantee to the host practice. For example, if in the first month of the agreement, collections and non-salary related costs attributable to the physician are $20,000 and $15,000, respectively, then (1) the host practice will pay $5,000 of the physician's monthly $10,000 salary out of the excess collections attributable to him, (2) the hospital will pay the host practice $5,000 pursuant to the income guarantee, and (3) the host practice will use this $5,000 from the hospital to cover the remaining portion of the physician's monthly salary.

Commentary: The recruitment arrangement must meet the host practice relocation requirements because the remuneration provided by the hospital (i.e., the income guarantee payment) flows "indirectly" to the recruited physician through payments made to the physician practice.

Example 10.7

This includes the same facts as Example 10.6, except the recruitment agreement provides that the hospital will pay monies pursuant to the income guarantee to the recruited physician (and not to the host practice). Thus, under the facts in Example 10.6, (1) the host practice will pay $5,000 of the physician's monthly $10,000 salary out of the excess collections attributable to him and (2) the physician will receive the remaining $5,000 directly from the hospital.

Commentary: The recruitment arrangement must meet the host practice relocation requirements because the remuneration provided by the hospital (i.e., the income guarantee payment) flows "directly" to the recruited physician (who has "joined a physician practice").

---

1. Written agreement requirement

The "written agreement" referenced in connection with solo relocations also must be "signed by the party to whom the payments are directly made."[19] This requirement is somewhat ambiguous. It would clearly require the host practice in Example 10.6 to be a party to (and execute) the agreement underlying the recruitment arrangement because payments are "directly made" to the host practice by the hospital under that arrangement. By its terms, however, it would not appear to require the host practice in Example 10.7 to be a party to the recruitment agreement because payments are not "directly made" to the host practice by the hospital under that arrangement.[20]

2. Pass through requirement

The Stark Regulations provide that "except for actual costs incurred by the physician or physician practice in recruiting the new physician," the remuneration at issue must be "passed directly through to" or "remain with" the recruited physician.[21] (*Note:* We will refer to this as the "pass through" requirement.)

This requirement also is somewhat ambiguous (and potentially problematic) because it is not entirely clear what can be included in "actual costs incurred" by the host practice "in recruiting the new physician."[22] Presumably, however, if a host practice incurs actual (out of pocket) costs in connection with recruiting a physician (such as headhunter fees; airfare, hotel charges, meals, and other costs associated with visits by the applicant and his or her family to the relevant geographic area; and moving expenses), then the hospital may reimburse the host practice for these costs as part of the recruitment arrangement, and the practice is not required to pass this reimbursement "directly through to" the recruited physician (which would make no sense, because the recruited physician did not incur the costs at issue).

Also somewhat ambiguous is how remuneration that does not fall into the "actual costs of recruitment" category fares under the pass through requirement. For example, in Example 10.6, is it really the case that the host practice would have to wait until it received the $5,000 from the hospital before it could pay the physician his full $10,000 monthly salary? This would seem neither fair (to the physician) nor necessary to achieve the exception's policy objectives. Similarly, does the host practice have to pay the recruited physician using the "same" $5,000 that the practice received from the hospital? This would seem overly burdensome to the host practice, which would have to create a separate bank account just for monies exchanged under a particular recruitment agreement and (once again) unnecessary to achieve the objectives of the physician recruitment exception.

Furthermore, if construed narrowly, the pass through requirement arguably cannot be met in the case of any recruitment agreement involving an income guarantee, where—as is frequently the case—there are one or more months where collections attributable to the recruited physician are not sufficient to cover his or her non-salary-related costs. Two examples help demonstrate this point.

Example 10.8

This includes the same facts as Example 10.6, except the collections and non-salary related costs attributable to the recruited physician are $5,000 and $15,000, respectively. Pursuant to the recruitment agreement, the sponsoring hospital would pay the host practice $20,000 ($10,000 to make up the difference between the collections and non-salary related costs attributable to the recruited physician, and $10,000 to cover the physician's salary).

Commentary: Because the entire $20,000 paid by the hospital to the host practice would not be "passed directly through to" the recruited physician (i.e., the $10,000 serving to reimburse the practice for its non-salary related costs attributable to the physician would remain with the practice), the arrangement arguably would not meet the pass through requirement (if construed narrowly).

Example 10.9

This includes the same facts as Example 10.7, except the collections and non-salary related costs attributable to the recruited physician are $5,000 and $15,000, respectively. Under the recruitment agreement, the sponsoring hospital would pay the recruited physician $20,000 (i.e., $10,000 for the difference between the collections and non-salary related costs attributable to the physician and $10,000 to cover the physician's salary). The recruited physician, in turn, would "upstream" $10,000 to the host practice to cover the shortfall between his collections and non-salary-related costs.

Commentary: Because the entire $20,000 paid by the hospital to the recruited physician would not "remain with" the recruited physician (i.e., the $10,000 intended to reimburse the host practice for the recruited physician's non-salary related costs would be passed through to the host practice by the recruited physician), the arrangement arguably would not meet the pass through requirement (if construed narrowly).

---

3. Incremental cost requirement

That CMS did not intend such a narrow interpretation of the pass through requirement is suggested by the third host practice relocation requirement, which provides that, "in the case of an income guarantee made by the hospital to a recruited physician who joins a physician or physician practice, the costs allocated by the physician or physician practice to the recruited physician" must "not exceed the actual additional incremental costs attributable to the recruited physician."[23] (*Note:* We will refer to this as the "incremental cost" requirement.)

This requirement contemplates that recruitment agreements may involve income guarantees and, in order to effectuate such guarantees, non-salary-related costs attributable to the recruited physician will need to be determined. Having effectively "blessed" income guarantees as a valid recruitment benefit, it is unlikely that CMS would have essentially made it impossible to provide such a guarantee through a narrow interpretation of the pass through requirement. Nonetheless, the healthcare industry would benefit greatly from a confirmation/clarification by CMS in this regard.

In any event, the incremental cost requirement is important beyond its interpretive value with respect to the pass through requirement. Most notably, the requirement provides that, in the case of an income guarantee, the costs allocated to the recruited physician may not exceed the "actual additional incremental" costs to the host practice attributable to the recruited physician.[24] CMS rejected an alternative "*pro rata*" approach because many host practice expenses are "sunken costs" incurred regardless of the number of physicians in the practice. As such, an income guarantee using a *pro rata* approach risks making the host practice more than "whole," with the excess possibly serving as an inducement or reward for referrals. Once again, an example helps demonstrate the application of this requirement.

Example 10.10

On January 1, 2004, a relocating physician joined a four-physician practice group as an employee at a salary of $120,000. As part of the recruitment package, the sponsoring hospital agreed to provide the recruited physician with a one-year income guarantee of $120,000. In 2005, the host practice's total non-salary related costs were $450,000 (up from $400,000 in 2004). The recruited physician's *pro rata* share of the host practice's non-salary related costs in 2005 were $90,000 (i.e., $450,000 divided evenly among five physicians). The additional incremental non-salary related cost to the practice attributable to the recruited physician in 2005 was $50,000. Collections attributable to the recruited physician in 2005 were $120,000. Thus,

• using an "incremental costs" formula, the hospital would pay the host practice $50,000 under the income guarantee, and
• using a "*pro rata* costs" formula, the hospital would pay the host practice $90,000 under the income guarantee.

The hospital pays the host practice $90,000.

Commentary: The recruitment arrangement does not meet the incremental cost requirement.

---

4. Practice restriction requirement

The next host practice relocation requirement provides that the host practice "may not impose additional practice restrictions on the recruited physician other than conditions related to quality of care."[25] (*Note:* We will refer to this as the "practice restriction" requirement.) According to CMS, this requirement makes clear the agency's "original intent that recruitment payments not be used to lock physicians into using the recruiting hospital . . ."[26]

CMS interprets the phrase "additional practice restrictions" to include "non-compete agreement[s]"[27] and, as such, has advised—in guidance issued on July 14, 2004—that parties to existing host practice relocation arrangements should void all non-compete clauses and document that such clauses will not be enforced.[28] CMS's interpretation and guidance raise many questions and issues.

First, if CMS's objective is to avoid "locking physicians into using the recruiting hospital," it is not clear how prohibiting non-compete agreements accomplishes this. If, on the other hand, a non-compete serves to induce the recruited physician not to leave the host practice, then—pursuant to the other requirements of the recruitment exception (discussed below)—the agreement must allow the physician to refer patients to the sponsoring hospital and to any other hospital. If, however, the recruited physician *leaves* the host practice (notwithstanding the non-compete), then upon the physician's departure, there is nothing to prevent the physician from referring patients to any hospital. Simply put, there is no direct nexus between the purported policy objective of the practice restriction requirement and the operation of non-compete agreements.

A more logical (but unarticulated) reason for prohibiting non-competes might be that an enforceable non-compete could preclude the recruited physician from continuing to furnish services to the community if he or she leaves the host practice. The Stark Law's recruitment exception, however, does not require the existence of "community need." In any event, the prohibition of commercially reasonable restrictions on a recruited physician's ability to compete with a host practice is likely to reduce the willingness of some physician groups to participate in future hospital-sponsored recruitments. Moreover, by directing parties to void commercially reasonable non-compete components of their existing recruitment arrangements, CMS has placed sponsoring hospitals, in particular, in a difficult position. The following are the hospital's principal options:

- The hospital can ask the host practice to delete the non-compete provision from the agreement voluntarily. Because non-competes have economic value, however, the practice may not honor this request.

- The hospital can rely on a "change of law" clause or a "void against public policy" argument and ask a court to nullify the non-compete at issue. However, this could be an uphill battle. Among other things, the hospital arguably could honor its contractual duties under the recruitment arrangement without violating the Stark Law simply by not billing for DHS it furnishes to Medicare patients referred by the recruited physician.

- The hospital could offer to "buy out" the non-compete for a price that is consistent with fair market value. This option also is not without complications, however, as it involves the exchange of money between the hospital and the group, as well as the provision of value to the recruited physician.

Finally, some have suggested that a solution lies in the use of "springing non-competes" (i.e., non-competes that only take effect after the recruitment agreement's financial support period ends or after the recruitment agreement as a whole expires). As a practical matter, these provisions would not address situations where the recruited physician leaves the host practice before the support period ends or the agreement expires. As a legal matter, it is not clear what CMS's position is with respect to such provisions. Thus, until and unless CMS clarifies matters, the most conservative course will be to ensure that host practices do not include any type of non-compete provisions in their agreements with recruited physicians.

5. Additional requirements

The final three host practice relocation requirements are as follows. First, the "remuneration from the hospital under the arrangement" must not "be determined in a manner that takes into account (directly or indirectly) the volume or value of any actual or anticipated referrals by the recruited physician or the physician practice (or any physician affiliated with the physician practice) receiving the direct payments from the hospital."[29] Second, the recruitment arrangement must not violate the anti-kickback statute or federal or state law or regulations governing billing or claims submission.[30] Third, "records of the actual costs and the passed through amounts" must be "maintained for a period of at least [five] years and made available to [CMS] upon request."[31]

6. Indirect compensation arrangement definition and exception

There is a question concerning the applicability of the indirect compensation arrangement definition (Chapter 5) and indirect compensation arrangements exception (Chapter 9) to host practice relocations where the remuneration at issue does not flow directly from the sponsoring hospital to the recruited physician, but instead flows from the sponsoring hospital, through the host practice, to the recruited physician. (*Note:* In the case of a solo relocation or a host practice relocation where the remuneration at issue flows directly from the sponsoring hospital to the recruited physician, this question is not relevant because the hospital and recruited physician will have a direct compensation arrangement.)

As discussed in Chapter 5, CMS takes the position that any time remuneration flows from a DHS entity (e.g., a sponsoring hospital) to a physician (e.g., a recruited physician) through an "intervening" entity (e.g., a host practice), the only type of financial relationship that may exist between the DHS entity and the physician is an "indirect compensation arrangement." As discussed in Chapter 5, however, such an arrangement will exist only if three conditions are satisfied.

The first of these conditions is that if the recruited physician is an employee or contractor of the host practice, then the recruited physician must receive "aggregate compensation" from the host practice "that varies with, or otherwise reflects, the volume or value of referrals or other business generated by" the recruited physician for the sponsoring hospital.[32] If the host practice-physician arrangement does not meet this condition, then the sponsoring hospital and recruited physician do not have a financial relationship and, as such, the parties do not need to rely on either the physician recruitment exception or the indirect compensation arrangements exception.

The second condition of the indirect compensation arrangement definition requires the sponsoring hospital to have "actual knowledge" or act "in reckless disregard or deliberate ignorance" of the fact that the recruited physician receives aggregate compensation from the host practice that varies with, or otherwise reflects, the volume or value of referrals or other business generated by the recruited physician for the sponsoring hospital.[33] Again, if this condition is not met, then the recruited physician and sponsoring hospital do not have a financial relationship and, as such, the parties do not need to rely on either the recruitment exception or the indirect compensation arrangements exception.

Further, even assuming that an indirect compensation arrangement is created where the remuneration at issue flows from the sponsoring hospital, through the host practice, to the recruited physician, the parties would, at least arguably, have the option of complying with either the recruitment exception or the indirect compensation arrangements exception (Chapter 9).[34] We use the term "arguably" because CMS has not addressed this issue directly.

On one hand, it might be argued that permitting sponsoring hospitals, host practices, and recruited physicians to use the indirect compensation arrangements exception could, in some cases, undermine the policy objectives that CMS was attempting to achieve when it created the incremental cost, practice restriction, and various other host practice relocation requirements of the recruitment exception. On the other hand, CMS has been clear that (1) the indirect compensation arrangements exception may protect any indirect compensation arrangement[35] and (2) where remuneration passes from a DHS entity to a physician through any intervening entity, the only type of financial relationship that the entity and physician may have is an indirect compensation arrangement.[36]

Under these circumstances, the better argument is that (1) where, pursuant to a recruitment arrangement, remuneration flows from a sponsoring hospital, through a host practice, to a recruited physician, this can only result in one type of financial relationship—an indirect compensation arrangement—and (2) where such a relationship is, in fact, created, it may be protected by either the recruitment exception or the indirect compensation arrangements exception. Until CMS confirms that this is the case, however, the most conservative course will be to ensure that physician recruitment arrangements meet the requirements of the Stark Law's recruitment exception.

7. Non-recruited physicians

Finally, a host practice relocation may create (1) a financial relationship between the recruited physician and the sponsoring hospital as well as (2) an indirect compensation arrangement between the hospital and any other physician who has an ownership interest in or compensation arrangement with the host practice. Whether a relocation arrangement creates an indirect compensation arrangement between the sponsoring hospital and any such "affiliated" physician requires an application of the indirect compensation arrangement definition (Chapter 5). If the relocation creates such an arrangement, the indirect compensation arrangements exception (Chapter 9) or an all-purpose exception (Chapter 6) may protect it.

II. Physician retention exception

The Stark Law does not have an exception for payments made by a hospital to a physician that are intended to induce the physician to *remain* in the hospital's community or service area. Before 2004, the Stark Regulations also had no such exception. In the Stark II, Phase II Regulations, however, CMS created a very narrow exception that permits payments made by a hospital or FQHC "directly" to a physician on the hospital or FQHC's medical staff "to retain the physician's medical practice" in the GSA served by the hospital or FQHC, provided that the arrangement meets the following requirements[37]:

1. The arrangement is set out in writing and signed by both the hospital/FQHC and the physician.

2. The arrangement is not conditioned on the physician's referral of patients to the hospital/FQHC.

3. The hospital/FQHC does not determine (directly or indirectly) the amount of the remuneration to the physician based on the volume or value of any actual or anticipated referrals by the physician or other business generated between the parties.

4. The physician is allowed to establish staff privileges at any other hospital/FQHC and to refer business to any other entities.[38]

5. The GSA served by the hospital/FQHC must either be in a health professional shortage area (HPSA), regardless of the physician's specialty, or in an "area with demonstrated need for the physician," as determined by CMS in a Stark Law "advisory opinion."[39] Because (1) most hospitals/FQHCs are not in a HPSA, (2) the Stark Law's advisory opinion process (Chapter 12) has yet to be established in earnest, and (3) even if it were, CMS has indicated that it expects to approve retention payments only in "unusual and compelling circumstances,"[40] this requirement will be very difficult for most hospitals/FQHCs to meet.

6. The physician at issue must have "a *bona fide*, firm, written recruitment offer" from a hospital/FQHC "that is not related to the hospital or [FQHC] making the payment."[41] This competing offer must (1) specify "the remuneration being offered" and (2) "require the physician

to move the location of his or her practice at least 25 miles and outside of the geographic area served by the hospital or [FQHC] making the retention payment."[42] (*Note:* CMS may waive this "relocation" requirement "if the retention payment arrangement otherwise complies with all of the conditions of [the physician retention exception]."[43])

Example 10.11

A urologist has been practicing medicine in Hospital A's GSA, which qualifies as an HPSA, for five years. Hospital B is located 50 miles from Hospital A. Hospital B does not have any urologists on its staff and contacts the physician to try to induce her to relocate her practice to Hospital B's GSA. Hospital A learns that Hospital B has contacted the physician and begun preliminary negotiations.

Commentary: Hospital A may not pay the physician remuneration to keep her practice in Hospital A's GSA because the physician has not yet received a *bona fide* written relocation offer from Hospital B.

---

7. The "retention payment" must be the lower of the following amounts:

- The amount obtained by subtracting (1) "the physician's current income from physician and related services" from (2) "the income the physician would receive from comparable physician and related services in the *bona fide* recruitment offer," "provided that the respective incomes are determined using a reasonable and consistent methodology, and that they are calculated uniformly over no more than a 24-month period."[44]

- The "reasonable costs" the hospital/FQHC "would otherwise have to expend to recruit a new physician to the geographic area served by the [hospital/FQHC] in order to join the medical staff of the [hospital/FQHC] to replace the retained physician."[45]

Example 10.12

A primary care physician (Physician A) is considering relocating out of the GSA of Hospital A. Physician A's current income for physician and related services is $200,000. A second hospital (Hospital B), located 1,000 miles from Hospital A, attempts to recruit Physician A, offering him a $220,000 income guarantee. Hospital A contacts a second primary care physician (Physician B), who practices 2,000 miles from Hospital A. Physician B indicates that she will relocate to Hospital A's GSA provided that Hospital A will cover her moving expenses, which are expected to be approximately $10,000.

Commentary: Hospital A cannot offer Physician A a retention payment that exceeds $10,000.

8. Finally, (1) the retention payment must be subject "to the same obligations and restrictions, if any, on repayment or forgiveness of indebtedness as the *bona fide* recruitment offer,"[46] (2) the amount and terms of the retention payment may not be altered during the term of the arrangement in any manner that takes into account the volume or value of referrals or other business generated by the physician,[47] (3) the arrangement may not violate the anti-kickback statute or any federal or state law or regulation governing billing or claims submission,[48] and (4) the hospital/FQHC may not enter into a retention arrangement with a particular referring physician more frequently than once every five years.[49]

Notes

1. 42 United States Code (USC) §1395nn(e)(5).
2. 42 Code of Federal Regulations (CFR) §411.357(e).
3. 42 USC §1395nn(e)(5).
4. 42 CFR §411.357(e)(1).
5. 42 CFR §411.357(e)(5).
6. 42 CFR §411.357(e)(1).
7. 42 CFR §411.357(e)(1).
8. 42 CFR §411.357(e)(1).

9. 42 CFR §411.357(e)(2). The Stark Regulations provide that for the initial "startup" year of the recruited physician's practice, the 75% test "will be satisfied if there is a reasonable expectation that the recruited physician's medical practice for the year will derive at least 75% of its revenues from professional services furnished to patients not seen or treated by the physician at his or her prior medical practice site during the preceding three years." 42 CFR §411.357(e)(2)(ii).

10. 42 CFR §411.357(e)(2).

11. 42 CFR §411.357(e)(2).

12. 42 CFR §411.357(e)(1)(i).

13. 42 CFR §411.357(e)(1)(iii).

14. 42 CFR §411.357(e)(1)(ii).

15. 42 CFR §411.357(e)(1)(iv). There is an exception for referrals that "may be restricted under a separate employment or services contract that complies with" 42 CFR §411.354(d)(4).

16. Stark II, Phase II Regulations (Preamble), 69 *Federal Register* (*FR*) 16054, 16095 (2004).

17. 42 CFR §411.357(e)(4).

18. 42 CFR §411.357(e)(4).

19. 42 CFR §411.357(e)(4)(i).

20. Note, however, that separate from the requirements of the recruitment exception, sound business and compliance practices may dictate that the host practice execute the agreement underlying the recruitment arrangement at issue.

21. 42 CFR §411.357(e)(4)(ii).

22. 42 CFR §411.357(e)(4)(ii).

23. 42 CFR §411.357(e)(4)(iii).

24. Stark II, Phase II Regulations (Preamble), 69 *FR* 16054, 16096 (2004).

25. 42 CFR §411.357(e)(4)(vi).

26. Stark II, Phase II Regulations (Preamble), 69 *FR* 16054, 16095 (2004).

27. Stark II, Phase II Regulations (Preamble), 69 *FR* at 16054, 16096-16097 (2004).

28. CMS Frequently Asked Questions Answer ID 3163 set forth on the CMS Web site at *www.cms.hhs.gov.*

29. 42 CFR §411.357(e)(4)(v).

30. 42 CFR §411.357(e)(4)(vii).

31. 42 CFR §411.357(e)(4)(iv).

32. 42 CFR §411.354(c)(2)(ii). If the relocating physician also was an owner of the group, then the host practice would have to receive "aggregate compensation" from the hospital "that varies with, or otherwise reflects, the volume or value of referrals or other business generated by" the recruited physician for the sponsoring hospital. See Chapter 5.

33. 42 CFR §411.354(c)(2)(iii).

34. 42 CFR §411.357(p).

35. 42 CFR §411.357(p).

36. 42 CFR §411.354(a)(2).

37. 42 CFR §411.357(t).

38. 42 CFR §411.357(t)(1)(i). Again, there is an exception for referrals that "may be restricted under a separate employment or services contract that complies with" 42 CFR §411.354(d)(4).

39. 42 CFR §411.357(t)(1)(ii).

40. Stark II, Phase II Regulations (Preamble), 69 *FR* 16054, 16097 (2004).

41. 42 CFR §411.357(t)(1)(iii).

42. 42 CFR §411.357(t)(1)(iii).

43. 42 CFR §411.357(t)(2).

44. 42 CFR §411.357(t)(1)(iv)(A).

45. 42 CFR §411.357(t)(1)(iv)(B).

46. 42 CFR §411.357(t)(1)(v).

47. 42 CFR §411.357(t)(1)(vi).

48. 42 CFR §411.357(t)(1)(viii).

49. 42 CFR §411.357(t)(1)(vi).

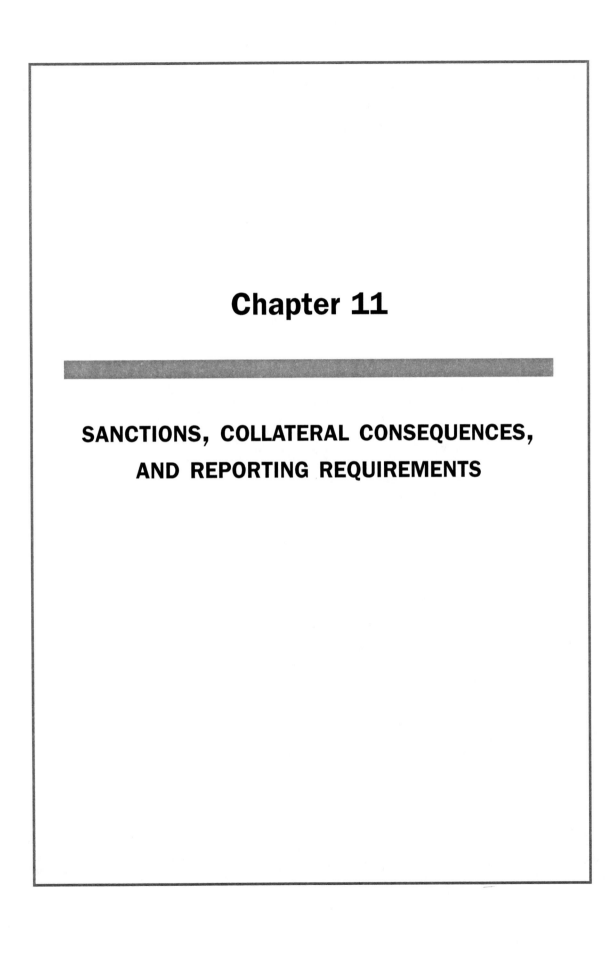

Chapter 11

SANCTIONS, COLLATERAL CONSEQUENCES, AND REPORTING REQUIREMENTS

Chapter **11**

SANCTIONS, COLLATERAL CONSEQUENCES, AND REPORTING REQUIREMENTS

As discussed in Chapter 1, the Stark Law has two basic prohibitions: a referral prohibition and a billing prohibition. This chapter addresses the sanctions the government may impose on physicians and entities that violate these prohibitions, the collateral consequences that may result from a violation of the Stark Law, and the Law's reporting requirements.

I. Sanctions

A. Denial of payment rule

The Stark Law provides that "no payment may be made [under the Medicare program] for a designated health service which is provided in violation" of the referral and billing prohibitions.[1] Similarly, except as provided below, the Stark Regulations provide that "no Medicare payment may be made for a designated health service that is furnished pursuant to a prohibited referral."[2] We will refer to this as the "denial of payment rule."

Example 11.1

A physician serves as the medical director of a clinical laboratory and, as such, has a financial relationship (in the form of a direct compensation arrangement) with the laboratory. This arrangement does not meet an exception. The physician refers a Medicare beneficiary to the laboratory for services reimbursable by Medicare, and the laboratory submits a claim to Medicare (seeking $125) for these services.

Commentary: Medicare can reject the claim pursuant to the denial of payment rule.

The Stark Regulations provide one exception to the denial of payment rule. Under this exception, "payment may be made to an entity that submits a claim for a designated health service" if (1) the entity "did not have actual knowledge of and did not act in reckless disregard or deliberate ignorance of, the identity of the physician who made the referral of the designated health service to the entity" and (2) the claim "otherwise complies with all applicable federal and state laws, rules, and regulations."[3]

Logically, if payment may be made to an entity pursuant to this exception—because the entity furnishing the designated health services (DHS) is unaware of the identity of the referring physician—the entity also should not be subject to the refund obligation or the civil monetary penalty (CMP), assessment, or exclusion sanctions discussed in this chapter. Unfortunately, the regulations that govern these sanctions neither adopt nor cross-reference this exception. As such, it is not entirely clear what, if any, effect the exception to the denial of payment rule has on these other sanction provisions under the law.

B. Refund obligation

The Stark Law provides that if a person "collects any amounts that were billed in violation" of the billing prohibition, "the person shall be liable to the individual for, and shall refund on a timely basis to the individual, any amounts so collected."[4] The Stark Regulations modify and expand this sanction somewhat, providing that an "entity that collects payment for a designated health service that was performed under a prohibited referral must refund all collected amounts on a timely basis,"[5] which is defined as within 60 days "from the time the prohibited amounts are collected" by the entity.[6] We will refer to this as the "refund obligation." *Note:* As discussed in the next section, a failure to comply with the refund obligation may give rise to CMPs and other sanctions.

Example 11.2

This includes the same facts as Example 11.1; however, instead of rejecting the claim for reimbursement submitted by the laboratory, Medicare reimburses the laboratory in the amount of $125.

Commentary: The laboratory is obligated to refund this $125 to Medicare on a timely basis (i.e., within 60 days of receipt of payment).

C. Civil money penalties, assessments, and exclusion

In addition to the denial of payment rule and refund obligation, the Stark Law provides for several types of CMPs and assessments, as well as for exclusion from participation in Medicare, Medicaid, and other federal healthcare programs.

1. Presenting claims CMP

The Stark Law provides that any person who "presents" or "causes to be presented" a "bill or a claim" for a service that such person "knows or should know" is for a service "for which payment may not be made" by Medicare—because the service was provided in violation of the Stark Law's referral prohibition—is subject to a CMP of not more than $15,000 for each such service and an assessment of up to three times the amount claimed for the service at issue (in lieu of damages).[7] In addition, the government may exclude the person from participation in all "federal healthcare programs."[8] For purposes of these statutory provisions:

- The term "should know" means "that a person, with respect to information" either (1) "acts in deliberate ignorance of the truth or falsity of the information" or (2) "acts in reckless disregard of the truth or falsity of the information."[9] However, "no proof of specific intent to defraud is required."[10]

- The term "federal healthcare programs" means "any plan or program that provides health benefits, whether directly, through insurance, or otherwise, which is funded directly, in whole or in part, by the United States Government" (other than the Federal Employee Health Benefit Program).[11] Most notably, "federal healthcare programs" include Medicare and Medicaid.

Although the Stark Regulations do not have companion CMP, assessment, or exclusion provisions, the general healthcare fraud sections of the Code of Federal Regulations (CFR) (i.e., the "CMP Regulations") have incorporated these provisions. The CMP Regulations provide that any person who "has knowingly presented, or caused to be presented, a claim" that is for "a payment that such person knows, or should know, may not be made under [the denial of payment rule]" is subject to a CMP of up to $15,000 for each improperly referred service, and an assessment of up to three times the amount claimed for the service at issue (in lieu of damages).[12] In addition, the government may exclude the person from participation in Medicare, Medicaid, and other federal healthcare programs.[13] We will refer to these sanctions collectively as the "presenting claims CMP."

In sum, although not a model of clarity, the presenting claims CMP provides as follows: If an individual or entity either "presents" or "causes to be presented" a claim that the person "knows" or "should know" is for a DHS that was furnished in violation of the Stark Law's referral prohibition, then the person is subject to a CMP of up to $15,000, an assessment of up to three times the amount claimed, and exclusion from participation in all federal healthcare programs, including Medicare and Medicaid. Thus, DHS entities that bill Medicare directly are subject to the presenting claims CMP, as are any referring physicians who have "caused" such claims to be presented.

Example 11.3

This includes the same facts as Example 11.1.

Commentary: Provided that the laboratory knew or should have known that the physician at issue had an unexcepted financial relationship with the laboratory—and, as such, that his DHS referral to the laboratory violated the Stark Law's referral prohibition—the laboratory would be subject to a CMP of up to $15,000, an assessment of up to $375 (3 x $125), and exclusion from participation in federal healthcare programs. The physician also may be subject to such sanctions.

---

2. Failure to refund CMP

The Stark Law also provides that any person who "presents" or "causes to be presented" a "bill or a claim" for a service that such person "knows or should know" is "for a service . . . for which a refund has not been made" is subject to a CMP of not more than $15,000 for each such service and an assessment of up to three times the amount claimed for the service at issue (in lieu of damages).[14] In addition, the person may be excluded from participation in all federal healthcare programs."[15] We will refer to these sanctions collectively as the "failure to refund CMP."

On its face, the failure to refund CMP makes no sense because an entity cannot make a "claim" for a "service" for which a "refund" has not been made. Put somewhat differently, an entity can only fail to refund a payment for a service if the government already paid it; conversely, if the government already paid it, then there is no claim for the provider to submit.

The CMP Regulations fix this particular problem but create another. First, the fix: The CMP Regulations provide that the Office of Inspector General (OIG) may impose a CMP of up to $15,000 (per improperly referred service) against any person who "has not refunded on a timely basis . . . amounts collected as the result of billing an individual, third party payer, or other entity for a DHS that was provided in accordance with a prohibited referral."[16] The CMP Regulations also provide for an assessment of up to three times the amount claimed for the service at issue.[17] Unlike the Stark Law, however, the CMP Regulations do not provide for exclusion.

Now, the problem: The CMP Regulations omit a critical requirement of the Stark Law (i.e., that the failure to refund CMP can only be imposed on a person who "knows or should know" that the payment to be refunded was for an improperly referred service). It appears that this is an oversight on CMS's part. Part 1003 of Title 42 of the CFR codifies the CMP Regulations. The first section of Part 1003—Section 1003.100 ("basis and purpose")—provides that the "purpose" of Part 1003 is to provide "for the imposition of CMPs and, as applicable, assessments against persons who," among other things, "have collected amounts that they know or should know were billed in violation of [the Stark Regulations] and have not refunded the amounts collected on a timely basis."[18]

As noted above, however, Section 1003.102 ("basis for civil money penalties and assessments") drops this "knows or should know" language, providing simply that the OIG may impose a CMP against any person who "has not refunded on a timely basis . . . amounts collected as the result of billing an individual, third party payer, or other entity for a DHS that was provided in accordance with a prohibited referral . . ."[19]

Although not entirely clear, CMS appears to have been counting on an amendment to the term "timely basis" to sweep the Stark Law's state-of-mind requirement back into the Regulations' failure to refund CMP. In the preamble to the 1998 Proposed Stark II Regulations, CMS stated that it was proposing to define "timely basis" by cross-referring to §1003.101 in the [CMP Regulations]. While §1003.101 currently defines this term as "the 60-day period from the time the prohibited amounts are collected by the individual or entity," the OIG is planning to issue shortly revised final regulations that will amend this term. Under the amended version, the 60-day time frame for a refund will begin when the individual or entity knew or should have known that the amount collected was related to a prohibited referral. We plan to adopt this revised definition as well.[20]

Unfortunately, the OIG never amended the definition of "timely basis," which (as noted above) continues to provide that this term means within 60 days "from the time the prohibited amounts are collected by the individual or the entity."

In sum, whereas Congress (in the Stark Law), CMS (in the preamble to the Proposed Stark II Regulations), and the OIG (in the introductory section to the CMP Regulations) all appear to have intended the failure to refund CMP to include a "knows or should know" state-of-mind requirement, the current CMP Regulations do not include this requirement, providing simply that the OIG may impose a CMP against any person who "has not refunded on a timely basis" (i.e., within 60 days) "amounts collected as the result of billing an individual, third-party payer, or other entity for a DHS that was provided in accordance with a prohibited referral."

3. Circumvention/cross-referral CMPs

Finally, the Stark Law provides that "any physician or other entity that enters into an arrangement or scheme (such as a cross-referral arrangement) which the physician or entity knows or should know has a principal purpose of assuring referrals by the physician to a particular entity which, if the physician directly made referrals to such entity, would be in violation of this section," shall be subject to (1) a CMP of not more than $100,000 for "each such arrangement or scheme" and (2) an assessment in lieu of damages.[21] In addition, the government may exclude the person from participation in all federal healthcare programs.[22]

This provision is almost indecipherable. What does it mean for an arrangement to be designed to ensure referrals by a physician to an entity that "would be in violation" of the Stark Law "if the physician directly made referrals to such entity"? The use of the term "directly" suggests that Congress was concerned about certain "indirect" referrals. But what is an "indirect" referral (as used in this CMP)? The provision's cryptic reference to "cross-referral arrangements" does not shed much light on the subject either. There is nothing "indirect" about an arrangement pursuant to which Physician A agrees to refer patients to Physician B, if Physician B agrees to reciprocate.

Even more problematic, however, is that this CMP seems to stand for the following proposition: "We enacted a very broad referral prohibition, but we're concerned that there might be some ways around it. So even if a referral does not actually violate the referral prohibition, if it would have violated the prohibition, we will sanction it nonetheless, in the form of a $100,000 CMP." Unfortunately, the CMP Regulations, which effectively create two distinct CMPs—a "cross-referral CMP" and a "circumvention CMP"—do not provide physicians and DHS entities with an easy way out of this potential no-win situation.

a. Cross-referral CMP

The cross-referral CMP provides for a $100,000 CMP against any physician or entity that enters into "a cross-referral arrangement, for example, whereby the physician owners of entity 'X' refer to entity 'Y,' and the physician owners of entity 'Y' refer to entity 'X' in violation of [the referral prohibition]."[23] The cross-referral CMP also provides for an assessment of up to three times the amount claimed for the service at issue, but it does not provide for exclusion.[24] As with the related Stark Law section, this provision is not a model of clarity. Consider the following questions:

- Is it saying that if (1) there is a cross-referral arrangement and (2) referrals under this arrangement violate the referral prohibition, the government may impose the CMP? If so, this provision simply increases the CMP from $15,000 to $100,000 for prohibited referrals made as part of a cross-referral arrangement (as opposed to some other arrangement).

- Does the provision stand for the proposition that any referrals made as part of a cross-referral arrangement are subject to a $100,000 CMP, regardless of whether they violate the referral prohibition? If so, then this regulatory provision suffers from the same infirmity as its statutory parent: It provides for a Stark Law violation even where there is no prohibited referral.

Exacerbating the problem, the regulators once again also forgot to incorporate the Stark Law's state-of-mind requirement into the cross-referral CMP. The Stark Law clearly provides that the CMP only applies if the physician or entity "knows or should know" that the arrangement at issue "has a principal purpose of assuring referrals by the physician to a particular entity which, if the physician directly made referrals to such entity, would be in violation of this section."

b. Circumvention CMP

The circumvention CMP provides for a $100,000 CMP against any physician or entity that enters into any "arrangement or scheme that the physician or entity knows, or should know, has a principal purpose of circumventing [the Stark Regulations' referral prohibition]."[25] The circumvention CMP also provides for an assessment of up to three times the amount claimed for the service at issue, but it does not provide for exclusion.[26] Although this provision includes the requisite state-of-mind requirement, as with the parallel Stark Law provision, it is both vague and ambiguous. Most notably, perhaps, one person's "compliance" with the Stark Law and Stark Regulations may be another person's "circumvention" of them.

An example helps demonstrate the point. If an entity wishes to receive services from a particular physician who is employed by a physician group, it may be possible for the entity to either avoid creating a financial relationship with that particular physician altogether or to fit the financial relationship into an exception—and, in either case, avoid violating the Stark Law—if the entity enters into a compensation arrangement with the physician group and not the individual physician. The majority of health fraud and abuse practitioners would take the position that this is perfectly appropriate and consistent with an effort to comply with the Stark Law. Others, however—such as private whistleblowers—might argue otherwise.

D. Temporary noncompliance exception

In response to the Stark II Proposed Regulations, a number of commenters asked CMS to create a "grace period" for arrangements that either (1) "[f]all out of compliance with aspects of an exception through events outside their control" or (2) "are unable to comply with an exception for temporary periods of time."[27]

In the 2004 Stark II, Phase II Regulations, CMS—"persuaded that a specified and limited exception for certain arrangements that have unavoidably and temporarily fallen out of compliance with other exceptions is warranted and consistent with the overall statutory scheme and the obligations the statute imposes on providers"[28]—created such an exception.[29]   According to CMS, the temporary noncompliance exception:

> should address a number of situations that present special and temporary compliance problems, including conversion of publicly-traded companies to private ownership; loss of rural or health professional shortage areas (HPSA) designations; or delays in obtaining fully-signed copies of renewal agreements.[30]

Pursuant to the "temporary noncompliance exception," an entity "may submit a claim or bill and payment may be made to an entity that submits a claim or bill for a DHS," provided several conditions are met:

- First, the "financial relationship between the entity and the referring physician" must have complied with a Stark Law exception "for at least 180 consecutive calendar days immediately preceding the date on which the financial relationship became noncompliant with the exception."[31]

- Second, the financial relationship must have "fallen out of compliance with the exception for reasons beyond the control of the entity," and the entity must "promptly take steps to rectify the noncompliance."[32]

- Third, the financial relationship cannot violate the anti-kickback statute and must otherwise comply with all applicable federal and state laws, rules, and regulations.[33]

The Stark Regulations further provide that this exception is only available with respect to "DHS furnished during the period of time it takes the entity to rectify the noncompliance, which must not exceed 90 consecutive calendar days following the date on which the financial relationship became noncompliant with an exception."[34] Moreover, the exception may only be used by an entity once every three years with respect to the same referring physician.[35]

Finally, the temporary noncompliance exception does not apply if the exception with which the financial relationship previously complied was the (1) compensation under $300 per year exception or (2) medical staff incidental benefits exception.[36] According to CMS, to "provide otherwise would effectively negate the limits set in those exceptions."[37]

II. Collateral consequences

A. Civil False Claims Act

Under the federal civil False Claims Act (FCA), a person who "knowingly" "presents" or "causes to be presented" a "false" or "fraudulent" "claim for payment" to the U.S. government is liable for a civil penalty of up to $11,000 per claim, plus three times the amount of damages sustained by the government.[38]

The FCA defines "claim" to include any "request" for "money" that is made to a "contractor" if the U.S. government provides any portion of the money that is requested.[39] Thus, for example, when a lab furnishes services to a Medicare beneficiary and seeks reimbursement for these services from a Medicare carrier, the lab has submitted a "claim" for purposes of the FCA. The FCA defines the term "knowingly" to mean that the person (1) has actual knowledge of the information, (2) acts in deliberate ignorance of the truth or falsity of the information, or (3) acts in reckless disregard of the truth or falsity of the information.[40]

B. Stark Law violations and the FCA

According to CMS, "violations of the physician self-referral prohibition may also be pursued under the FCA."[41] The OIG[42] and the Department of Justice (DOJ) share this view. Indeed, the DOJ has filed multiple pleadings in federal court with respect to this issue,[43] arguing that the "overwhelming" weight of federal case law establishes "that the appropriate inquiry for a court considering whether the violation of a statute, regulation, or contract provision gives rise to FCA liability is whether a nexus exists between the statute, regulation, or contract provision, and the defendant's claim for payment, i.e., whether compliance is a prerequisite to payment or the right to retain payment."[44]

According to the government, such a "nexus" exists between the Stark Law and claims submitted to Medicare for DHS. More specifically, the government takes the position that where (1) a physician refers a Medicare patient to an entity for the furnishing of DHS, (2) the physician and entity have a financial relationship, (3) the relationship does not meet any Stark Law exception, and (4) the entity seeks reimbursement from Medicare for the DHS at issue, the entity has "presented" a "claim for payment" to a government contractor (i.e., the carrier or intermediary), and this claim is "false" for FCA purposes. The claim is not "false" for the traditional reasons (e.g., the services at issue were not provided or were not medically necessary). Rather, the claim is "false" because, pursuant to the denial of payment rule, Medicare will not pay for DHS furnished in violation of the Stark Law's referral prohibition.

Note that the conversion of regulatory violations into FCA violations is a very complicated area of law, particularly regarding FCA actions premised on Stark Law violations, where the jurisprudence is evolving and there are no Supreme Court cases directly on point. However, several lower federal courts have sided with the government, concluding that, where a provider submits a claim for services that were furnished pursuant to a referral that violated the Stark Law, the submission may constitute a "false claim" for purposes of the FCA.

C. Private whistleblowers

Even assuming that the government may proceed under the Stark Law or under the FCA if an entity submits a claim to Medicare for DHS furnished in violation of the referral prohibition, the sanctions provided for under the FCA (i.e., a fine of up to $11,000 per claim plus treble damages) arguably are less imposing than those provided for under the presenting claims CMP discussed in this chapter (i.e., a penalty of up to $15,000 per service, plus an assessment of up to three times the amount claimed). Moreover, by "bootstrapping" the Stark Law to a FCA claim, the government must prove not only each element of the FCA violation (including its state-of-mind requirement) but also each element of the underlying Stark Law violation.

Notwithstanding these limitations, however, the FCA poses perhaps the greatest Stark Law compliance challenge and risk for DHS providers, suppliers, and physicians. This is not because CMS, the OIG, or the DOJ are necessarily interested in pursuing FCA cases based purely on Stark Law violations. (Again, for Stark Law violations, the government has CMPs that allow for greater recoveries and may be easier to prove than FCA violations.) Rather, the FCA poses a significant challenge because, unlike the Stark Law's CMP assessment and exclusion sanctions, the FCA empowers private citizens to bring qui tam actions for violations of the FCA.[45]

Congress enacted the qui tam provisions of the FCA to assist the government in ferreting out fraud.[46] It deemed the assistance of private citizens necessary because of the perception that the government could not possibly discover all of the fraud—and, in particular, the submission of false claims—being perpetrated against it. Thus, to encourage private citizens to come forward with information, Congress provided them with a financial incentive in the form of a specified percentage of any monies ultimately recovered in the action, along with reasonable attorneys' fees.

Under the current statutory framework, a qui tam plaintiff—commonly known as a "relator" or "whistleblower"—may recover as much as 30% (but more typically between 15 and 20%) of the proceeds of the action.[47] The precise percentage depends on whether the government intervenes/joins in the action, the contribution the relator makes in prosecuting the case, and the significance of the information provided by the relator, among other things.[48] If the relator's contribution is substantial and the investigation or litigation proceeds primarily on the basis of his or her information, the relator will receive 15%–25% of any recovery if the government joins the action, or 30% if the government does not. If the relator's contribution is insubstantial or if the relator was part of the alleged wrongdoing, the award cannot exceed 10% of the recovery.[49] Adding to the attraction of a qui tam action are the civil FCA's fee-shifting provisions. If the relator prevails, the defendant must pay the relator's reasonable attorneys' fees and expenses.[50]

D. FCA and Stark Law qui tam cases

Because the FCA provides for treble damages and a civil penalty of up to $11,000 per claim, a qui tam action can be extremely lucrative for a successful relator. For example, the whistleblowers in the $1.7 billion settlement between HCA, Inc., and the government received a reported $151 million as their share of the settlement,[51] and the whistleblower in Gambro Healthcare's $350 million settlement with the government received a reported $56 million.[52] Not surprisingly, settlements such as these have caused a tremendous increase in the filing of qui tam actions. In the five years between 1987 and 1991, a total of 53 healthcare qui tam cases were filed (i.e., cases in which the Department of Health and Human Services (HHS) was the primary agency); by comparison, in the five-year period between 2000 and 2004, more than 1,000 healthcare qui tam cases were filed.[53]

The case of United States ex rel. Johnson-Porchardt v. Rapid City Regional Hospital[54] illustrates the threat posed by Stark Law-driven qui tam actions. That case involved a lease arrangement between a hospital ("Hospital") and a community-based medical oncology practice group ("Group"), pursuant to which the Group paid the Hospital $19,000 per year in lease payments. When the Hospital relocated its cancer center to a new building, the Group moved as well, occupying much larger and newer premises. Upon relocation, however, the Hospital and Group neglected to execute a new lease. As a result, the Group continued to pay the Hospital the "old" rent ($19,000 per year) for both different and much larger premises. Concluding that the Hospital was transferring to the Group more than $100,000 in discounted space and other forms of remuneration, the former administrator of the cancer center initiated, and the government intervened in, a qui tam action alleging that the arrangement gave rise to an unexcepted financial arrangement and, as such, to improper referrals and billings in violation of the Stark Law. The action ultimately was settled, with the Hospital paying $6 million and the Group $525,000.

In the future, it is likely that an increasing portion of the qui tam cases filed will allege Stark Law violations[55] for the following reasons:

1. If a relator is looking to convert a regulatory violation into an FCA violation, the Stark Law is an excellent candidate. Unlike most regulatory statutes, a physician and entity can violate the Stark Law's referral prohibition even if they did not intend to do so.

2. The Stark Law and Stark Regulations, the healthcare industry, and the nature and scope of arrangements between and among physicians, hospitals, and other DHS entities are ubiquitous and exceedingly complex. As a result, the likelihood of "technical" Stark Law violations—the classic example being the personal services or lease agreement that one party inadvertently fails to execute—is high. Although the federal government, exercising its discretion, may choose not to pursue such cases under the FCA, there is no reason to believe that relators and their counsel, lured by the type of settlements referenced above, would decide not to proceed.

3. With the promulgation of the Stark II, Phase II Regulations in 2004, CMS has put in place the last major piece of the regulatory puzzle. Although CMS will undoubtedly supplement and revise the Stark Regulations over time, the issuance of the 2004 Regulations clarified much of the uncertainty relating to CMS's interpretation of numerous critical issues (e.g., the definition of "indirect compensation arrangements"). With this clarification comes a corresponding reduction in litigation risk for potential qui tam relators.

IV. Reporting requirements

Adding to the burden of physicians and DHS entities, the Stark Law provides that every entity that furnishes items or services covered by Medicare (and not simply entities that furnish DHS) must provide HHS with "information concerning the entity's ownership, investment, and compensation arrangements," including (1) the "covered items and services provided by the entity," (2) the names and unique physician identification numbers (UPIN) of all physicians (and IFMs) with an ownership or investment interest in the entity, and (3) the names and UPINs of all physicians (and IFMs) with a compensation arrangement with the entity.[56] The Stark Law also provides that this "information shall be provided in such form, manner, and at such times" as HHS (through CMS) shall specify.[57]

At one time, it appeared that these reporting requirements would impose a monumental administrative burden on hospitals and other DHS providers. After a long and tortuous regulatory history, however, CMS—through the 2004 Stark II, Phase II Regulations—has essentially converted the Stark Law's reporting requirements into document retention requirements. Specifically, the Stark Regulations provide that, if requested, an entity that furnishes Medicare-covered services must provide certain information to CMS or the OIG concerning the entity's "reportable financial relationships."[58] *Note:* Entities that furnish 20 or fewer Part A and Part B services during a calendar year and Medicare-covered services furnished outside the United States are exempt from this requirement.[59]

CMS defines a "reportable financial relationship" as any direct or indirect compensation arrangement or any direct or indirect ownership or investment interest (except those that satisfy the exceptions for publicly traded securities and mutual funds).[60] The information that CMS or the OIG may request includes the covered services furnished by the entity; the name and UPIN of each physician who has a reportable financial relationship with the entity (or who has an IFM with a reportable financial relationship with the entity); and, with respect to each of these physicians,

> the nature of the financial relationship (including the extent and/or value of the ownership or investment interest or the compensation arrangement) as evidenced in records that the entity knows or should know about in the course of prudently conducting business, including, but not limited to, records that the entity is already required to retain to comply with the rules of the Internal Revenue Service and the Securities and Exchange Commission and other rules of the Medicare and Medicaid programs.[61]

With respect to the form and timing of reports, the Stark Regulations provide that entities must "submit the required information, upon request, within the time period specified by the request."[62] However, all entities will be "given at least 30 days from the date of the request to provide the information."[63] CMS has not developed an official reporting form for responding to requests for information under the Stark Law.

The Stark Regulations further provide that entities "must retain the information, and documentation sufficient to verify the information, for the length of time specified by the applicable regulatory requirements for the information, and, upon request, must make that information and documentation available to CMS or OIG."[64] Finally, in addition to the CMPs discussed in this chapter, the Stark Regulations provide that any person "who is required, but fails, to submit" any required information is subject to a CMP of up to $10,000 per day until the requested information is provided.[65]

Notes

1. 42 United States Code (USC) §1395nn(g)(1).
2. 42 CFR §411.353(c).
3. 42 CFR §411.353(e). The exception was added in 2001 in response to CMS's 1998 "proposed presumption that a physician has referred his or her patient to an entity for the furnishing of DHS" as long as "the patient obtains the services from the entity with which the physician has a financial relationship." Stark II, Phase I Regulations (Preamble), 66 *Federal Register (FR)* 856, 872 (2001). (Chapter 4

discusses this issue.) Specifically, a commenter asked whether the entity in the following scenario would have Stark Law exposure: "A physician orally tells a patient or another person that the patient needs a DHS. The patient obtains the service from an entity with which the physician has a prohibited financial relationship. The entity does not know (and cannot know) that the physician orally told the patient (or other person) that the service was needed." Stark II, Phase I Regulations (Preamble), 66 *FR* 856, 872 (2001).

4. 42 USC §1395nn(g)(2).

5. 42 CFR §411.353(d).

6. 42 CFR §1003.101.

7. 42 USC §1395nn(g)(3), cross referencing 42 USC §1320a-7a(a).

8. 42 USC §1395nn(g)(3), cross referencing 42 USC §1320a-7a(a).

9. 42 USC §1320a-7a(i)(7).

10. 42 USC §1320a-7a(i)(7).

11. 42 USC §1320a-7b(f)(1).

12. 42 CFR §1003.102(a)(5) (authorizing CMP and assessment), 42 CFR §1003.103(b) (indicating maximum amount of CMP), and 42 CFR §1003.104(a)(2) (indicating maximum amount of assessment).

13. 42 CFR §1003.105(a)(1).

14. 42 USC §1395nn(g)(3), cross referencing 42 USC §1320a-7a(a).

15. 42 USC §1395nn(g)(3), cross referencing 42 USC §1320a-7a(a).

16. 42 CFR §1003.102(b)(9) (authorizing CMP and assessment).

17. 42 CFR §1003.104(a)(2) (indicating maximum amount of assessment).

18. 42 CFR §1003.100(b)(1)(ix).

19. 42 CFR §1003.102(b)(9).

20. Proposed Stark II Regulations (Preamble), 63 *FR* 1659, 1695 (1998).

21. 42 USC §1395nn(g)(4), cross referencing 42 USC §1320a-7a(a).

22. 42 USC §1395nn(g)(4), cross referencing 42 USC §1320a-7a(a).

23. 42 CFR §1003.102(b)(10)(i) (authorizing CMP and assessment) and 42 CFR §1003.103(b) (indicating maximum amount of CMP).

24. 42 CFR §1003.104(a)(2) (indicating maximum amount of assessment).

25. 42 CFR §1003.102(b)(10)(ii) (authorizing CMP and assessment) and 42 CFR §1003.103(b) (indicating maximum amount of CMP).

26. 42 CFR §1003.104(a)(2) (indicating maximum amount of assessment).

27. 31 USC §3729(a).

28. Stark II, Phase II Regulations (Preamble), 69 *FR* 16054, 16056-57 (2004).

29. Stark II, Phase II Regulations (Preamble), 69 *FR* 16054, 16057 (2004).

30. 42 CFR §411.3531(f).

31. Stark II, Phase II Regulations (Preamble), 69 *FR* 16054, 16057 (2004).

32. 42 CFR §411.3531(f)(1)(i).

33. 42 CFR §411.3531(f)(1)(ii).

34. 42 CFR §411.3531(f)(1)(iii).

35. 42 CFR §411.3539(f)(2).

36. 42 CFR §411.3539(f)(3).

37. 42 CFR §411.3539(f)(4).

38. Stark II, Phase II Regulations (Preamble), 69 *FR* 16054, 16957 (2004).

39. 31 USC §3729(c).

40. 31 USC §3729(b).

41. Stark II, Phase II Regulations (Preamble), 69 *FR* 16054, 16125 (2004).

42. OIG Supplemental Hospital Compliance Program Guidance, 70 *FR* 4858, 4862 (2005).

43 *United States ex rel. Maria Urbank et al.*, United States' Statement of Interest on Relators' Motion for Partial Reconsideration (No. 00-CV-4863, U.S. Dist. Ct. East. Dist. Pa.); *United States of America, ex rel. Scott Barrett, et al.*, United States' Second Statement of Interest on Defendants' Motion to Dismiss (No. 99-3304, U.S. Dist. Ct. Dist. Columbia); *United States of American ex rel. A. Scott Pogue v. Diabetes Treatment Centers of America, Inc., et al.*, Memorandum Opinion (No. 99-CV-3298, U.S. Dist. Ct. Dist. Columbia).

44. *United States ex rel. Maria Urbank et al.*, United States' Statement of Interest on Relators' Motion for Partial Reconsideration (No. 00-CV-4863, U.S. Dist. Crt. East. Dist. Pa.).

45. 31 USC §§3730(a)-(b). The term "qui tam" comes from the Latin phrase *qui tam pro domino rege quam pro sic ipso in hoc parte sequitor*, which means "who as well for the king as for himself sues in this matter." *United States ex. rel. McDowell v. McDonnell Douglas Corp.*, 755 F. Supp. 1038 n.1 (M.D. Ga. 1991). Thus, as the name implies, a qui tam action is an action brought by a private citizen, acting as private attorney general, on behalf of the United States.

46. *United States ex rel. Williams v. NEC Corp.*, 931 F.2d 1493, 1497-98 (11th Cir. 1991).

47. 31 USC §3730(d)(1)-(2).

48. 31 USC §3730(d)(1)-(2).

49. 31 USC §3730(d)(1)-(2). The award can be reduced further if the relator "planned and initiated" the submission of the false claims at issue and eliminated altogether if the relator is convicted for his or her role in submitting the false claims. 31 USC §3730(d)(3). The civil FCA further protects relators by providing them with a private federal cause of action for any adverse employment action that is taken against them as a result of their qui tam action. 31 USC §3730(h).

50. 31 USC §3730(d)(1). The reverse, however, applies only if the government does not intervene in the action and the action was "clearly frivolous, clearly vexatious or brought primarily for purposes of harassment." 31 USC §3730(d)(4). Where the government intervenes, the prevailing defendant may still apply for attorneys' fees and expenses under the provisions of 28 USC §2412(d). 31 USC §3730(g).

51. "Largest Health Care Fraud Case Settled; HCA Inc. to Pay Record Total of $1.7 Billion," BNA Health Care Fraud Report (Vol. 7, No. 14) (July 9, 2003).

52. "Whistleblower to Receive $56 Million From $350 Million Gambro Settlement," BNA Health Care Fraud Report (Vol. 9, No. 8) (April 13, 2005).

53 Fraud Statistics—Health & Human Services (October 1, 1986–September 30, 2004), Civil Division, U.S. Department of Justice.

54. *United States ex rel. Johnson-Porchardt v. Rapid City Regional Hosp.*, 01-CV-5019 (D.S.D.) (Settlement announced in 2002).

55. Indeed, over the past several years, there has been a steady increase in FCA settlements involving alleged Stark Law violations. Since 2002 through August 2005, for example, Rapid City Regional Hospital (South Dakota) (discussed above), McLeod Hospital (South Carolina), Jackson General Hospital (West Virginia), Metropolitan Health Corp. (Colorado), Good Samaritan Hospital (Nebraska), and North Ridge Medical Center (Florida), have entered into settlements ranging from $1.2 million to $22.5 million arising from allegations of Stark Law-based FCA violations.

56. 42 USC §1395nn(f).

57. 42 USC §1395nn(f).

58. 42 CFR §411.361(a),(e).

59. 42 CFR §411.361(b).

60. 42 CFR §411.361(d).

61. 42 CFR §411.361(c).

62. 42 CFR §411.361(e).

63 42 CFR §411.361(e).

64. 42 CFR §411.361(e).

65. 42 CFR §411.361(f).

Chapter 12

ADVISORY OPINIONS

Chapter **12**

ADVISORY OPINIONS

I. Background

A. Anti-kickback statute

One of the Stark Law's "cousins" is the federal healthcare program anti-kickback statute.[1] In general, this statute prohibits the intentional offer, payment, solicitation, or receipt of any form of remuneration (i.e., anything of value) in return for the referral of Medicare, Medicaid, or other federal healthcare program patients or business. The anti-kickback statute is discussed further in Chapter 2.

The anti-kickback statute is so broad that many commonplace arrangements risk violating it. Recognizing this problem, Congress and the U.S. Department of Health and Human Services Office of Inspector General (OIG) have created more than two-dozen statutory "exceptions" and regulatory "safe harbors" (collectively, safe harbors).[2] An arrangement that fits into one or more of them is protected from prosecution.

Unfortunately, safe harbors do not exist for every type of legitimate arrangement that may implicate the anti-kickback statute. Moreover, the existing safe harbors tend to be quite narrow, and the OIG affords immunity only to those arrangements that precisely meet all of a safe harbor's conditions.[3] Material or substantial compliance with such requirements is insufficient.[4]

Because the anti-kickback statute is so broad and the protection offered by its safe harbors so limited, Congress has created and the OIG has implemented an "advisory opinion" program. Under this program, individuals and entities may submit proposed arrangements to the OIG and request, in effect, a "case specific" safe harbor. As of October 2005, the OIG had issued more than 120 such advisory opinions. In most cases, the requestor's proposed arrangement arguably implicated the anti-kickback statute but could not meet a safe harbor. More often than not, however, the OIG concluded that the arrangement (1) did not implicate the statute's principal policy objectives, (2) did not pose a material risk of program abuse, and (3) as such, would not be sanctioned.

B Stark Law

As discussed in the Introduction, in addition to the overbreadth of the Stark Law's referral and billing prohibitions, the proliferation of exceptions, and the complexities of both, a fourth factor has made compliance with the Law difficult for healthcare organizations: The Centers for Medicare & Medicaid Services (CMS) has provided only sporadic and relatively limited Stark Law guidance to the provider and physician communities.

Seeking, at least in part, to address this paucity of guidance, in 1997, Congress created a Stark Law advisory opinion program (to be operated by CMS) that largely mirrored the pre-existing anti-kick-back statute advisory opinion program operated by the OIG.[5] Unlike the OIG's program, however, this newer program has, for all intents and purposes, been non-existent. Between January 1998 (when the program first went into effect) and September 2005, CMS issued just three advisory opinions (two in 1998 and one in 2005) addressing issues other than the narrow issue of whether the requester at issue met the "under development" requirement of the specialty hospital moratorium.[6]

II. Advisory opinion scope and process

A. Scope

Pursuant to the Stark Regulations, as part of the advisory opinion process, any individual or entity (i.e., "requester") may ask CMS to determine whether an arrangement between one or more physicians and one or more entities that furnishes designated health services (DHS) creates any "financial relationships" that could potentially restrict physician referrals to the DHS entity (or entities) and, if so, whether the arrangement qualifies for one or more Stark Law exceptions.[7] The scope of the advisory opinion process has four principal limitations:

1. The request at issue must concern an existing arrangement or an arrangement into which the requester will enter (contingent upon receiving a favorable advisory opinion).[8]

2. The requester must be a party to the existing arrangement or, in the case of a proposed arrangement, must be an individual or entity that will be a party to the arrangement.[9]

3. CMS will not consider requests that present general questions of interpretation, pose hypothetical situations, or involve the activities of third parties.[10]

4. CMS will not address whether fair market value was (or will be) paid or received for any goods, services, or property, or whether an individual was or is a bona fide employee under relevant Internal Revenue Code provisions.[11]

B. Process

1. How to request an advisory opinion

When submitting a request to CMS for a Stark Law advisory opinion, the requester must provide a complete description of the arrangement at issue, including the following:

- The purpose of the arrangement.

- The nature of each party's contribution to the arrangement.

- The direct or indirect relationships between the parties, with an emphasis on the relationships between the physicians (or immediate family members) involved in the arrangement and the entity (or entities) furnishing DHS.

- The types of services for which the physicians wish to refer.

- Whether the referrals will involve Medicare or Medicaid patients.[12]

In addition, requesters must provide copies of relevant documents affecting the arrangement (e.g., employment contracts, financial statements, and leases), descriptions of any oral or collateral under-standings, and complete information about the identities of those involved in the arrangement (either directly or indirectly), including name, address, legal form, ownership, structure, and, if relevant, Medicare and Medicaid provider number.[13]

CMS also recommends that the requester raise any specific issues that it would like the agency's opin-ion to address, including any arguments supporting the requestor's belief that the Stark Law's referral prohibition is not triggered by the arrangement or that one or more exceptions apply to the arrange-ment.[14] In addition, the requester should indicate whether it is seeking, or plans to seek, an advisory opinion from the OIG.[15]

Note that every request for an advisory opinion also must include the following signed certification:

> With knowledge of the penalties for false statements provided by 18 United States Code (USC) §1001 and with knowledge that this request for an advisory opinion is being sub-mitted to the Department of Health and Human Services, I certify that all of the informa-tion provided is true and correct, and constitutes a complete description of the facts regarding which an advisory opinion is sought, to the best of my knowledge and belief.[16]

The requester must sign the certification if the requester is an individual. If the requester is a corpora-tion, partnership, or limited liability company (LLC), the chief executive officer, managing partner, or managing member (respectively) must sign the certification.[17]

Finally, a $250 non-refundable deposit must be included with each request for an advisory opinion.[18] By submitting a request for an opinion, the requester also agrees to pay for all of CMS's costs in preparing the opinion, including fees for expert opinions from outside sources, if required.[19] The requesting party, however, may specify a "triggering dollar amount," as further outlined in the Stark Regulations, in an effort to limit its expenses.[20]

2. How CMS processes advisory opinion requests

Pursuant to the Stark Regulations, CMS must determine within 15 days of receiving a request whether to accept or decline the request or whether additional information is required.[21] Once it has accepted a request, CMS has 90 days—subject to certain tolling periods—to issue an advisory opinion.[22] If a request involves a complex arrangement, however, CMS will issue an advisory opinion within a "reasonable period."[23] If the OIG advisory opinion process is any guide, a "reasonable time period" may be as long as one year, and perhaps longer.

Requesters may withdraw a request for an advisory opinion at any time before CMS issues the opinion.[24] Once it issues a formal advisory opinion, CMS will make a redacted version of it available to the general public on its Web site.[25]

C. Protection offered by advisory opinions

The protection afforded by a favorable advisory opinion extends only to the parties who request the opinion and only to the specific facts and circumstances that form the basis of the opinion. As a result, third parties are not bound by—and cannot rely on—advisory opinions.[26]

CMS advisory opinions do not limit the investigatory or prosecutorial authority of the OIG, the Department of Justice (DOJ), or any other agency of the government.[27] Requesters should also understand that in connection with a request for an advisory opinion, CMS, the OIG, or the DOJ may conduct whatever independent investigation it deems appropriate.[28] Finally, any advice given by CMS is without prejudice to the right of the agency to reconsider the questions involved and when, the public interest requires, CMS may rescind or revoke the opinion.[29]

Notes

1. 42 USC §1320a-7b(b).
2. 42 USC §1320a-7b(b)(3); 42 CFR §1001.952.
3. OIG Advisory Opinion No. 98-5 (Apr. 24, 1998).
4. 56 *FR* 35952, 35954 (July 29, 1991).
5. 42 USC §1395nn(g)(6).

6. The first opinion, AO-98-001, released in October 1998, involved a variety of issues faced by an LLC proposing to operate an ambulatory surgical treatment center (ASTC). Specifically, the opinion addressed (1) whether the investment in and ownership of an ASTC by physicians who refer patients to (and perform surgeries at) the ASTC would violate the Stark Law; (2) whether the proposed location of the ASTC qualified as a rural area under the Stark Law's rural provider exception, and whether this exception would apply to the proposed arrangement; and (3) whether non-surgeon physician investors in the ASTC could refer patients to the ASTC without violating the Stark Law's referral prohibition. The second opinion, AO-98-002, released in November 1998, involved the issue of whether the partners and physician employees of a proposed partnership may, under the Stark Law's in-office ancillary services exception, refer Medicare patients to the partnership for eyeglass prescriptions filled subsequent to cataract surgery with the insertion of an intraocular lens. The third opinion, AO-2005-08-01, released in August 2005, involved the issue of whether stock held by physician-shareholders in a nonprofit, tax-exempt multi-specialty group medical practice constitutes an ownership or investment interest for purposes of the Stark Law. All three of these opinions can be found on CMS's Web site at *www.cms.hhs.gov/physicians/aop/opinion.asp*. CMS issued a notification on March 19, 2004 stating that the agency would use its advisory opinion program to issue determinations regarding whether a hospital is subject to the moratorium on physician referrals to specialty hospitals in which they have an ownership or investment interest, which was established by Section 507 of the Medicare Prescription Drug, Improvement and Modernization Act of 2003. CMS Pub. 100-20, Transmittal 62, Change Request 3036 (March 19, 2004). The 10 opinions concerning this issue can be found on CMS' Web site at *www.cms.hhs.gov/physicians/aop/opinion.asp*.

7. 42 CFR §411.370(b).

8. 42 CFR §411.370(b).

9. 42 CFR §411.370(b)(2).

10. 42 CFR §411.370(b)(1).

11. 42 CFR §411.370(c)(1)(2).

12. 42 CFR §411.372(b).

13. 42 CFR §§ 411.372(b)(4) and (5).

14. 42 CFR §411.372(b)(6).

15. 42 CFR §411.372(b)(7).

16. 42 CFR §411.373(a). An additional certification is required if the arrangement is a proposed, rather than an actual, arrangement. 42 CFR §411.373(b). If CMS believes it needs additional information in order to render an opinion, it may request whatever additional information it deems necessary.

17 CFR §411.372(c).

18 CFR §411.372(b)(8).

19. 42 CFR §§ 411.375(b); 411.375(d); 411.377.

20. 42 CFR §411.375(c).

21. 42 CFR §411.379.

22. 42 CFR §§ 411.379(e); 411.380.

23. 42 CFR §411.380(c)(1).

24. 42 CFR §411.378.

25. 42 CFR §411.384.

26. 42 CFR §411.387.

27. 42 CFR §411.370(f).

28. 42 CFR §411.370(f). Thus, parties contemplating the submission of a Stark Law advisory opinion request should realize that the information submitted to CMS may later be used against them. As such, individuals or entities should consult legal counsel to help weigh the risks and benefits of seeking a CMS advisory opinion.

29. 42 CFR §411.382.